*Every Other Saturd*

*Linfield, the Irish League, and the Chan*
*Football 1986-2016*

Daniel Brown

*Every Other Saturday:*

*Linfield, the Irish League, and the Changing World of European Football 1986-2016*

**About the Author**

Daniel Brown has taught sports history and modern American history at Queen's University Belfast. He studied British history for his masters, and in 2012 completed his PhD in American history. Whilst the focus of his studies has traversed back and forth across the Atlantic, his passion for Linfield Football Club and the Irish League has remained a constant. In this, his first book, Daniel examines his beloved Blues through the changing footballing, social, political and economic climate in Northern Ireland and beyond.

First published in November 2016

Publisher: Motelands Publishing

Copyright © Daniel Brown, 2016

All rights reserved

ISBN 978-0-9934434-3-5


Printed and bound by

CPI Group (UK) Ltd, Croydon, CR0 4YY

# Acknowledgements

Writing a book on Linfield Football Club has been without doubt the most enjoyable venture I have undertaken. It was also something that I was only able to complete with the help of a number of individuals. First and foremost, Linfield trustee Dr Cameron Ramsey was a driving force of the project. Cameron opened up the club archives, and was the perfect person to bounce ideas off. His feedback on writing was invaluable. Then when it came to putting the book together, he was once again to the fore. Cameron made this book possible.

Thanks must go to Linfield Football Club for providing access to archives, and also to individual directors for their help with research and putting the book together: to club president Peter Lunn, honorary treasurer Richard Johnson, trustees Paul Weir, Jack Grundie and Stuart Gilmore, to vice-chairman Billy Kennedy, to Andy Conn and Roy McGivern. Also to club secretary Ken Greer and to Pauline Anderson.

Ian Carser lent his entire catalogue of *Look at Linfield* programmes to aid research, and I cannot thank him enough for this. Newspaper research was crucial in this project, and an extremely enjoyable six months was spent in Belfast Central Library's newspaper holdings. Special thanks go to Brian Girvin (with all his tales of Pippa), Billy Walker, as well as Al Gregg. Thanks go to Edna Hatton for giving me sight of Sammy Hatton's archive, as well as to Brian Leth for his translation from Danish of the 1993 Copenhagen programme.

Undertaking oral interviews was vital for this project, and Gary Eccles facilitated this. Whoever I wanted to speak to, Gary was always able to put me in touch with them. Thanks go to Roy Coyle, Eric Bowyer, Trevor Anderson, David Jeffrey, Warren Feeney, David Healy, Lindsay McKeown, Alan Dornan, Noel Bailie, Michael Gault, Andy Waterworth, Jamie Mulgrew, Peter Dornan, George Dunlop, Martin McGaughey, Lee Doherty, Dessie Gorman, Pat Fenlon, William Murphy, Glenn Ferguson, Gavin Arthur, Phil Charnock, Peter Thompson and Sean Ward. Special thanks must go to David Jeffrey for providing the book's foreword.

Comments on the various drafts of the chapters were invaluable, and I must thank a number of people for this. As well as to directors

Cameron Ramsey, Stuart Gilmore and Billy Kennedy, thanks must go to Graham Brownlow, Anthony Stanonis, Pete Shirlow, Sean O'Connell, James Greer, Liam Kelly, Jen Davison, Dominic Bryan, Marian Duggan, Gordon Gillespie, Leslie Crowe, Rodney Brown and Kenneth Brown.

Thanks go to Marie Coleman for her inspiration for the book, and to Andrew Holmes who allowed me to teach sports history to first-year students. The module was invaluable when gathering my thoughts for the book. Thanks to Brian Kelly for teaching me the historian's craft.

Thanks to Jane Garton who undertook proofreading of the book and helped finesse the writing. Furthermore she was always understanding on deadlines. Thanks go to Colin McKeown for his work on the book cover, and to Bill Morrison for facilitating the publishing of the book. Bill provided invaluable insights along the way.

An earlier version of some of the material from the second, third and fourth chapters appeared in the journal *Soccer and Society* as the article 'Linfield's "Hawk of Peace": pre-Ceasefires reconciliation in Irish League football'. Thanks go to the editor Boria Majumdar for allowing the work to be reproduced. Also to Conor Curran and David Toms, the editors of the special journal edition that the article appeared in.

The illustrations used throughout have been provided by a number of sources, and I am indebted to each. Thanks go to Colin McMaster, to PressEye and to Pacemaker Press. Also to Linfield Football Club for allowing use of pictures from the club website, programmes and other personal archives, as well as to Gary Galbraith.

Thanks of course go to the many Linfield fans whom I have sat beside at matches and at times bored with tales of my research – you all know who you are.

Lastly thanks go to my mother, father, sisters, brothers-in-law, nephews, uncles, aunties and grandparents, as well relatives who are no longer here. Thanks go to my Uncle Bobby for inspiring me with tales of Tommy Dickson, my Grandfather Irvine for faithfully getting me *Ireland's Saturday Night*, and to my Grandmother Brown, even though she teased me every time Glentoran beat the Blues.

All of the above have helped in different ways with the book. Any mistakes that appear in the pages that follow are my own.

Audaces Fortuna Iuvat (Fortune Favours the Brave)

# Picture Index

Chapter 11
1. Peter Thompson with Irish Cup, courtesy of Colin McMaster
2. Celebrations after a third straight Double, courtesy of Colin McMaster
3. Hostile atmosphere in Zagreb, courtesy of William Cherry, Press Eye

Chapter 12
1. Noel Bailie's 1,000th appearance, courtesy of Colin McMaster
2. Philip Lowry, courtesy of Pacemaker Press
3. Title 2011/12 celebrations, courtesy of Colin McMaster

Chapter 13
1. Linfield at Ibrox, courtesy of Colin McMaster
2. Malcolm Brodie recording David Jeffrey, courtesy of LFC
3. Aaron Burns celebrates against Xanthi, courtesy of Aleksander Djorovic, Press Eye
4. The 'old' Windsor Park, courtesy of Colin McMaster
5. View from 'old' South Stand, courtesy of Colin McMaster

Chapter 14
1. Warren Feeney, courtesy of Colin McMaster
2. Andy Waterworth celebrates against AIK, courtesy of Colin McMaster
3. David Healy, courtesy of Pacemaker Press
4. Roy Carroll, courtesy of Colin McMaster

Cover photo courtesy of Pacemaker Press

*Every other Saturday's my half day off*

*And it's off to the match I go*

*Happily I walk along the Donegall Road*

*Me and ma wee pal Joe*

*I love to see the lasses with their blue scarves on*

*I love to hear the boys all roar*

*But I don't have to tell you what's the best of all*

*I love to see the Linfield sc-o-o-o-ore!*

# Contents

# Foreword by David Jeffrey

When I think about Linfield, my first thoughts are through the eyes of a little lad in his blue scarf. As that young boy grew into a man, Linfield became a big part of his life. It was a thrill to be part of Roy Coyle's dominant 'team of the 1980s'. Yet more than this, I travelled the world with Linfield. There were European ventures to the Balkans, Portugal, Greece, Switzerland, Scandinavia and to the USSR. Then there were North America tours. These were all some fantastic experiences!

There were also times when football was put into perspective. The joy of winning the 1988/89 League title at Glenavon paled into total insignificance as news of the unfolding Hillsborough disaster came through. On such an occasion you think to yourself, what's this all about? I experienced a rollercoaster of emotions whilst a player at Linfield. But I could always rely on the friendships formed at the club to help me through the tough times, as well as to celebrate the good.

Linfield also gave me the opportunity to manage. Make no mistake about it – the challenges of management were tough. It would take three and a half seasons to win my first Gibson Cup as Linfield boss. But doing so in 2000 – after finishing runners-up the previous two seasons – was so sweet. I'll never forget the day we won it, up at Coleraine, and sitting in the bath at the Showgrounds talking and talking until the water turned cold. Just winning one title was great, but then to do back-to-back Leagues, an all-Ireland Cup, a Clean Sweep and back-to-back Doubles – unbelievable!

It wasn't just the trophies that made managing Linfield so special, it was the people who were there through it all. There were confidants like Gary Eccles, Terry Hayes, Kenny McKeague, Andy Kerr and Dennis Shields, as well as my management team of Bryan McLaughlin and Alfie Wylie. And of course there were the many Linfield supporters who always encouraged me – they were just brilliant.

For over 30 years I served the club as a player and a manager, then suddenly that was over. Leaving Linfield was never going to be easy, because Linfield had been my footballing life. I always knew it wouldn't go on forever. Nevertheless it was so tough to get used to. My last night as manager was like a wake, with all the players down in the Windsor boot room. It was heartbreaking, and I'm not ashamed to admit there were many tears shed.

Getting back into football when the Ballymena job became available, I was struck by the number of "Good luck" messages sent from Bluemen. They were so good with me, just as they had been when I was at the Blues. Furthermore, all the things I learnt at Linfield, I have taken with me. Linfield has shaped my understanding of football, and there couldn't have been a better club for that.

At Linfield I had tremendous experiences, travelled to places I would never otherwise have been, was part of unprecedented success, and formed some fantastic friendships.

But the biggest thrill of all – that wee lad in the blue scarf lived the dream. In the pages that follow, I hope that the reader can live (or indeed relive) the dream too.

**September 2016**

# Every Other Saturday

# Linfield, the Irish League, and the Changing World of European Football 1986-2016

# *Introduction*

Billed as "a 'MUST' for everyone with a drop of blue blood in his or her veins", *Linfield 100 Years* went on sale in the autumn of 1985. Written by veteran reporter turned historian Malcolm Brodie, the book chronicled the first century of Belfast's most famous and most successful club. Tales of 'Clean Sweeps' (when all available pieces of domestic silverware were lifted), League domination and legendary European nights were all recollected. As Brodie maintained, the "high standards... set by the pioneers who created the tradition that is Linfield... have been continued through the [the club's] 100 years". Given the Blues' trophy-laden history, this triumphant tone was only natural. Yet as the club entered its 1986 centenary season, it did so at a time when Irish League football and the British game more generally were on an unsure footing.[1]

---------

Only a matter of months before *Linfield 100 Years* hit the shelves, Brodie declared that he had attended the "most amazing [Irish Cup] final". However, his observation had nothing to do with the game served up by Linfield and Glentoran at the Oval. In fact, he maintained that from a footballing perspective, "it was one of the worst finals for years". His match report for *Ireland's Saturday Night* exclaimed that there was, "Too much hard tackling, too much anxiety [and as] a result, we had a completely frenetic 90 minutes" – the game would end in a 1-1 draw. What had made for the spectacle were the "dozens of arrests [in the stands], the petulant players [on the pitch], and a bizarre start delayed by six minutes because of a pig and a cockerel".[2]

That 4 May 1985 Irish Cup final would forever be remembered for what the press described as "farmyard jinks". As the Linfield and Glentoran teams lined up before kick-off, the attention of the crowd was drawn toward a blue-painted pig that had made its way onto the

1

pitch, and a cockerel that appeared to be running the line. Glentoran fans had released both animals onto the playing area: the cockerel represented their club's emblem, whilst the pig painted blue was an insult, poking fun at their Linfield rivals. Setting aside this symbolism, the sight of a pig and a cockerel wandering round the Oval was farcical.[3]

It was embarrassing that the animals had made their way on to the field, and to make matters worse, both stayed on for the entirety of the 90 minutes. The pig was temporarily removed before proceedings got underway, but he was back by the time the game had started. When "Porky" (as *Ireland's Saturday Night* named him) returned, Linfield goalkeeper George Dunlop, Glentoran trainer Teddy Horner and a police officer all gave chase to catch him once again, but their efforts were in vain. It was all rather absurd, especially the sight of Horner unsuccessfully diving in an attempt to grab him. Aside from the spectacle served up by the farmyard animals, the only other real action seemed to have taken place on the terraces. Ugly confrontations unfolded when rival supporters clashed in the Oval's unreserved stand as fists and missiles were exchanged with venom. Projectiles also rained down on the playing area, and a stone struck a linesman on the back of the head. His injury was not serious and after receiving medical attention, he was able to run the line. Yet this was scant consolation. In keeping with footballing culture across the United Kingdom, the final had been defined by trouble.[4]

Hooliganism appeared to be on the rise, and the 'beautiful game' looked to be in crisis. Earlier that season a UK-wide television audience had watched on as an English FA Cup tie between Luton and Millwall descended into anarchy. Match commentator John Motson described the scenes as "the worst outbreak of hooliganism [he] ever saw on a domestic ground". In the game's aftermath, Prime Minister Margaret Thatcher established a 'War Cabinet' to address the issue of football-related violence. Despite her efforts, British football plunged further and further into crisis that spring of 1985. In mid-May, hooligans at a Birmingham City vs Leeds United game rioted with deadly consequences – amidst the chaos, a teenage fan died when a wall collapsed on him. Then later that month, 39 people were killed in similar circumstances when Liverpool and Juventus met in the European Cup final, at Brussels' Heysel stadium. Disaster was seemingly following disaster, and it appeared that the game had reached a nadir. This was something that Nick Hornby captured in *Fever Pitch* (his autobiographical musings on football), when he wrote, "post-Heysel there was simply nothing going on". Critics were only too keen to slate the sport, and attendances were on the decline.[5]

It was against this widespread despondency that Peter Dornan – chairman of the Northern Ireland Players' Football Association (PFA) – penned a scathing assessment of the Irish League. At the outset of the 1985/86 campaign, Dornan, who had recently retired after a successful career with Linfield, contributed an editorial for *Ireland's Saturday Night* in which he berated the local game as "stagnant". He lamented that "violence [was] rearing its ugly head" at matches, and complained that "the big crowds [were] gone". Worried by these trends, he warned that if there wasn't change, "the death knell of local football will surely sound". The picture painted was depressing, and what made it even tougher to accept was that – to use Dornan's words – "Those halcyon days seem not far gone." Only two decades beforehand, Linfield, the Irish League's powerhouse, were attracting home crowds in excess of 15,000. Those days were over. For years, Blues fans had sung: "Every other Saturday's my half day off, and it's off to match I go." Yet with every passing season, more and more of them were finding other ways to pass match-day afternoons.[6]

----------

When researching this book – which picks up Linfield's story where Brodie's *Linfield: 100 Years* left off – the author was struck by Dornan's words. The dire prediction of local football's "death knell" could have come at any time in the years that followed. I was still to reach my first birthday when Dornan penned his editorial. But by the early-to-mid 1990s when I was watching and attending games, talk of Irish League decline was commonplace. The major difference by then was that football on the mainland was on a much stronger footing. The English Premier League was revolutionising perceptions of the sport and – contrary to the Northern Irish experience – attendances were on the up. Continued Irish League decline, set against rejuvenation of the game elsewhere, is a story in itself, and is something this book considers.

Yet despite the negativity that has often hung around the Irish League, the local game always captivated me and following Linfield has been my passion. Researching and writing a book on the Blues has been a labour of love, and over the pages that follow I trust this comes through. Recording successes achieved under Roy Coyle, Trevor Anderson and David Jeffrey was a thrill, whilst situating the club in Northern Ireland's changing social and political landscape was something I relished. This was also the case when coming to terms with how the club fared as European football was restructured. Given that the gap between the 'haves and have-nots' has grown considerably, it was at times sobering to recount. That said, it is salient to do so.

I believe the story of Linfield from its 1986 centenary to the present day is an important one to tell. The club's many detractors are only too quick to blacken the reputation of the Blues with spurious claims. Conveying a full and open history of this Northern Irish institution – warts and all – is needed.

Chapter 1

# *Celebrating a Centenary*

Amidst the gloom that had enveloped 1980s football, Linfield were experiencing a particularly successful patch of their distinguished history. Ahead of their 1986 centenary, the Blues had won four straight League titles. They had just missed out on a League and Cup Double in the 1984/85 season – after defeat in the replayed 'Pig and Cockerel' final. Thus there was no question of Linfield's supremacy in the local game, and what was more, the Blues could boast of a presence on the world stage. Lucrative North American tours formed part of the club's itinerary, and its players were receiving prestigious international accolades. Although British football was enduring a tough time, the Belfast Blues seemed to be making the most of the difficult conditions.

Under the stewardship of manager Roy Coyle, Linfield had amassed a very talented group of players, and Coyle knew how to get the best out of them. Going into the 1985/86 campaign however – when it was expected Linfield would mark their centenary with a fifth consecutive League victory – one of Coyle's star performers was sidelined. A cruciate ligament injury, sustained at the end of the previous campaign, prevented forward Martin 'Buckets' McGaughey from playing football for an entire year. Coyle would thus have to prepare for the centenary season without the striker he had described as "invaluable".[1]

In footballing parlance, hyperbole is often used to describe the ordinary. This was not the case when the Blues boss spoke about McGaughey. During the 1984/85 campaign, the forward had scored 56 goals in 50 games for the Blues, 34 having come in League appearances. Buckets recalled that, "everything seemed to click" that season and "it felt like I could score at every opportunity". The return earned him Province-wide acclaim, but also propelled the forward onto the international stage. He won a Northern Ireland cap in a game with Israel, and even more  significantly, the UEFA European 'Silver Boot' –

a tribute which denoted McGaughey as the second most deadly finisher in Europe. Only FC Porto's Fernando Gomes (with 39 League goals) had bettered Buckets' tally.[2]

In November 1985, an injured McGaughey would fly to France to collect his award at a glitzy Parisian ceremony. There he rubbed shoulders with the cream of European football as they quaffed the finest champagne. McGaughey maintained it was "an unbelievable experience... Franz Beckenbauer presented me with the 'Silver Boot'... the night was a tremendous occasion". It all seemed a far from cry from the part-time league that Buckets plied his trade in. But on that autumn night, the elite of European football were saluting his exploits.[3]

Completing a fifth consecutive League title without the services of such a player was never going to be easy, but Roy Coyle – who had always striven to maintain Linfield's dominance – was not going to sit back and wallow in the loss of a player. Instead, during that 1985/86 campaign Coyle gave his side a push by implementing an extra weekly training session. Before Christmas, Blues chairman David Campbell met with players to discuss the possibility, only to report the reaction "had not been enthusiastic". Yet undeterred, the club moved ahead with 10 players who agreed to a trial period. From 28 February 1986, Linfield supplemented their two training nights per week with an extra session on a Friday afternoon. Midfielder Lee Doherty explained that the manager "wanted to improve the players technically". Doherty pointed out that the extra hours were beneficial, but ultimately limited in what they could achieve. Not long after it started, Coyle had to acknowledge that "it wasn't to be... the players couldn't buy into it". Work commitments prevented some from attending, whilst others could only make it intermittently.[4]

Finance would always hinder such ventures and ultimately would thwart Coyle's ambition to make the playing side of the club more professional. That said, his efforts helped to ensure that Linfield remained the Irish League's number one side. In mid-April, the Blues won their fifth consecutive League at a canter. Despite the loss of McGaughey, the goals had continued to flow. Veteran striker Trevor Anderson hit the net on 31 occasions, Robert Barr weighed in with 22 goals and young Mark Caughey struck 16 times. Indeed, Caughey's performances would earn him a place in Billy Bingham's Northern Ireland World Cup squad.

The quality up front was matched at the back, with a miserly defence conceding only 22 goals in 26 League games. In front of goalkeeper George Dunlop, sat the likes of Lindsay McKeown, David Jeffrey, John Garrett, Gary McCartney, Darrin Coyle, Colin Crawford and Paul Mooney. Then in the midfield, Lee Doherty, Tom Sloan, Stephen McKee and Billy Murray were all integral cogs in the side's engine. Throughout the team there was quality, and when the title was secured on 19 April with a 1-0 win away to Portadown, Coyle credited his players on their efforts. He exclaimed, "it's particularly fabulous and it's particularly pleasing as it's our centenary year". Defender David Jeffrey recalled the pressure on Coyle was immense that season: "Given the anniversary, [players] felt under strain as well as pressure, so dear knows what Roy Coyle was feeling."[5]

Whatever stress Coyle had been feeling – and the release that came after taking the title – he did not have much time to dwell on his emotions. In the week after the win, Linfield's players were on their travels to the United States. For the second year running, the Blues would tour North America. At the end of the previous season the club had endured a disappointing trip, with the *Belfast Telegraph* labelling it a "playing disaster". The results of that tour had included a 4-0 defeat to the Tulsa Roughnecks, followed by a 4-1 loss to San Jose Earthquakes. All told there was a sole victory, one draw and four defeats. Yet whilst the team was humbled on the pitch, financially there had been much to gain. A fee of $6,000 per game was used to lure the Blues stateside.[6]

Back then, football was not the thriving success it would go on to become in the United States. When Linfield toured in the mid-1980s, the North American Soccer League – that had played host to Best, Beckenbauer and Pele – was defunct. Indeed, since the launch of that league in 1968, no team had ever made a profit. Spiralling debts, organisational mismanagement, a lack of home-grown talent and the failure to establish a large enough fan base all accounted for its demise. In the years that followed, football in the country was in the doldrums, with occasional tournaments and exhibition games arranged to maintain a profile. Linfield's two tours of the 1980s were part of this. Malcolm Brodie, though, took a dim view of the potential of such ventures: "If football – or soccer as they call it – is ever to succeed in the US, and frankly I don't see that happening in the immediate future... I rate the chances minimal, certainly for the next two decades."[7]

Considering the state of the North American game at the time, Brodie's pessimism seemed well placed. Furthermore, Linfield's underwhelming showing in the 1985 tour only lent credence to a narrative of Irish League decline. In 1986, however, the Blues produced performances that were a credit to Northern Irish football. In a three-team tournament, held at the Miami Orange Bowl, the Blues put on impressive showings against Columbian and Argentinian sides. On 23 April, the Blues drew 0-0 with Columbian team Athletico Junior, then four days later went down 2-1 to Independiente from Buenos Aires. The 2-1 defeat had come at the hands of a team that had two years earlier triumphed over Liverpool to lift the World Club Championship. Both results were significant, and also added to the achievement of lifting the League title in the centenary campaign.[8]

Within the club there was understandably great pride at Linfield's recent achievements as well as the long-sustained success. Outside of Blues circles, there were claims that the club's achievements were built on an unfair relationship with the Irish Football Association (IFA). Some rivals pointed to the controversial 1984 contract between Linfield and the association as indicative of a cosy relationship. This contract ensured the Northern Ireland international team would play home games at Windsor for a 104-year period. In return, Linfield would receive 15 per cent of all international gate receipts, television rights, and commercial rights from games.[9]

As soon as the ink on the contract had dried, controversy flowed forth, with supporters from other clubs querying whether this was a level playing field. One letter printed by *Ireland's Saturday Night*, in the aftermath of Linfield's centenary title articulated this grievance. A Mr McAllister of Ballymacarrett Glentoran Supporters Club, bemoaned

Linfield's dominance and linked it directly to the IFA deal. McAllister advocated a "push for a National Stadium for all sports" instead of the current arrangement, arguing that the IFA could "divide the profits of the football events equally among all the teams in the league". McAllister's sentiment was widely shared, and this ensured that the upkeep of Windsor would always be a controversial subject.[10]

During 1986 that controversy was laid bare, as debate raged over the IFA's award of £50,000 toward required ground improvements at Windsor. Stadium safety regulations had dramatically changed after the May 1985 Bradford City fire – in which 56 people died attending the Yorkshire side's Third Division match against Lincoln City. The resulting Popplewell inquiry recommended that: "the Fire Authorities should… prohibit and restrict the use of any stands, which in their view constitute a risk to spectators". At Windsor Park, this saw prohibition notices served on both the South and Railway Stands. The work on the international stadium was thus essential, yet Irish League clubs squabbled over the IFA's decision to provide one-fifth of the £250,000 needed for the upgrades.[11]

Glentoran's IFA representative David Chick queried whether "everything which is going to be done at Windsor Park will have a contribution from the IFA?" Chick argued: "Linfield derive a lot of money from the (newly built) North Stand at international games. We allowed a percentage to go to them from the seats in that stand. Now we are providing another stand from which they can get money." Chick was painting a picture of Linfield dependence which gave the Blues an unfair advantage over their competitors. This was not an accurate representation of Linfield's relationship with the IFA. As Linfield Management Committee member David Crawford indicated, the North Stand (property of the IFA) had cost the Blues £100,000. He also pointed out that during the Troubles, the Blues had kept Windsor at international standard – an onerous task in the midst of widespread civil unrest and reduced income from falling attendances. Thankfully, on this occasion, the arguments put forward by Crawford and Linfield would win the day, and the required upgrades would receive IFA funding. The controversy it had aroused though, gave an indication of just how sensitive issues around such funding could be.[12]

The required renovations were completed and the prohibition orders were lifted by the middle of August 1986. This was just in time for one of the centenary year's highlights. On 19 August, Flamengo of Brazil arrived at Windsor to take part in an exhibition game – billed as the centrepiece of the celebrations. Unfortunately Flamengo travelled without their two star attractions. Socrates and Zico – footballing royalty in Brazil, and worldwide household names after their exploits at the 1986 World Cup – were both ruled out by knee injuries. Still the Brazilian side was loaded with talent, including the 22-year-old forward Bebeto, who eight years later would be one of the stars of the 1994 Brazilian World Cup winning team.[13]

In the lead-up to the game, Roy Coyle promised: "Ulster fans are in for a treat." This was a prediction that came true, with all in attendance enjoying Flamengo's skill and technique – the Brazilians would run out 4-0 victors. For Coyle, the match was the highlight of the centenary year. He later explained, "It was a very special evening… the quality of the Brazilians… was from a different world." Goalkeeper George Dunlop was of a similar opinion, as he marvelled at how the Flamengo players could make the ball move in the air. Dunlop recalled that for one of their goals he had gone one way, only for the ball to sail the other into the net.[14]

On the pitch, there was no question that the Flamengo game had proved a success; off it, the match had been a financial disaster. The Blues had released details of the game in early May, anticipating a sell-out attendance. Yet in the days before the fixture it became apparent that the crowd might fall considerably below what was originally expected. Prior to the match, chairman David Campbell pointed out that Linfield had paid a "substantial guarantee" to Flamengo, and he was not sure if this would be recouped. The chairman commented, "If we break even financially, then we'll be happy enough." When the gate receipts were counted, however, the club was well short.

A sizable number of forged tickets were handed in at the turnstiles. Still, forgeries alone did not account for the loss of over £18,000 – all told, a crowd of 4,392 was recorded for the game. Linfield secretary Derek Brooks lamented, "It was a financial disaster. Never in our wildest dreams did we envisage a crowd of under 5,000 for a match against opposition of this calibre."[15]

Aside from their two star names who were missing, Flamengo did not possess talent that was instantly recognisable in Northern Ireland; they were never going to pack out Windsor. It was thus understandable that the game – billed as the pinnacle of the centenary year – had in financial terms proved catastrophic. In retrospect, the decision to invite the Brazilians would appear questionable and Linfield officials were obviously despondent about what had unfolded.

Then, out of the blue, came an opportunity to make some of the losses back. A couple of weeks later, Linfield received a phone call from Les Olive, secretary of Manchester United. Olive was enquiring if a match could be arranged at short notice, as United wanted a fixture to test Bryan Robson and Remi Moses in comebacks from injury. Linfield jumped at the opportunity, and less than a week after the call, the game – a third against United in five years – took place.[16]

On the night of 10 September the two clubs met, with the Blues captained by defender David Jeffrey. He had cut his teeth with the Manchester club, but after leaving United in 1982, had returned to the Province to play for the Blues. Then in the years that followed Jeffrey established himself as a no-nonsense centre-back and a crowd favourite. However, on that September night, there was little that he and his fellow defenders could do to stop the class of the Manchester side – the Reds won by a decisive 3-0 scoreline. The contrast to the flop of a few weeks earlier could not have been starker. Even at short notice, the allure of Manchester United (who were not enjoying a glorious period in their history) packed over 12,000 into Windsor. A net profit of £14,455 was raised from the game, and this would go some way to clawing back the losses from the Flamengo fiasco.[17]

When Linfield had faced United and Flamengo, they did so with nothing but pride riding on the games. The next time they faced opposition from outside the Irish League, there was much greater significance attached. As the previous season's title winners, the Blues entered the European Cup, and in the first round were paired with Rosenborg BK of Norway. When the draw was made, a naive local press was fully expectant that the Blues would win against "unknown" Rosenborg. Furthermore, Roy Coyle was in confident mood and claimed the draw "gives us the incentive to produce our best and get in among the attractive teams for the second round. I'm pretty happy."[18]

European Cup ties were two-leg affairs, and in this particular tussle Rosenborg began with the home advantage. Out in Norway Linfield lost 1-0, yet Coyle was undeterred in his belief that Linfield would progress, claiming: "the players approach the next leg in an optimistic mood – confident they can win". Unfortunately, this did not bear fruit, as the Blues failed to replicate their strong domestic showing on the European stage. At Windsor the two teams played out a 1-1 draw and Rosenborg went through to the next round with a 2-1 aggregate win.[19]

After the Blues had crashed out, Malcolm Brodie exclaimed: "Linfield have hit an all-time low." Given that he could recall many of the clubs famous European performances, his disappointment was understandable. He had after all witnessed the club make it to the quarter-finals of the 1967 European Cup and also defeat Manchester City in the 1970 Cup Winners' Cup. Brodie could thus attest to a widening gap between the Irish League and the rest of Europe in the nearly two decades that had passed since then. Yet the condemnation of such defeats was even stronger from within the club. Roy Coyle deemed Linfield's loss an abject failure, and reflected: "Players just looked on European football as a bonus for winning the League. They looked at it as a wee trip away for a few days in a different country. I don't think they took it that seriously… We should have been doing better, no question about that."[20]

The charge that players could have given more and prepared with greater diligence might have had some truth in it. On the other hand, progression past the early rounds of European competition was an extremely tall order. Linfield were competing with teams on a different level. There was professionalism at Rosenborg that the Blues could not match. Rosenborg were backed by local businesses and trained five times a week. The Norwegians had the luxury of club cars and the use of facilities that surpassed those that Linfield could offer. George Dunlop recalled conversations with Rosenborg players who explained they were allowed out of their work to train. That did not happen at Linfield. There was not the backing to operate on such a level. The likes of Rosenborg may have at first sight appeared an easy draw, but in reality the Norwegians were on a much stronger footing than the Blues.[21]

Linfield's 1986/87 European involvement was a chastening experience, but solace was soon found on the return to domestic football. After a shaky start, the Blues were once again top of the League by 1 January 1987. From then until the end of the Gibson Cup campaign (as the League title is otherwise known), only one game was lost. That loss came on 10 January, in an away fixture at Coleraine. The match against Coleraine stood out for two reasons. Firstly, it was the club's only defeat during an impressive three-month spell. Secondly, an attendance of 7,000 was recorded – the largest at a domestic game in Coleraine for a decade. Both home and away, the Blues were enjoying considerable support. Windsor's South Stand was regularly filled to capacity and *Look at Linfield* was encouraging supporters to arrive at games "early to ensure a seat". Whilst crowds across the League were falling, the numbers recorded at the Coleraine game – and at Windsor – were testament to the pulling power of a strong Linfield team.[22]

Cheered on by this sizeable support, Linfield captured a sixth straight Gibson Cup. The achievement was both remarkable and groundbreaking. No Irish League side had ever before won six successive titles. Coyle's mid-1980s side was thus setting new standards, and – it must be stressed – the success was fully deserved.

As George Dunlop maintained, the Blues got the simple things right: "We had a good squad of players, we were strong at the back, and we had the likes of Martin McGaughey upfront scoring goals for fun." Lee Doherty concurred with Dunlop's summation, stressing that this Linfield side "had players who were able to consistently perform, they knew how to win… The team had the desire to compete, right through the 90 minutes and beyond." Martin McGaughey maintained that there were no "weaknesses in the team… in every position we had the first or second best player in the League", and furthermore there was a great rapport in the squad. Masterminding it all was Roy Coyle, a man who club captain David Jeffrey described as "driven, absolutely driven". The Linfield team of the mid-1980s was both fearsome and well drilled – the success they achieved was no accident.[23]

The Blues had clinched the title with a 6-0 victory over Distillery on 7 February, during what was the penultimate week of the League programme. In a farcical state of affairs, the administrators of the local game had decided that the Gibson Cup would conclude with three months of the season still to be played! There was no apparent logic to the scheduling, and *Look at Linfield* quite rightly queried the decision that left "clubs three months to chase after less prestigious and appealing trophies". Going further, the editorial called the governance of local football into question, maintaining that "there has been far too much tampering with the traditional format of the game in recent years". For example, during the previous campaign the Irish League had slapped a ban on 3pm kick-offs. Ruling that clubs were not allowed to make use of floodlights, the League decreed that all kick-offs were to take place at 2:30pm. Yet when this proved financially disastrous, the 3pm time was reinstated. Governance of the local game seemed devoid of any planning, and the criticism that came its way was justified.[24]

During the surreal final three months of the season, the Blues endured indifferent results. Linfield fell to Coleraine at the first hurdle in the Irish Cup. Then in the Gold Cup the team made the final, only to suffer defeat to rivals Glentoran. Success would eventually arrive right at the very end of the campaign. On 9 May, a scrappy win over Crusaders brought the League Cup back to Windsor. Yet instead of revelling in the triumph, keeper George Dunlop spoke out afterwards, bemoaning the season's calendar. Dunlop maintained: "It is wrong to have such a tournament at the end of the season… the players have become stale. It is unfair to… the public and the players… This season has been a daft one – absolutely ridiculous, and it is ruining the game." Without League games, the domestic season had drifted along for three months. Dunlop could thus barely muster the enthusiasm to celebrate the club's success. Instead he was more concerned with the poor administration of the local game.[25]

The fixture programme for that 1986/87 campaign was absurd. However, setting aside the timing of it all, there were questions to be asked about the value that the lesser competitions added to the local game. Linfield had in the past rightly boasted about their two Clean Sweeps – when they lifted seven trophies. That said, the League title and the Irish Cup were by far and away the two most important pieces of silverware. During the 1986/87 campaign, the Blues played a total of

61 games, and less than half of these had come in either the League or the Irish Cup. The fact that the local game seemed to be flooded with unimportant matches was a major problem.

Football as a 'good' – something that spectators pay to watch – has always been built on habit. Thus as crowds were falling across the board, it would have been an idea to streamline the sport. Instead of prizing quantity over quality and turning people off, the Irish League should have been proactive about protecting its currency. This was of course what the English Premier League did when it came into existence in the early 1990s. The top flight was reduced from 22 teams to 20, and the commercial success that was partly generated by a less congested fixture list was clear for all to see. In Northern Ireland the local game seemed to limp on without addressing a major issue. In the early 1980s there were calls in *Look at Linfield* to consider the "glut of games". Ten years later, the programme was still lamenting the demands of "fulfilling… additional fixtures in knock-out competitions".[26]

If frustration had characterised the end of the 1986/87 season, Linfield's 19-year-old forward George O'Boyle was experiencing very different emotions. Having just finished his first campaign with the club – during which he hit 20 goals in 46 games – O'Boyle had been snapped up by French side Bordeaux. The striker signed a three-year deal with a flat and a car thrown in as sweeteners. The only downside for O'Boyle was that he didn't have a driving licence. Upon signing his contract, he quipped: "My priority now is to get lessons in Belfast before I leave."[27]

Two significant things can be drawn out of O'Boyle's move to the continent. In the first place, it came about because of a friendly game against the French side – and such matches were very common at this time. During their centenary season, Linfield had played against Sunderland, Newcastle United, Flamengo, Manchester United, Tottenham Hotspur and Bordeaux. The club had also twice toured North America. Secondly, O'Boyle's move to a team in the top flight of a much-respected league was not out of the ordinary back then. In December 1985, defender Darrin Coyle transferred to Everton in the English First Division. Then in March 1988, reserve goalkeeper Tommy Wright also made the move to the English First Division with Newcastle United. On a regular basis, managers of top European teams were prepared to take a chance on Linfield players. The club could thus pride itself on the esteem in which its players were held. Indeed, the

Blues could boast of an international presence in the mid-1980s. For all the negativity around football in the Province and beyond, Linfield commanded respect on the world stage.[28]

Chapter 2

# *Out of Africa*

The sale of players such as George O'Boyle to the likes of Bordeaux indicated a healthy respect for the top performers in the Irish League. On the other hand, the stagnation of clubs like Linfield in European competition was doing little to enhance the overall reputation of the League. Unfortunately this was a well-established trend by the mid-1980s – despite the consternation of the local press at most European losses. Furthermore it was clear to see – at least for those who were prepared to accept the glaring realities – that the stagnation would continue. Whether the established trend of Linfield dominance of the local game would also continue was another matter altogether.

After the scheduling farce of the 1986/87 season, local football's calendar returned to a more recognisable format the following year. The League campaign would stretch right to the end of April and not to late winter. Regrettably this did not mean that the administrators of the local game would fare any better in promoting Irish League interests. One game in Linfield's early-season fixtures stood out for all the wrong reasons, and made embarrassing national headlines. On 25 August 1987, the Blues played away to Coleraine in the quarter-finals of the Ulster Cup. The Bannsiders would win by the odd goal in a 3-2 scoreline. That 'goal', supposedly headed into his own net by Linfield forward Stephen Baxter, was odd in more ways than one. As Ulster Television commentator Jackie Fullerton maintained: "It wasn't a goal... The ball went over the bar, hit the top and went down the back... incredible."[1]

Over the coming days the local press was awash with comment on the incident. Linfield called for a replay of the game, arguing that all "fair-minded soccer people... will agree that we were terribly wronged". Yet the Irish League and IFA stood by referee Andy Ritchie, who had awarded the goal. League secretary Mervyn Brown stated that, "A decision made by the referee on points of fact connected with play shall be final so far as the result of the game is concerned." David Bowen, the secretary of the IFA, backed Ritchie and sympathising with referees, he maintained they "had to make a split second decision", adding that there was no place for "trials by television".[2]

Bowen was reacting against a fuss that had understandably been kicked up by the Blues and the local press. Yet this was small fry compared to the exposure the incident was soon receiving on UK-wide television. On the Saturday that followed the tie, footage of the 'goal' appeared on the ITV show 'Saint and Greavsie'. The programme, hosted by former players Ian St John and Jimmy Greaves, was popular with football fans across the nation, though at times it was criticised for its irreverent look at the footballing world. Their light-hearted approach gave way to accusations that the pair trivialised the game, and this was very much the view of Irish League president, John Crossen. He reacted furiously to the airing of the 'goal', complaining that the "only time Irish soccer is shown nationally is when there is something controversial".[3]

Clearly not a believer that all publicity was good publicity, the Irish League president slapped a ban on Ulster Television (part of the ITV network) cameras at local grounds. This lasted all of 24 hours, as an apology – with an assurance that the likes of this would not happen again – was forthcoming. UTV cameras were allowed back, but the whole debacle was far from edifying. Indeed, Crossen's knee-jerk move to block a media network displayed far more than a lack of humour – shutting down publicity indicated that there was a shortage of both foresight and awareness at the top of the Irish League.[4]

Unfortunately, this lack of awareness seemed to characterise Irish League perceptions of where Northern Irish football stood at the time. For the second season running, the Blues drew Norwegian opposition in the European Cup, and once again, misplaced optimism reared its head. In the 1987/88 edition of Europe's premier tournament, Linfield were pitted against Lillestrom, with Roy Coyle predicting that his team had "every chance of getting a good result". A first leg 1-1 draw away from home seemed to lend some credence to that confidence. Yet in Belfast, Coyle's men went down 4-2. In the aftermath, Coyle lamented that his side had "committed football suicide", whilst captain David Jeffrey wondered, "When will we ever learn?"[5]

Experiencing defeat was never easy, and the frustration expressed was only to be expected. That said, once again, Linfield were competing against a club with greater resources and a more professional set-up. Scandinavian football was progressing to another level, whilst Irish League football was standing still. In retrospect, it should have come as no surprise that players from a part-time club could not match professional opposition. Yet the expectations on local sides gave no consideration to the realities that they were facing. With this mindset, and without the resources to compete, the Blues (and the rest of the part-time Irish League) were destined to stagnate at European level.

The disappointment dealt by defeat was not the only concern of Linfield's 1987/88 European foray. On two separate occasions the Windsor fixture was stopped when a stone then a bottle were aimed at Lillestrom keeper Arne Amundsem. IFA secretary and UEFA member David Bowen predicted that the incidents could result in a fine of approximately £1,000, but this was wildly off the mark. Linfield were handed a two-game home ban in European competition, with a stipulation that these matches would take place at least 150 kilometres (over 90 miles) from Belfast. Linfield's next two 'home' European games would thus take place outside Northern Ireland, and the Blues would lose out on major revenue. Complaining that the club was paying a heavy price for the actions of "a few mindless morons", chairman David Campbell estimated the ban would result in a loss of £50,000.[6]

When Linfield returned to domestic duties, the fallout from what had essentially been a disastrous European campaign left a gloom over the club. Indeed, success in the shape of a Gold Cup did little to extinguish the pervading sense of dejection. This was especially the case as the Blues were enduring an indifferent start to the League. However, in Troubles-afflicted Northern Ireland, the events on a sports pitch would all too often pale into insignificance against the sectarian slaughter that was taking place. During the autumn of 1987, the Province experienced one particularly dark day. On 8 November, the Provisional IRA set off a bomb in Enniskillen beside the town's war memorial. The attack happened at 10:45am, minutes before the beginning of the town's annual Remembrance Sunday ceremony. In total 11 people were killed and a further 63 injured in the resulting carnage. These events greatly impacted upon Glentoran and Northern Ireland midfielder Jim Cleary, who hailed from Enniskillen and knew some of the victims. Struck by the devastation, he resolved to help by bringing Linfield and the wider Irish League family on board in a benefit match. Cleary organised a fundraiser that pitted a combined Glentoran and Linfield team against an Irish League select.[7]

On the evening of 3 December, the game took place at Windsor and the 'Big Two' side emerged with a 7-1 victory. Cleary's help in the aftermath of the bomb demonstrated the positive impact the Irish League could have during the bleak days of the Troubles. The funds raised by the game gave practical assistance to those directly impacted by the catastrophe. More than this, the gesture demonstrated that local football was at times a release from a depressing climate of fear. This is not to say that it escaped from the cultural baggage of the Troubles. Critics of the game in Northern Ireland were never shy about pointing a condemnatory finger at the ills of local football; sectarian chanting being an obvious manifestation of this. Nevertheless, the game carried on through the worst of times, providing welcome respite away from the madness of sectarian butchery.[8]

Normal competitive service resumed after the fundraising game, and it was the two teams that had come together to face the Irish League select that fought it out for the title. By the New Year, the Blues had weathered their early-season poor form, and when they faced off against Glentoran on 16 January 1988, they sat in second place, just one point behind the East Belfast side. Going into the showdown, Glentoran keeper Alan Paterson was protecting a 10-match run of clean sheets. Nevertheless, Linfield were able to breach his goal on two occasions, and at the start of the second half held a 2-1 lead. That was before referee Alan Snoddy called a halt to proceedings in inclement weather. Fog had rendered conditions unplayable and the game was abandoned, meaning that a relieved Paterson still had his clean-sheet record intact. He reflected afterwards: "I'm beginning to think we might lead a charmed life this season."[9]

The luck Paterson spoke of was certainly to the fore in the rearranged fixture. On the evening of 2 February, Windsor was again beset by horrific weather conditions. This time, the game was played to conclusion, and ended with a 2-0 victory for Glentoran. Writing in the *Belfast News Letter* (hereafter referred to as the *News Letter*), Denis O'Hara questioned the logic of completing that fixture, whilst the *Belfast Telegraph* reported that a "gale howled [and] the rain cascaded in Niagara torrents". Whether or not the match should have finished, all that mattered was that Glentoran had taken the initiative in the title race.[10]

Having won six straight League titles, Coyle and his Linfield team were not going to relinquish the Gibson Cup without a fight. There were still 12 League games remaining, and in these, Linfield managed 10 victories, one draw and succumbed to only one defeat. This fine run took the title race to the last day of the campaign, but alas it was in vain. Glentoran held their nerve and took the title to East Belfast. To compound the misery for Linfield fans, the Glens added the Irish Cup to complete a Double. For the first time since 1980/81, no major trophy would reside at Windsor Park, and this was considered a failure. To quote *Look at Linfield*, it was "simply not good enough".[11]

In light of the side's failings, Coyle promised to revitalise his squad with new players. Furthermore, he stated an intention to look outside the local game, maintaining: "I just won't be held to ransom by other Irish League managers." His search took him to Belgium, where he watched a friendly in which Club Brugge KV were showcasing players for loan moves. Two players caught Coyle's eye, and he recommended that the Blues acquired both for the following season. Over the weeks that followed the club chased up deals for the two, and in early June, one of them – Abdeli Khammal, a 20-year-old winger from Morocco – was secured. Khammal would soon acquire the nickname 'Sam' from teammates on account of hailing from Casablanca. In the 1942 romantic drama *Casablanca*, the character 'Isla Lund' uttered the phrase "play it Sam" when asking a piano player and singer to perform 'As Time Goes By'. Isla's words – often misquoted as "play it again Sam" – entered popular culture, and gave the young winger his nickname.[12]

Roy Coyle described Khammal as being "in a different class from anything in the Irish League". This was enough to whet the appetite of fans for the new season ahead, yet there was more to come that June day. Another transfer coup (unconnected with the Belgium scouting trip) was secured, with former forward George O'Boyle signing on loan. O'Boyle's side Bordeaux had just finished second in the French league and were buying in new talent. Realising his opportunities would be limited, the Shankill Road man resolved to come home for the year. Given that O'Boyle was a known quantity, and Coyle's praise for Khammal was effusive, there was a flurry of excitement that greeted both recruitments. This though, was nothing compared with the stir caused by the signing of Antoine ('Tony') Coly, a 24-year-old Senegalese international.[13]

Coly was the second Club Brugge KV player that Coyle had recommended, and news of his joining was relayed on Monday 4 July. Six days later, one of the Sunday papers led with a front page 'exclusive' on the deal. The *Sunday News* plastered "A TWELFTH WEEKEND MESSAGE FOR LINFIELD FANS" headline that screamed: "YOUR NEW STAR IS A CATHOLIC!" Mike Scrivener of the paper warned that Coly faced a "hot reception from the soccer club's true blue fans". The journalist backed up his story with a quote from an unnamed supporters club committee member who thought that the signing would be unpopular with fans, as "We were under the impression that [Coly] wasn't a Catholic." When a bewildered Roy Coyle read the newspaper, his first thought was that the club had signed a player without informing him. Coyle was unaware of Coly's faith, and "didn't ask the lad, 'By the way what religion are you?'". Coyle never ascertained a player's place of worship before a transfer took place, and he was never instructed to do so. That said, Coly's arrival at Windsor Park was significant. Linfield had not fielded a Catholic player since well before the Troubles began.[14]

According to local journalist Denis O'Hara, the gates at Windsor had "slammed shut… on Catholic players" at the end of the 1940s. Before then Linfield could list a host of Catholics that had turned out for the club. Yet their representation on the playing staff was virtually non-existent in the 40 years that followed. O'Hara explained that there was one notable exception to this: Imre Hidvegi – a Hungarian who had turned out for Linfield Swifts. Hidvegi was a refugee fleeing in the aftermath of the 1956 Hungarian Uprising. This revolt against Soviet domination of the country was short-lived, and soon after the protests began, tanks rolled into Budapest, delivering brutal repression, with thousands killed. Approximately 200,000 were, however, lucky enough to escape as refugees, and Hidvegi was one of them. He made his way to the Northern Irish seaside town of Bangor, and was part of a group who ended up in the town's Crofton Hotel. It was here Hidvegi divulged his footballing pedigree, telling staff that back home he was a member of the Budapest club Honved. Upon hearing this, a member of staff informed him, "You must go to Linfield." Heeding the advice, Hidvegi headed to Windsor, and gained a place with the Swifts. He would spend two years with them before transferring to Cliftonville.[15]

Hidvegi's involvement aside, no Catholic had played for Linfield since the late 1940s. The signing of Coly was therefore significant. In

Northern Ireland, the politics of religion and identity mattered, and Linfield had received considerable criticism for its record on fielding Catholic players. Local entertainer James Young famously poked fun at this with his novelty song, 'I'm the only Catholic in the Linfield team'. The 40 years without Catholic representation in the first team, allied to the club's Protestant/unionist identity, had thus led to accusations that the club was sectarian.

Critics who maintained that Linfield was sectarian drew parallels with Glasgow Rangers. At the time of Coly's move to Linfield, no Catholic had represented Rangers since the 1920s. By the second half of the twentieth century this was a phenomenon that, according to journalist Ronnie Esplin and academic Graham Walker, was "widely perceived as unacceptably discriminatory". However, things were soon to change at Rangers, with the 'Souness Revolution' transforming the Gers on and off the field. In July 1989, Souness stunned the footballing world with the signing of Maurice 'Mo' Johnston. Johnston was Catholic and joined from French side Nantes. The news sent the media into a frenzy. Yet despite some isolated histrionics, the vast majority of supporters took the transfer in their stride. Fans voted with their feet as they packed out Ibrox to witness Johnston and Rangers claim the 1989/90 league title. At the start of that season Souness had been warmly received at the club AGM, when he explained that he bought Johnston to cement Rangers' position as Scotland's top team. Alan Montgomery, Rangers' chief executive, was afforded a similar reception when he articulated that sectarianism in Scotland was not confined to football. Montgomery maintained that religious bigotry was a societal issue that stemmed from separate schooling.[16]

Glasgow Rangers was confident in asserting its position during the media circus that had resulted from the Johnston signing. The same was not the case for Linfield during the furore caused by the *Sunday News* story. Officials at the Blues were uncomfortable in making comment on the religious angle of the Coly transfer. A week after the *Sunday News* headlines, the paper complained that Linfield had "BLACKBALLED" their reporters. A disgruntled article stated: "Club secretary Derek Brooks was said to be 'not available' to Sunday News." The shunning of reporters was indicative of the club's reluctance to engage in discussion on this sensitive subject. Instead of rebutting claims that the club operated a sectarian transfer policy, Linfield officials kept their counsel.

The silence on the matter left a vacuum for others to consolidate a narrative that portrayed the club in an uncomplimentary light.[17]

After riding out the *Sunday News* controversy with silence, the focus at Linfield switched to locating a ground for European 'home' games. The Blues – who had qualified for the 1988/89 UEFA Cup on account of their previous season's second-place finish – needed to find an alternative home venue, given the ban issued after the Lillestrom defeat. The club looked in England, Scotland, Belgium and the Netherlands, but drew a blank. During the trying search, chairman David Campbell admitted to feeling "completely despondent [over] the entire issue". Then with less than a month until European commitments were due to get underway, Wrexham FC stepped into the breach, offering use of their Racecourse Ground. The gesture from Wrexham was much appreciated, but considering the Blues had drawn unfashionable Turun Palloseura of Turku in Finland, the financial implications looked disastrous. The costs of travelling to Turku (about 100 miles west of the capital Helsinki) were, according to *Ireland's Saturday Night*, "astronomical". When the expenses of playing the 'home' tie in Wales were added, the club would rack up nearly £30,000 worth of debt. This was a hefty price to pay for a venture that ultimately ended in elimination on the away-goals rule.[18]

Once again Europe provided no joy for the Blues, but domestically Linfield were resurgent in 1988/89, and the two African players were central to this. Right from the off that season, 'Sam' Khammal was flaunting speed and trickery on the wing. The Moroccan had jumped at the chance to play for Linfield, and settled very quickly into Northern Irish life. His performances earned him the 'Guinness Player of the Month' award for September and high praise from his manager. Roy Coyle explained that: "Normally when you get foreign players with language difficulties they find it hard… However Sam has been able to cope with the situation. He is a good player and quite a character… The fans… have really taken to him and his mate Tony Coly."[19]

Both were flourishing in the Irish League and the pair revelled in the team spirit at Windsor. On and off the pitch, they were greatly appreciated by their teammates. David Jeffrey described the pair as "two fantastic lads", whilst Lee Doherty singled out Coly for his outgoing character and infectious humour. Doherty recalled that after games Coly joined teammates at 'Pip's International' on the Dublin Road, lighting up the place with his personality (but also with a resplendent white suit).[20]

Coly and Khammal would collect their first pieces of silverware on the evening of 1 November 1988. That night, Linfield defeated Portadown 1-0 in the Gold Cup final. A Lindsay McKeown penalty separated the two teams, though in the following day's press it was the two African players who stole the headlines. Malcolm Brodie peppered his *Belfast Telegraph* report with superlatives describing the players. Khammal was commended for "his wing artistry, his control, his pace, his dazzling runs and those perfect tantalising crosses". Then turning the attention to Coly, the veteran journalist extolled how the Senegalese player "strolls… and struts majestically around the pitch yet with a purpose… study his movements closely and you'll notice he never wastes a ball. Don't expect him to be in a game for 90 minutes but when he does move into action he does so with great effectiveness and such a graceful way."[21]

At the end of November the two players would line up in another decider. Unfortunately in this instance, in the League Cup final against Glentoran, they did not have the same impact. In front of a 10,000-strong crowd, the Glens took the cup in bizarre circumstances. With just four minutes left on the clock and the match level at 1-1, Glentoran keeper Alan Paterson punted the ball high into the Belfast sky; it bounced once in Linfield's half and in doing so looped over the head of stranded keeper George Dunlop to finish in the net. The *Irish News* hailed the goal as a "DREAM WINNER". For Dunlop it was a nightmare blunder. Inconsolable after defeat, he lamented, "I can't go on costing the club trophies... I feel like calling it quits." His opposite number, Alan Paterson, was in no mood to gloat. As a fellow member of the 'goalkeepers' union', Paterson held that Dunlop was "too good a goalkeeper to contemplate packing it in". Importantly, Roy Coyle was in agreement and maintained full confidence in his keeper, refusing to drop him. Indeed, during the following month Dunlop went on to record his 500th appearance in a Linfield shirt.[22]

Dunlop's reaction was only to be expected. The freakish nature of the winner was never going to be easy for a goalkeeper to live down. Yet in the days after Glentoran's triumph, it was not his howler that dominated the post-match analysis. Instead, it was the actions of Glentoran supporters in the home stands that came under considerable scrutiny. Throughout the 90 minutes of football, bananas and mandarin oranges rained down on the pitch. The projectiles were aimed at Khammal and Coly, the two non-white players on the field, with the *Belfast Telegraph* reporting that they had endured "a virtual 90 minute banana-throwing onslaught [on top of] jeering and taunting". Coly's performance was notably below par and in the 66th minute he had been substituted.[23]

Condemnation of the abuse was swift. Officials from both clubs, as well as the press, launched scathing attacks on those who had jeered and pelted the players with objects. In the denunciations, two themes were prominent. Firstly, there was little surprise that the racial abuse had taken place. Secondly however, there was shock at the sheer amount of fruit thrown. Blues chairman David Campbell admitted that he "expected it could have happened, perhaps when the teams were running out or at the finish", but he had not anticipated the sustained nature of the antagonism. Glentoran chairman John Crossen added: "[I thought] maybe they would have their fun at the start, but that wasn't the case."[24]

The League Cup final at the Oval was the first Big Two matchup of the season. This meant it was the first time that Coly and Khammal had faced Glentoran, and this played a role in the sustained abuse – reminiscent of that endured by English player John Barnes in his first Merseyside derby. After moving to Liverpool in the summer of 1987, the winger experienced his first game against Everton on 28 October, at home in the League Cup. The third-round tie was settled in Everton's favour, but the evening was remembered for the behaviour of the crowd. Each time Barnes received the ball he was met with a chorus of boos, and he was showered with spit and bananas when he ventured in front of the Everton support. As the authors of *The Changing Face of Football* have stated, "It was precisely the fact that John Barnes was making his *first* appearance in a Merseyside derby that encouraged the… response he received."[25]

The ferocity of abuse Barnes would suffer in subsequent Liverpool games never matched his derby debut. Similarly, the torrent of abuse that Coly and Khammal experienced at the Oval in late November was never replicated (though that is not to say they would never again endure racist taunts). The high-profile nature of both games, and the historical lack of black players in the respective derbies, had combined to create the infamous atmospheres at the Oval and Anfield. It must be pointed out that the experiences of Coly and Khammal were not unique at Irish League grounds. Joey Cunningham, who turned out for Portadown, regularly suffered taunts. Cunningham endured verbal abuse and was also pelted with bananas on numerous occasions.

For Cunningham, racial abuse from the stands was a weekly occurrence, and as was also the case in England at the time, it was considered 'part of the game'. Paul Elliot who played for Celtic and Chelsea maintained it was something this generation of black players simply had to "put up with". Those who abused black players did so safe in the knowledge that in the main, no consequences would follow. Yet the high-profile nature of a League Cup final was a different matter. Six weeks after the game, the IFA slapped a £250 fine on Glentoran and warned the club about the future conduct of its supporters. Furthermore, an IFA committee stated that future misdemeanours could "result in [Glentoran] being refused permission to play in

Europe". Though the likelihood of the IFA following through on such a threat was minimal. Back then there was no appetite amongst football authorities to stamp out this sort of behaviour. The English FA (one of the first footballing authorities to tackle the issue) did not make a concerted effort to rid the game of racism until the mid-1990s.[26]

Football in Northern Ireland effectively turned a blind eye to racism, and this was abundantly clear in the way in which match sponsors made light of the events. Shortly after the final, Linfield travelled to Larne for a League game sponsored by the well-known razor blade manufacturing company, Wilkinson Sword. During half-time, representatives of the company threw more than 500 Wilkinson razors into the crowd as an advertising gimmick. Wilkinson's Northern Ireland manager, John Woods, joked: "It's better than banana skins, isn't it? Really, I thought it would be a nice gesture to the punter considering the bad publicity the game has been getting." Woods was right to highlight the "bad publicity" local football had received. Yet his gimmick belittled the seriousness of the crowd's actions that late November night.[27]

A *Look at Linfield* interview questioned Coly about how that night had impacted on him, and his answer was brief. He stated that he had never witnessed anything quite like it, and went on to say he was "more determined than ever to do his best for the Club". Coly was good to his word. In the second half of the season he was a standout performer, scoring eight goals including memorable long-range strikes against Ards, Larne and Glentoran, as well as contributing with numerous assists. He was a flair player who brought something unique onto the pitch. At times other members of the team were frustrated that he didn't care so much for tackling or tracking back, and it was not uncommon for exasperated teammates to give Coly an earful. Yet invariably his response was, "Feed me chocolate." According to Lee Doherty, this translated as, "Be nice and I'll play better." Coly was a luxury player, but he played in a team that allowed him to express himself.[28]

There was balance throughout the side – many of the players had, of course, been part of the team that had won six consecutive Leagues. At the back, the Blues had the significant experience of George Dunlop, then in front of him were players of considerable quality. Captain David Jeffrey, Darrin Coyle and Lindsay McKeown were rocks at the heart of the defence, whilst fullbacks Alan Dornan and Paul Mooney complemented this strong defensive line-up. In the midfield, Lee

Doherty held play together. His hard work allowed Khammal, Coly and Sid Burrows to take the game to opponents. Then up front, Stephen

Baxter contributed 28 goals, whilst George O'Boyle netted 19 times. And of course, as was always the case, Martin McGaughey weighed in with his fair share. He scored 26 times that year. Remarkably, almost a quarter of Linfield's goals during the 1980s came via McGaughey![29]

With quality throughout the team, Linfield comfortably won the League. The Championship was secured away to Glenavon on 15 April, with three games still to play. A McGaughey strike at Mourneview made sure of the win and brought the Gibson Cup back to Windsor. With the title won, George Dunlop became the first player in Irish League history to collect nine League Championship winners' medals. Indeed his manager, Roy Coyle, had won a staggering 10 Leagues in just 12 seasons.

In normal circumstances, the away dressing room would have hosted an almighty party. Coyle and his players had put right the disappointment of the previous season. Yet macabre events in Yorkshire on 15 April 1989 overshadowed the Gibson Cup triumph. As Linfield players left the Mourneview pitch, they learned of horrifying reports coming from Hillsborough Stadium in Sheffield. That afternoon, police crowd mismanagement during the FA Cup semi-final between Liverpool and Nottingham Forest had led to tragedy. Ninety-six men, women and children never returned home from a game of football. The full horror of the events was not clear by 5pm on the Saturday afternoon, but enough was known to end a party atmosphere.[30]

As the season closed, Linfield supporters were anxious to learn whether Coly and Khammal would return for another year. Sadly this would not come to fruition – there was no option from Brugge for another year of their services. Coyle thanked the two players in the press, and paid tribute to each individually: "Khammal was exciting, like a breath of fresh air... Coly made a great impact in quite a few matches, scored some memorable goals, but above all he introduced techniques to the players they hadn't known." Blues chairman David Campbell was equally effusive, and proudly stated: "At Linfield we introduced something new, something different into Irish League football... I think the two players gave a lot of people much enjoyment."[31]

Khammal and Coly thus left as crowd favourites, but it was expected that the holes they left in the team would be filled by the start of the following campaign.

Chapter 3

# *Sixes and Seven*

Having won eight League titles and two Irish Cups during the 1980s, it was safe to say that Linfield were the team of the decade. Directing their achievement throughout was manager Roy Coyle. He had assumed

charge of the club in 1975, and though success was not immediate, within a few seasons he had brought a winning mentality to the Blues. By the end of 1988/89 he had amassed 30 trophies at the club. Indeed, that final full season of the decade proved particularly memorable. The Blues dominated the League and won the title playing attractive football. However, two of the stars of the campaign, midfielders Abdeli Khammal and Antoine Coly, left in the immediate aftermath. Later that summer another key loan player, forward George O'Boyle, followed them out of the club, in his case to join Dunfermline. Replacing the likes of Coly, Khammal and O'Boyle would be a tall order.[1]

Supporters waited patiently, wondering who would take the place of the players that had left. Then less than a week before the 1989/90 season began, Linfield made a double signing. On 14 August, the Blues announced the capture of Algerian players Hocine Yahi and

Abderrahmeme Dehnoun. Both were signed on a full-time basis. *Look at Linfield* described the pair as "highly accomplished with wide experience in the game"; Yahi had represented Algeria on 50 occasions, including at the World Cup finals in 1982. Coyle extolled: "Both play the game [in] the European style, with techniques and flair that set them apart." The Blues boss was especially hopeful that their experience would aid the club's performance in Europe. Yet one week before the first round of the European Cup, Linfield lost Yahi to injury. Cartilage damage sustained during training ruled the player out for at least two months. This compounded what was an already stern test – the Blues had to contend with Dnipro Dnipropetrovsk from the USSR (modern-day Ukraine). John Laverty, writing in the *Belfast Telegraph*, commented that Linfield faced "a little known – and virtually unpronounceable – side on a mission impossible".[2]

Linfield would 'host' Dnipro in the first leg of the tie on 13 September. Like the season before, the Blues availed themselves of Wrexham's hospitality and played the fixture at the Racecourse Ground. Going into what was the club's 50th game in European competition, though its first against Soviet opposition, Roy Coyle stated: "You do not become Russian champions unless you are a good team… they are an outstanding side." Unsurprisingly then, Dnipro emerged with a win; that said, Linfield had managed to keep the score down to a respectable 2-1. Malcolm Brodie, contending that the Blues were lucky to emerge with such a scoreline, wrote in the *Belfast Telegraph* that the Soviet side was on a "different planet… certainly the best I've seen against Irish opposition in Europe". Given Brodie's many years following local football, that assessment was high praise. The *News Letter* commented that Dnipro gave Linfield "a soccer lesson", and added that there "was no sign of the Glasnost spirit". '*Glasnost*' was a byword that referred to the greater openness and democracy that was taking hold in the Soviet Union. This in conjunction with reform of communism – '*perestroika*' – was dramatically changing the governance of the USSR and would ultimately herald its break-up. Linfield's game against Ukrainian opposition had thus come at a seminal juncture in Soviet and Ukrainian history.[3]

For the second leg, the journey to the Ukraine was an odyssey. The team left Belfast on Sunday 24 September for London Heathrow, where they waited four and a half hours before catching a flight to West

Berlin. There was then an overnight stay, followed by a coach ride which crossed the city's infamous Wall and arrived at Schönefeld airport

in East Berlin. Goalkeeper George Dunlop commented that there were significant changes as they travelled into the communist-controlled part of the city, and was struck by the cars on the far side of the city. Dunlop pointed out that in the West, "there were BMWs and Audis, then on the

other side there were Ladas". As the party journeyed across the city, the West's prosperity set against the poverty in the East came into view.[4]

From Schönefeld airport there was then an almost three-hour flight to Kiev, where the team would sample Soviet food for the first time. Derek Brooks recorded that this consisted of "cheese, salami, bread, chocolate, wafer biscuit, mineral water and tea or coffee, but without milk". For many, it was not to their liking. David Jeffrey described the food on the trip as "something else!" A short bus journey then followed to a domestic airport for a one-hour flight to Dnipropetrovsk. It was only by about midnight on Monday 25 September that the travel-weary Linfield party arrived at their hotel.[5]

The city of Dnipropetrovsk had been closed to foreigners until 1988, which made the venture quite an experience. Lee Doherty described the time in Ukraine as "the biggest eye-opener on a European trip". The team hotel was a former apartment block and it was basic. According to Doherty, the shower was "just a copper pipe with some water dripping out of it". Conditions were tough, but demonstrative of this *Glasnost* era the Ukrainian welcome was warm. Malcolm Brodie, who had visited the USSR on seven occasions, reported: "No team has ever had the red carpet rolled out for them quite like the Blues." Players were asked for photographs and autographs throughout the trip. The club's honorary treasurer, David Crawford, exclaimed: "The friendship of the [Ukrainians]... has amazed me".[6]

On the pitch, Dnipro would again emerge victorious, this time by a 1-0 scoreline. As in the first game, the result was not reflective of proceedings: the Ukrainians dominated from start to finish. In the days after defeat, a reflective Martin McGaughey pondered the merits of competing in European competition. The striker commented: "It's great to qualify for Europe. You hope to get a few days' enjoyment out of it, but these Eastern bloc countries provide nothing." Given all that McGaughey and his teammates had gone through, the reaction was understandable. Travel gripes were though, far from the only worry for the club after the tie. Just fulfilling the fixtures was a "concern" for the club's Finance Committee. In the two seasons that Linfield endured the European home ban, the club had incurred debts of £70,000. *Look at Linfield* acknowledged the high financial risks involved in European football, but argued that these were outweighed by the "opportunities... for Irish League players to raise their game and for fans to witness a higher grade of soccer". The programme was right to highlight the positives, but European football was definitely hard for local teams to compete in.[7]

Worryingly, domestic form was mirroring the depressing financial outlook after Europe. Linfield had begun the season as "odds-on" favourites for another League title, but performances in the first half of the season were indifferent. The Blues suffered comprehensive defeats in the season's first two clashes with Glentoran. A 4-0 thumping at Windsor in the League Cup followed a 3-1 loss in the Ulster Cup. Discontent and unease were prevalent on the terraces, even when the team won, demanding fans were deriding the manager and players. The

*News Letter* described the Windsor atmosphere as "puzzling and perplexing". Boos rang out even when victories were secured. Fans were not witnessing the dominant form that had brought 10 League trophies in 12 years, and criticism grew.[8]

A Gold Cup triumph in late autumn, which gave Coyle a staggering 31st trophy as manager, brought some respite, but it could not hide the fact that the club was enduring a crisis. Losing 3-1 to Glenavon on 2 December signalled the first time that Linfield had endured three successive home defeats in 14 years. This was soon followed by another loss to Glentoran, on this occasion in a Big Two Boxing Day game that had once again (after an 11-year absence) become part of the fixture list. All the passion and excitement of a Big Two was on show, but Linfield could not manage a win. Glentoran made the most of the home advantage and took the victory 3-2.[9]

At the turn of the year, Coyle expressed sympathy with the Linfield support. The manager explained that he and the players understood "why the fans [were] so unhappy" and stressed: "We are not enjoying the situation." Fan frustration was of course borne out of the faltering results, but also at the let-down of the Algerian signings. Linfield had reaped considerable success on the back of foreign signings during the previous season, but in 1989/90, the venture backfired. Dehnoun and Yahi never matched the exploits of Coly and Khammal. All told, Abdi Dehnoun made 18 appearances, and injury-hit Hocine Yahi just 11. The two players struggled to settle, but also joined a team that was in decline. As the 1980s gave way to the 1990s, Linfield's position as the dominant force in the Irish League came under threat.[10]

In a bid to arrest the slump, Coyle brought in another international player. With a last throw of the dice, the Blues boss signed US forward, John Kerr. The American striker had English First Division experience with Portsmouth, and was initially signed on a four-week contract. Kerr's impact was instant – he helped create four goals in his first six games, and the team enjoyed a welcome resurgence in form. Wins were easier to come by, and the Blues pushed their way up the table. The good form also translated into performance in the Irish Cup, with the club progressing to the sixth round. At this juncture, Linfield were paired away to junior opposition.[11]

Normally a meeting against such a side would herald relief. On this occasion though, the Blues drew West Belfast team, Donegal Celtic. It was a tie which both captured the imagination and instilled a sense of dread. The press immediately hearkened back to the "dim and distant... Forties," and previous Linfield tussles with "a different Celtic". That Celtic was, of course, the Belfast Celtic who had left the Irish League soon after the infamous December 1948 riot at Windsor. Given that the 1990 Irish Cup tie was set against the backdrop of the Troubles, there was a worry that the game had the potential to be another sordid episode.[12]

From the moment Donegal Celtic and Linfield were paired, security became a major consideration. The West Belfast side had been afforded home advantage by the draw, but this was changed by the IFA. After consultation with the RUC, the match was moved to Windsor. Unimpressed by the manner in which the venue switch was handled, Donegal Celtic officials took legal action. Celtic's lawyer Philip Magee made the case to the High Court that the IFA had acted in "an arbitrary and cavalier fashion". The case was heard on 15 February, two days before the scheduled tie. Yet no alteration was forthcoming, and the game was kept at Windsor. The court cited fear of "serious public disorder" as the reasoning behind the ruling. Celtic secretary John Hall was underwhelmed, and complained that "it seems the IFA can do what they like". Officials accepted police advice that bringing Linfield fans to their Suffolk Road ground posed a security risk. Still, there was disappointment that decisions had been taken without consultation. Hall added: "The IFA should have discussed with us other considerations about staging the game." That said, Celtic would abide by the ruling.[13]

With the venue settled, attention turned to what the *Belfast Telegraph* hoped would prove "a memorable occasion". On the eve of the game, the associated hype had reached fever pitch, and the respective managers were eager for proceedings to begin. Celtic manager Paddy Bonner said his players could "hardly wait for the match". Roy Coyle was similarly excited though he hoped that on the day "all other issues [would be] irrelevant". Sadly this did not come to fruition. It was the football that quickly became immaterial. The Blues won the game 2-1, with both goals coming from the head of Stephen Baxter. Celtic had rallied in the closing stages, and scored in the 84th minute via a long-range free-kick from Brendan Tully. But press as they did afterwards, no equaliser came. Normally a football ground would come to life as two teams battled it out in a close-fought affair, yet by the time the tie climaxed, the 10,000-strong crowd had shrunk.[14]

Earlier that afternoon, kick-off was delayed to accommodate the size of the crowd. *Ireland's Saturday Night* reported that the crowd was "reminiscent of an International or of yesteryear when Belfast Celtic visited Windsor". The huge numbers brought atmosphere and colour, but also what IFA secretary David Bowen described as "naked sectarianism". 'Party songs' were sung and obscenities chanted as an accompaniment to chaotic scenes in the stands. As soon as the rival sets of supporters began congregating, disturbances began. Six or so youths from the Donegal Celtic end (in the Kop) climbed floodlighting pylons to hoist the Irish Tricolour over the ground, then one began urinating

 on police below. The fans high in the Belfast skyline only climbed down after a PA announcement explained that the pylons were electrified. By kick-off, the rival sets of supporters were in closer proximity than the police had intended, after Linfield fans had broken through security cordons in the upper deck of the North Stand. Both sets of supporters then started hurling objects at each other in what was a febrile atmosphere.[15]

During the game's opening exchanges, a missile thrown from the Linfield support struck Celtic player David McVicker. Then near the end of the first half, one Linfield supporter managed to make it past stationed police officers and onto the field. A young man approached from the lower deck of the North Stand before running toward Celtic's Brendan Tully. The Linfield fan kicked out at Tully and ran back to the stand. Tully was left "shocked" and "dumbfounded", though able to continue. As this played out on the pitch, rioting took place on the terraces. Celtic fans in the Kop fought with the RUC, who fired back with plastic bullets. When the second half began, the clashes intensified. The *News Letter* reported that "a section of the perimeter fencing behind the Spion Kop goal was torn down [and] Fearing an uncontrollable field invasion" the Royal Ulster Constabulary (RUC) again used plastic bullets. In the midst of the madness, the PA system was used to dispel a rumour that a bullet had fatally injured a spectator. The police tactic did, however, result in serious injury. The Sunday papers carried a picture of one Celtic fan with a bloodied face after being hit on the mouth.[16]

All told it was estimated that 63 people were injured in the trouble, and there was no doubt that the cup tie was poorly handled. The RUC struggled to control the (volatile) crowd, and the use of plastic bullets incensed nationalist and republican politicians. SDLP councillor Dr Joe Hendron labelled the RUC's tactic "absolutely crazy and indefensible". Sinn Féin councillor Máirtín Ó Muilleoir lambasted the RUC for "the way they fired into such a large crowd", and claimed it was akin to "shooting fish in a barrel".[17]

There was certainly merit in questioning the police tactics. That said, comments contained within a Sinn Féin statement faxed to FIFA, and carried by the *Irish News* were perplexing. The call was made for "the severest penalties against the IFA and Linfield FC [in the game's aftermath], including suspensions and substantial fines". It was then added: "that the IFA should be stood down pending the outcome of the FIFA inquiry and that Linfield FC should be barred from all international competitions."[18]

*Irish News*, journalist Seamus Kelters noted that at "the peak of the violence a rainbow [had] settled over what was once Celtic Park – Celtic Park is gone. Windsor is still there. Belfast's illegitimisation of football goes on." Kelters' remarks support the argument put forward by historian Mike Cronin, that the cup-tie game (amongst other episodes) was proof that "Northern Irish soccer [couldn't] deal with teams coming from predominantly Catholic and nationalist areas". It must be noted that Irish League football had operated in extremely difficult circumstances throughout its history. These conditions of course blighted the game, yet it had carried on. Unfortunately, it was impossible to divorce society's ills from 'the beautiful game'. The Troubles played their part in Derry City's departure from the League in the early 1970s, as well as in Distillery's move from the Grosvenor Road. Wider societal problems all too often injured the game. Football was a sport played by all, therefore polarised communities were at times face-to-face within sporting stadia. The Donegal Celtic vs Linfield Irish

Cup tie only highlighted tensions and problems that existed within wider society. Football in Northern Ireland had been severely harmed by external factors – but it was certainly not illegitimate.[19]

*Look at Linfield* described the events of 17 February as a "horrible nightmare". That analogy though, was also apt for team performances throughout the rest of the 1989/90 season. The resurgence of form in early 1990 was lost in the hype surrounding the Donegal Celtic game. One week before the game, Linfield suffered a humbling 4-1 defeat at home to Cliftonville. Then two weeks after the Celtic tie, there was the humiliation of a 5-1 away defeat to Ballymena. Instead of bouncing back, Linfield endured a fourth straight defeat to rivals Glentoran in the Budweiser Cup final. On the night, Linfield went down 4-2. By late winter, the season was at crisis point. The 'team of the 1980s' had lost its way early on in the 1990s.[20]

Disillusioned supporters would, however, find some respite amidst the depressing run. On 23 March, Malcolm Brodie wrote in the *Belfast Telegraph* that the Blues had carried off "one of the greatest coups… in their history". That day it was reported that World Cup holders Argentina had agreed to play Linfield at Windsor the following month. When goalkeeper George Dunlop heard about the game, he thought, "You gotta be kidding!" Club chairman David Campbell was also very excited by the "tremendous boost" that such a tie brought, "not only for us but, indeed, for Irish football generally". His enthusiasm was somewhat tempered by recollections of the poorly attended centenary celebration game against Flamengo. Campbell explained: "I hope it will be supported by all of the soccer loving members of the [NI] public, and that we won't have the same let-down as when we brought former World [Club] Cup champions, [Flamengo] of Brazil, to Windsor."[21]

US-based (though Ulster-born) soccer promoter Noel Lemon organised the game. His company Mundial Sport offered Linfield the chance to face Argentina after complications arose in the South Americans' World Cup preparations. The Argentinians were in Europe preparing for Italia '90, and had matches lined up against Scotland and Barcelona. The game in Barcelona was scheduled for the opening of the new Olympic Stadium, but when it emerged that the stadium would not be ready on time, it was cancelled. As Argentina had the match in Scotland, there was a wish to continue preparations in the UK. At this point Lemon offered Linfield the game with the World Cup holders.[22]

The South Americans arrived in Belfast on 30 March, and during their stay they actually played two games. The first was a hastily arranged, behind-closed-doors match with the Linfield Swifts. On that occasion Argentina comfortably won by an 8-0 scoreline. Then came the friendly at Windsor. Going into the match, George Dunlop told the *News Letter* that it "should be great entertainment for the fans" and added his hope that "we don't let people down". Privately he thought,

"We're in for a bit of a tanking here." Dunlop's fears were not realised, as the Blues earned much credit on the evening of 3 April. Argentina won 1-0 – Linfield and the reigning World Cup Champions were only separated by a single goal. Later that summer, Lee Doherty sat watching the World Cup final between Argentina and West Germany and thought, "We played against those boys!" Argentina would go down 1-0 in the decider and surrendered the trophy. But to think Linfield had not embarrassed themselves against a side that came very close to winning back-to-back World Cups – that was something else.[23]

Sadly the positivity engendered by the Argentina game did not improve domestic fortunes. After the glamour friendly, an Irish Cup semi-final soon followed. By then there was next to no chance of a League title, therefore the season hinged on an Irish Cup triumph. In the semi-final, Linfield faced Glentoran. This was the fifth time in that campaign that Belfast's Big Two had met. In all previous encounters, the Glens had taken the victory. That sequence was not broken in the Irish Cup. At a sun-drenched Windsor, Gary McCartney opened the scoring before Raymond Campbell added a second to clinch a 2-0 win. Glentoran had risen to the occasion, whilst Linfield had bottled it. A frustrated Lindsay McKeown snapped afterwards: "Some players froze… I don't think any of us played to our best." After the defeat as Coyle had walked to the dressing room, he did so to the accompaniment of boos and cat calls.[24]

Two days after the cup defeat, the Management Committee "discussed at length with the Manager" the season's performances. The pressure Roy Coyle was under was rising. He pointed out in the press that with the League title gone, Linfield's aim was second place and UEFA Cup qualification. That required a consistent finish, and also what had eluded the Blues all season – a victory over Glentoran. On 17 April, Linfield and the Glens met for the sixth time. *Look at Linfield* exclaimed, "This is a game our team MUST win." Claiming all three points was the only acceptable outcome. However, yet again, Glentoran would emerge victorious. *Look at Linfield* despaired, maintaining "this season has been one of the worst since the end of the last war".[25]

Coyle had suffered abuse throughout the 1989/90 season, and it now reached a crescendo. Against this backdrop, he walked. On the night of the game, a termination of his contract was agreed. A couple of days later, an emotional David Campbell stated: "On behalf of Linfield I would take this opportunity to thank publicly Mr Coyle for the many honours and successes he had brought to Windsor Park during his period as manager… His record of trophy success is there for all to see." Coyle felt his departure was "in the best interests of both parties… certainly the time was right for me, [it was] my time to move on… you can be there too long, sometimes you need a different voice in the changing room." In a press conference at Ulster Television he sighed, "Sometimes it is unhelpful to be too successful." In just over 14 years, Roy Coyle brought remarkable success to Windsor Park. He delivered 31 pieces of silverware to the Linfield trophy cabinet – which was an unprecedented achievement.[26]

Club captain David Jeffrey "couldn't believe it" when he heard the news. That night, Jeffrey travelled to his former manager's house to speak with him. Coyle, however, was not home, having gone to visit friends and unwind after the stress of the ordeal. So Jeffrey wrote a few lines on a piece of scrap paper and pushed it through the letterbox. It read, "Boss... I called tonight to say thank you. We had our share of disagreements but you never bore a grudge. You brought me to Linfield, gave me an opportunity, gave me a responsibility, which led to many honours. You helped instil in me what I feel is your greatest quality – attitude and the will to win." Coyle was gone, but at Linfield there was an expectation that this "will to win" would remain.[27]

As the season drew to a conclusion, the players had one last opportunity for redemption. This came in the final of the County Antrim Shield, and another meeting (a seventh) with the Glens. The last Big Two of the season was played at the Oval, but neither team could grab a goal in 90 minutes. After 30 minutes of extra time the score was still 0-0, and the game went to a penalty shoot-out. In keeping with form that season, Glentoran won that too. Conor McCaffrey scored the decisive penalty, after an 18-year-old Noel Bailie had sent his left-footed penalty over the bar. When he missed his spot-kick, the young player threw his hands to his head before collapsing to his knees. His captain David Jeffrey then raced up to him, took him by the arm and brought him to his teammates. The teenager was inconsolable, and blamed himself for Linfield's shortcomings. At an extremely young age, Bailie displayed his will to win – and also a readiness to shoulder responsibility. Like Bailie, the whole team was at a low at the end of the 1989/90 season.[28]

It would be up to a new manager to revitalise the club.

Chapter 4

# *Opening Up*

Whoever took over as Linfield manager knew that a considerable job awaited them. Supporters would expect quick success – even though a major rebuild was required. Such a rebuild amidst the upheaval of a new man taking the reins was never going to be easy. Indeed, change at a football club can be a traumatic experience. Change, however, can open up new conversations and new possibilities. At times, this can be awkward, though it can allow an institution to confront issues that have for a long time haunted them. That was indeed how Linfield's new manager found life at the Park. There was a tough time on the pitch, but the new Blues boss would open up a discussion that allowed for self-examination at Linfield.

Throughout the 1980s, club AGMs had served as opportunities for reflection on trophy-laden campaigns. The first AGM of the 1990s stood in stark contrast. It was held after the Blues had  finished fourth in the League and endured one of the worst seasons in recent memory. At the 1990 gathering of Linfield members, criticism was the dominant theme. Supporters voiced frustrations and sought assurances that success would return. Chairman David Campbell stressed that the club hierarchy was doing all in its power to put things right. He informed members that Linfield would shortly appoint Roy Coyle's successor, then asked supporters to be patient. Campbell asserted: "I appeal to the members and supporters to give the new  manager a chance to rebuild." In reality time was (and always has been) in short supply at Windsor.[1]

The rebuild that Campbell spoke of was considerable. Linfield were in transition; big names were leaving the Park. Shortly after Coyle's departure, stalwart goalkeeper George Dunlop called time on a decorated career. The Northern Ireland international explained that "all good things must come to an end". Dunlop's reflection applied to himself, but was also analogous for the break-up of Coyle's 'team of the

1980s'. By 1990, the first-team squad needed revamped, and the expectations were that this would happen quickly. To take responsibility for rebuilding the squad – and doing so after the club's most successful manager – was to take a poisoned chalice.[2]

At the end of May, Linfield hired former captain Eric Bowyer as the man to undertake the sizeable challenge. Bowyer was steeped in the club, having spent over a decade at the Blues as a player in the 1960s and 70s. Malcolm Brodie described Bowyer the player as "a devoted servant of Linfield [and] a perfect sportsman". In 1975, Bowyer won the coveted 'Ulster Footballer of the Year' award, and on four occasions had won individual Linfield supporters clubs' player of the year awards. He viewed becoming manager as "a great privilege". Upon the club unveiling him as manager, he stated: "When the opportunity arose there was no option but to grasp it... there will be no one bringing more commitment to Linfield than I." He joined from Cliftonville where he had worked  as a coach under Billy Sinclair, and came from the North Belfast side with a glowing recommendation. Sinclair commented that Bowyer "knew the game, knew the local scene, and most important of all, [had] the respect of players".[3]

The new manager arrived on a part-time contract. Outside of his Linfield commitments he worked as a senior administrator in the Southern Area Health Board. This arrangement was different from the previous regime, when Roy Coyle was employed full-time, and the change in managerial status was not well received by the support. It was perceived as a backward step, an indication that Linfield lacked ambition. In Bowyer's first press conference he acknowledged this sense of frustration. The former captain pointed out that "a lot of Bluemen [were] disappointed" at the new arrangement. Following Roy Coyle and rebuilding the squad was an already difficult act. Doing so amidst a  feeling that the club was moving backwards made the task even tougher.[4]

By the start of the 1990/91 season, Linfield's first-team squad looked very different from the group of players that finished the previous campaign. Only half of the 1989/90 squad remained at Windsor, as the new manager replaced those who left with players described by the club programme as "young and enthusiastic". Goalkeepers Paul Prentice and Wes Lamont, defender Robert Carson, midfielders Craig McCandless and Alan Boyd, as well as strikers Ritchie Johnson and Alan Campbell had all arrived. The club gained these players without spending vast sums of money, which was only interpreted as another sign of stagnation. Linfield appeared unwilling to pay the fees needed to compete. In many ways, there were similarities with Manchester United in the days before Alex Ferguson. It was thought that the 'honour' of turning out for Linfield and Manchester United was enough to entice the best players. Yet as others around them were offering better terms and greater transfer fees, the talent was going elsewhere. The 'Bowyer Era' had thus begun in the midst of supporter frustration.[5]

The first competitive game under Eric Bowyer came on 18 August. That afternoon, Linfield lined up at Windsor for an Ulster Cup tie against Omagh Town. The occasion heralded new eras for both clubs. Not only did it signal the beginning of Bowyer's tenure; it was also the Tyrone club's first game in senior football. Linfield were expected to comfortably defeat Omagh (regardless of wider concerns about the direction of the club). Yet instead of an easy victory, the team laboured to a 1-1 draw. Only a Sid Burrows equaliser with five minutes left saved Blue blushes. In the weeks that followed, results remained disappointing. Aside from an end-of-August win over Glentoran, the Blues struggled to find form. The 1-0 win at the Oval, courtesy of a Stephen Baxter header, had brought the first win over the Glens in nine encounters against the East Belfast team. Yet this was little comfort in a depressing run.

Throughout September, the Blues failed to record a victory. *Look at Linfield* ventured that the unwanted September drought had "never happened before", and by the middle of October, Linfield faced Carrick Rangers in an Irish League bottom-of-the-table clash! The Blues narrowly emerged with the spoils, winning 2-1, but had hit what *Ireland's Saturday Night* described as a "nadir of mediocrity". Malcolm Brodie compared Linfield's struggles at the outset of 1990/91 to the 1951/52 season. In that early-fifties campaign, Linfield had finished third from bottom and only "narrowly escaped the humiliation of seeking re-election". At the beginning of November 1990, Brodie contended that Linfield were in serious danger. The team had played 16 games and only four had resulted in victory. The reporter stated, "It may be early days yet in the championship, but that fear [of seeking re-election] haunts many Bluemen." Results improved somewhat in the months that followed, but Linfield's form was at best described as indifferent.[6]

At Christmas the Blues sat in seventh place, 17 points behind leaders Portadown. League title hopes were gone, and like the season before, everything hinged on success in the Irish Cup. By March the Blues had made the quarter-finals and faced a trip away to Ards. Roy Coyle had taken over as manager of the Strangford club, and this gave the knock-out tie an even greater edge. When the draw was made, the press billed the match as a "confrontation between the old Windsor boss and the new one". For both clubs, it was much more than a personality contest. The Irish Cup provided the only path to European football next season. The tie was make or break, and Ards ended up winning 3-2. Effectively Linfield's season was over by late winter.[7]

No silverware was added to the Windsor trophy cabinet during 1990/91, which was hard for fans to digest. *Look at Linfield* maintained that "supporters quite rightly label [the campaign] as one of the worst in the 105-year history of our illustrious Club". Bowyer had found that first season in charge "hard". He inherited a squad that was in decline, and turning the club's fortune around was no small task. The manager reflected: "I was realistic enough to know I wouldn't have got the job had the club not been in transition." He also knew that a marked improvement was expected the following season. Yet Bowyer's depressing first campaign finished on something of a high. At the end of April, Linfield travelled to North America. This was the club's third visit to the States in seven years. That said the 1991 sojourn had a different feel to the two trips during the 1980s. In 1990/91 the Blues finished seventh in the League, and Eric Bowyer noted that the team was invited on the strength of its "reputation", not its current form. Furthermore, football in the United States was, ever so slowly, growing in prominence. The 1991 tour was staged in the run-up to World Cup '94, which was to be held in the US.[8]

It must be noted that the awarding of World Cup hosting rights had by no means transformed the fortune of football in the United States. The game's appeal was far from being at fever pitch in the years leading up to the tournament, and commentators within and outside the US poked fun at the American public's indifference to the sport. Author Ed Horton likened America hosting football's most prestigious competition to holding "a conference of atheists in the Vatican", but this mattered little to world football's governing body. Increasing American interest in football was not FIFA's motivation for awarding the US the '94 World Cup. Instead, money talked. Historian David Wangerin stated that placing the World Cup "in the hands of powerful Yankee entrepreneurs [was] geared to realising maximum commercial gain". Ever since João Havelange was elected president of FIFA in 1974, the organisation had headed in that direction.[9]

The World Cup was a cash cow, and cities across the US wanted some of the action. In total, 27 cities submitted bids to host matches at the '94 World Cup. Knoxville, Tennessee, was one of the interested cities (though its application was ultimately unsuccessful). The bid was organised by the Tennessee Soccer Development Association, which invited the Blues stateside. Linfield's reputation was something that Knoxville wanted to utilise. The Blues had endured a very disappointing season, but the club's name still carried currency.[10]

On 27 April, the Blues played an exhibition match in Knoxville at the city's Neyland Stadium. In front of a 12,500-strong crowd, Linfield took on the American Professional League All Stars. In a venue for College American Football that has averaged attendances well in excess of 60,000, the figure for Linfield's game was uninspiring, and was indicative of the interest level in 'soccer' at the time. Nevertheless, the All Stars were a side packed with quality – former England international Paul Mariner was leading the line. There was thus no shame when the Blues lost the game 1-0 – and despite the loss, Linfield had controlled large parts of the match. Three days later the tour concluded against Fort Lauderdale Strikers. Slack defending characterised this match and ensured a second defeat – this time going down 2-0.[11]

Even with the two defeats, Eric Bowyer was of the opinion that the tour was "a great experience", and at the 1991 AGM he added that the American organisers "said we were the best football team from Ireland to visit the States in recent years". This 1991 meeting of Linfield members stood in stark contrast to the 1990 gathering. *Ireland's Saturday Night* reported that, "Linfield members were in buoyant mood". After Eric Bowyer gave an "impassioned ten-minute speech", members backed their manager with "rapturous applause". Bowyer maintained that, "given the right breaks we will make an impact next season".[12]

In the manager's speech he extolled the virtues of having a young squad. The average age of his first team at the time was 22. That said, he also had a good blend of experience. Veteran campaigners such as Alan Dornan and David Jeffrey complemented young players like Noel Bailie. Up front, Martin McGaughey still scored goals with regularity. Indeed, early on during the 1991/92 season, in an October win over Distillery, Buckets notched his 300th goal for Linfield. Out of the victory came more than just a personal milestone for the striker; with it, Linfield returned to the top of the Irish League table for the first time in two years. In Bowyer's second year at the helm, confidence was returning, and as autumn gave way to winter, Linfield were riding high.[13]

At the beginning of December, Linfield remained on top of the League. The club had also made it to a first cup final under Bowyer's guidance. On 4 December the Blues played Omagh Town in the Budweiser Cup decider. Before the game, the manager was cautious, warning: "Omagh will be no pushovers... we have never had it easy against them." The local press, however, portrayed the final as a David and Goliath affair, and confidently predicted a Linfield victory. On the evening of the match, the *Belfast Telegraph* announced: "the sleeping giant of Linfield is ready to wake up".[14]

The opening sequences of the final followed the intended script. With 15 minutes gone, Martin McGaughey volleyed home to give Linfield an early lead. But then shortly after, the Tyrone side equalised. At half-time the game stood at one apiece. In the second half, Linfield had a golden opportunity to retake the lead from a penalty. Unfortunately Stephen Baxter missed, and with this the initiative was handed to Omagh. The Tyrone side scored two without reply, and won 3-1 to achieve a famous victory. For Eric Bowyer the experience was "awful". He lamented, "We should have won it." Next day at his nine-to-five job in the health service he felt "so depressed and so down". Linfield had fluffed the first opportunity under Bowyer to win a trophy. It was now over two years since the November 1989 Gold Cup victory – the club's last addition to the Windsor trophy cabinet.[15]

Defeat in the Budweiser Cup final heralded a slump in League form. Linfield only mustered two points over the next four League games. The inconsistency of the previous season had returned, and Bowyer (along with his players) was under pressure. *Look at Linfield* griped: "Patience and understanding... can be exhaustible commodities." Frustration also grew on the terraces. The front cover of the 1991 Christmas edition of the Linfield fanzine *One Team in Ulster* encapsulated this feeling. The publication led with a picture of Eric Bowyer (as a player) receiving the 1971 Ulster Cup. Above was a caption that read, "THIS IS WHAT A TROPHY LOOKS LIKE, LADS!!"[16]

THIS IS WHAT A TROPHY LOOKS LIKE, LADS !!

ERIC BOWYER TALKS TO OTIU-
AND WE CAN'T GET HIM TO SHUT UP!

SPECIAL 44 PAGE CHRISTMAS ISSUE

**Linfield Fanzine**

**No. 18**          £1.00

Fanzines – 'fan magazines' – were publications that gave supporters a chance to have their say. They were produced on photocopiers or small printing presses and sold outside grounds on match days. Fanzine culture on the UK mainland had its origins in the 1970s, though it was not until the mid-1980s that the phenomenon experienced a boom. According to author Steve James, fanzines "gave long-suffering fans a place to slag off the players, the prices of the pies and burgers, ticket arrangements, the chairmen and directors, replica kit prices and other teams and fans". In Northern Ireland, Cliftonville supporters led the way in fanzine culture. *The Wee Red* – the first Ulster-based fanzine – appeared in September 1987; though as historian Gordon Gillespie pointed out, it was not until two years later that Northern Irish fanzines began appearing in any number. Blues supporters were to the fore in this. At the start of 1989 two Linfield fanzines appeared, *Blue for You* (in January) and *One Team in Ulster* (in March). Gillespie identified the years that followed, until about 1993, as the "golden age" of local fanzines. In the years afterwards, the numbers of fanzines in production fell, and by the end of the 1990s they had ceased to appear at matches.[17]

At times the impact of fanzines was huge – indeed the 1991 Christmas edition of *One Team in Ulster* created a storm at Windsor Park. Below the front cover's picture of Bowyer the player was a reference to the fanzine's interview with Bowyer the manager. The tagline read: "ERIC BOWYER TALKS TO OTIU [*One Team in Ulster*] – AND WE CAN'T GET HIM TO SHUT UP!" The fanzine editorial acknowledged, "we've managed a bit of a scoop", then added, "we hope you'll find it interesting reading!" The entire interview was published over 13 pages and covered a variety of topics. Bowyer answered questions on the team's current form, his views of the press and the Irish League in general. He also answered on a topic that the Linfield hierarchy shied away from.[18]

Near the end of the interview Bowyer was asked, "How do you feel about the club's image as a sectarian club... Can you ever see that image changing?" When Tony Coly had signed in 1988, the Blues had shirked public comment on perceptions that the club was sectarian. Quotes were rattled off about not asking a player's religion before he signed, but no challenge was made against the supposed sectarian nature of the club. Three years down the line, Linfield was still dogged by accusations that the club did not want to field Catholic players. The signing of Tony Coly was portrayed in some quarters as an accident, and after this 'blip' normal service had returned. The club as a whole (supporters, members, players, coaches and Management Committee) was castigated as bigoted.[19]

Eric Bowyer realised that answering a question on "the club's [sectarian] image" was potentially explosive. Yet instead of ducking the issue, he gave a hard-hitting critique of Northern Irish society and how the Blues operated within it. The manager explained that the Troubles fostered conditions which made it difficult for Linfield to sign Catholics. In articulating this, he wanted to provoke debate. Bowyer recalled that "part of me wanted this to open up because I wanted to sign Catholic players... I didn't see any sense in cutting half of the footballing population off."[20]

Bowyer's recorded response started by explaining that he did not like "the whole idea of sectarianism". Then he continued:

> "I'm... a realist and I know that there are major
> problems in our society... To be realistic, I would
> sign Peter Murray [a Catholic player at Cliftonville]
> tomorrow, because I know how good a player he
> is – but that just wouldn't have worked. It
> wouldn't have worked for a whole variety of

reasons. It wouldn't have worked because Peter Murray couldn't have lived in Northern Ireland society. Even if he'd wanted to come here... The crowd mightn't have liked it, but the more important thing is that when he went back to live in North Belfast, his life would have been miserable. Getting shot would not be an impossibility. I mean, Mo Johnston's OK – he got a million and a half in his hand to live in Edinburgh after two years. You can't do that here! So, with the best will in the world, it would be almost impossible for us to sign Catholics."[21]

Very soon, Bowyer's provocative musings were gracing a much wider audience than the *One Team in Ulster* readership. In the first weekend of 1992, a *Sunday Life* headline read: "NO GO FOR CATHOLICS: Linfield boss spells out why he'll not be signing RC players." The Sunday paper carried quotes from Bowyer in which he explained, "If any man or boy from the nationalist community were ever to join us, their life would be unbearable and that's a simple fact... What I am saying is that in our society in Northern Ireland it would be idiotic to think differently." Bowyer reiterated the comparison with Mo Johnston and maintained that any Catholic who signed for the Blues "would not be able to escape the enormous pressures when he returned to his own community".[22]

The *Irish News* weighed in on the story on 6 January (the day after the *Sunday Life* headlines), claiming that Linfield "might be investigated by the Fair Employment Commission". An unnamed source in the Commission was quoted as saying: "Officials believe that what has happened here is that the club has decided to virtually flaunt the fair employment laws." The paper also included an opinion piece by editor Nick Garbutt, which let fly. Garbutt made the unwarranted accusation that: "Linfield FC... never wants any Catholics in its first team... By keeping the Taigs out, Linfield FC perpetuates sectarianism, and gives it a 'respectable' face... it is difficult to understand why UEFA continues to allow Linfield to play in European tournaments." The *One Team in Ulster* interview had opened debate, but in doing so brought denunciation of the club. At the start of 1992, Linfield's name was mired in controversy.[23]

Criticism of the Blues had spread to the other side of the Atlantic by the end of January. The Irish National Caucus (INC), an Irish-American lobby group, had read Bowyer's comments and initiated a campaign against Linfield. The Caucus demanded that the IFA cut all links with the club and Windsor Park on account of the Blues' supposed sectarian policies. Father Sean McManus (described by *Sunday Life* as a "controversial" figure) headed up the Caucus and the campaign. He contended that: "Linfield must be expelled from all soccer games... [the club's] publicly stated position is the equivalent of an American sports coach saying he could not hire a black or a Jew."[24]

IFA secretary David Bowen was quick to refute this "outrageous and totally unjustified attack". Acknowledging "the problems facing Linfield in this most difficult of countries", Bowen maintained that the IFA did not "regard Linfield as a sectarian club in any way". However, his intervention made little difference, as the INC continued its efforts with gusto, and its message struck a chord within the United States' political establishment. The US Congressional Committee for Irish Affairs wrote to FIFA in support of the Caucus' position, calling for the Irish League to throw Linfield out of the competition. In a short period of time, the campaign had gained considerable traction.[25]

By mid-February the Caucus was claiming a first scalp in its campaign. An *Irish News* headline declared: "Pressure group claims victory after Linfield lose sponsorship." The story referred to Thorn Security, whose company logo had adorned the Linfield kit in that 1991/92 season. The newspaper informed readers that a "major American electrical company announced yesterday that it has withdrawn its sponsorship of Linfield Football club... it was revealed last night that an Irish-American pressure group met Thorn Security's parent US company two weeks before the multi-national announced it would stop sponsoring the Windsor Park side." Against the backdrop of the Caucus campaign, the costly loss of Thorn's backing was embarrassing.[26]

There was, though, no correlation between loss of sponsorship and the lobby group's crusade. Months before the news broke, Linfield's Board was aware that Thorn would not fulfil its sponsorship deal. In late November 1991, the Finance Committee had discussed a Thorn Security decision, which indicated that the company was "unable to honour its agreement with the Club for season 1991/92". Then after the story broke, Thorn's public relation's officer, Julia Kisch, stressed that the Caucus' adverse publicity played no part in matters. Kisch maintained that the company had taken "a purely commercial decision and no other factors came into account". In *Look at Linfield*, the club expanded further on the loss of sponsorship. An editorial explained that after new management assumed control of Thorn Security, "redundancies at the Belfast branch of the company made the sponsorship deal... untenable".[27]

Caring little for the nuances of the story, Father McManus was quick to capitalise on the withdrawal of sponsorship. He called on "all fair minded companies" that backed Linfield to follow Thorn's lead. McManus outlined that the Caucus wanted to "pressurise major companies to stop supporting... Linfield until they change the policy of discrimination". Businesses that sponsored the Northern Ireland national team were also targeted. According to McManus, the IFA's defence of the Blues placed the body "right up to its neck" in terms of guilt. Therefore the INC approached companies like General Motors and Coca-Cola that gave financial backing to Northern Ireland. The lobby group's expressed aim was to dry up sponsorship for both teams. Father McManus argued: "The way to stop discrimination in its tracks is to find the connection between discrimination in Northern Ireland and US funding."[28]

Yet for all the bluster of McManus, the INC struggled to get sponsors to back its stance. As St Patrick's Day approached, the Caucus' leader informed the press that the INC would step up efforts. He promised that the body would "make life uncomfortable" for companies that did not support the campaign and Coca-Cola was singled out. The soft drink manufacturer had advertising hoardings on the North Stand, and was not prepared to remove them. On 15 March, McManus issued a call for a boycott of Coca-Cola products. All "Irish Americans, as well as all lovers of peace and justice" were urged to join this action. Coke, New Coke, Sprite, TAB, Fanta, Five Alive and Bacardi Tropical Mixers were amongst an extensive list of products that the INC blacklisted. But Coca-Cola did not give in to the boycott; the company's North Stand hoardings remained at Windsor. The INC was not successful in forcing companies to withdraw sponsorship from Linfield or the Northern Irish international team.[29]

Throughout this period, the adverse publicity caused considerable discomfort for the Linfield Management Committee. The press coverage and the Caucus campaign were regularly discussed at Board level. However, the club was reluctant to make official comment. Linfield's hierarchy did not like engaging in debate over the perceived sectarian image of the club; the press debacle over Tony Coly's signing had demonstrated this. The 1992 controversy was, though, very different in nature to the 1988 *Sunday News* furore. In 1988, the bad press about the club had died down quickly. This time, a political lobby group kept the story in the public eye. The club could not stick its head in the sand and hope everything would blow over. Action was needed, and this came on 18 March. That evening, Linfield's Board issued a lengthy response to refute the claims.[30]

The statement made clear the "known fact that there never has been a bar on Roman Catholics playing for Linfield at any time in its history including the present... More than 70 Roman Catholic players... have worn the famous royal blue colours of the club." Examples of Linfield greats who happened to be Catholic were then listed. Included were two former goalkeeping captains, Sylvester Bierne and Tommy Breen. The highly popular Gerry Morgan was also named. As a member of Linfield's 1921/22 seven-trophy side, Morgan was a revered Linfield player. Yet Gerry Morgan was more than an acclaimed footballer. For 20 years, from 1939 until he died in 1959, Morgan – who was known as 'Mr Linfield' – was the first-team's trainer. The statement drove home the point that Catholic players and coaches were steeped in the history of Linfield Football Club.[31]

After rejecting claims that the club had ever employed a sectarian player-recruitment policy, the statement addressed the reasons for the lack of Catholic players in recent years. Blame was apportioned to the "climate created by the present Ulster troubles". Against this backdrop, Linfield had struggled to attract Catholics on account of its "distinctly British and Ulster ethos". The Blues Board made no apology for this "quite legitimate ethos... which [was] just as strong today as it was in the early formative years" when Linfield was established "by a group of millworkers in the strongly Protestant district of Sandy Row".[32]

It should be pointed out that the club was far from unusual in identifying with a particular tradition – this was a common phenomenon in football globally. That said, the Management Committee was willing to accept the difficulties that Linfield's identity had posed whilst trying to entice Catholics to join during the Troubles.

Anecdotal evidence from "the early 1970s" was provided to illustrate such complications. "Back then... Linfield signed a promising young Roman Catholic player from West Belfast, but after he and his family reassessed the situation in the light of the serious civil unrest... the move was abandoned." This failed bid was not unique. "Other attempts [had] been made to sign Roman Catholic players of proven ability, but they were [also] unsuccessful." According to the Management Committee, the Troubles hamstrung Linfield's transfer dealings.[33]

Northern Irish society was, as the Management Committee stated, polarised "along religious and political lines". The Troubles had raged since the late 1960s, and by 1992 there was no sign of any let up. In the three-month period between Bowyer's interview and the Board's statement, the Province witnessed two particularly tragic days. On 17 January, the Provisional IRA murdered eight Protestant workers in a bombing at Teebane Crossroads, County Tyrone. Then on 5 February, the loyalist paramilitary grouping, the 'Ulster Freedom Fighters' (UFF) killed five Catholics in a bookmakers shop on the Ormeau Road, Belfast. This "civil unrest" spilled into every aspect of life, and local football was very much afflicted. The 1990 Irish Cup game with Donegal Celtic had highlighted this, as had a Linfield vs Cliftonville Budweiser Cup semi-final during the 1991/92 season. On that occasion, loyalist paramilitaries attacked Reds fans by throwing a shrapnel grenade in their direction. No injuries resulted, but the attack's life-threatening potential was obvious. Furthermore, it gave credence to Bowyer's assertions about the potentially toxic mix of the Troubles and sport.[34]

Yet despite these very real concerns, the fact that Bowyer had opened up discussion of Linfield signing Catholics appeared to have moved matters along. In the days after Linfield released their statement, the press was awash with reports of a bid for Jim McFadden of Cliftonville. McFadden was a North Belfast Catholic, who had worked with Eric Bowyer at the Reds. The New Lodge man was, however, unreceptive to the bid from the Blues. The *Irish News* reported that he turned down a move to Linfield that offered "three or four times" his current salary. McFadden denied he rejected the deal because of the Caucus campaign. Speaking to the press, he explained that "the climate was simply not right... It would be difficult to envisage any Catholic player from Northern Ireland signing for Linfield, although I could see a Scottish or English Catholic playing for them." Linfield had launched a bid for McFadden four weeks prior to the news breaking. The move was therefore not linked to the increased pressure from McManus and the INC. It was, however, an indication that Bowyer's provocative fanzine interview had opened up the "almost impossible". Jim McFadden would not break the mould at Linfield, but the speculation over his potential transfer suggested that change might be on the way.[35]

While controversy reigned off the pitch, Linfield's players had a job to do on it, and they did so with relative success. After the slump in form over the Christmas period, the Blues recovered in the second half of the campaign. The club was still a distance off challenging for the title, but was there was improvement on the season before. An

impressive end of season led the team to a third-placed League finish. During this time, Linfield gained their first trophy under Bowyer. A 3-0 win over Larne secured the League Cup. Eric Bowyer commented that it was "nice to get that first trophy out of the way", but he was hungry to add more, and in May, an opportunity to do so presented itself. For the first time since 1985, the Blues had reached the final of the Irish Cup: Bowyer's men thus had the opportunity put a gloss on a testing season.[36]

The last time the Blues had won the Irish Cup was way back in 1982, and *Look at Linfield* asserted: "Ten years is too long for Northern Ireland's premier club to go without an Irish Cup triumph." Standing between the Blues and cup glory was a strong Glenavon team who had waited even longer – it was 31 years since their last Irish Cup win. The mid-Ulster club also had insider information on Linfield, as former Linfield stalwart Alan Fraser managed the team. Fraser had represented the Blues in a distinguished career that lasted well over a decade. He also had detailed knowledge of the current Linfield squad. In October 1991, Fraser had resigned as assistant to Eric Bowyer to take up the Glenavon job. Both managers were good friends, but both were driven by the will to win.[37]

On 2 May the two teams faced off, and it was the Belfast Blues who scored early on through the ever-clinical Martin McGaughey. With this, the Linfield section of the 14,000-strong crowd was sent into raptures. In the midst of the celebrations, about 100 individuals staged a pitch invasion – causing a short suspension of the game. When the officials were happy to resume, Linfield's early dominance dissipated. Eric Bowyer felt that the break "changed the impetus" of the game, and *Ireland's Saturday Night* was in full agreement. The paper reported that as the first half wore on, "Glenavon came more and more into the game". Then as the first half approached the close, a mistake from Linfield defender Jeff Spiers presented Glenavon with a chance to equalise. Geoff Ferris pounced, and the teams went in all square at half-time.[38]

The cup final only had one goal left in it, and it fell to Glenavon. The winner would come on 56 minutes from the right foot of 18-year-old Gerard McMahon. A free-kick was rolled to the youngster, who struck the ball past goalkeeper Alan Patterson. A deflection off the Linfield wall helped wrong-foot the keeper, and it ended in the net. The Belfast Blues pressed for an equaliser, but despite coming close it remained elusive. At full time, Bowyer reflected: "It wasn't to be our day." Alan Fraser though was obviously delighted with his side's success, but also had "sympathy for Linfield… I still have a lot of friends at the club." Fraser maintained that the "real Blue-men [had] stayed behind on the terraces to congratulate our players… but sadly those sort of things rarely get the headlines". Instead the cup final had generated more bad publicity for the club. The pitch invasion (which resulted in 31 banning orders for Linfield fans) ensured that the club's run of bad press continued.[39]

The first half of 1992 had proven tough for the Blues. Bad publicity had become a recurring theme at Windsor, and until tangible evidence of change appeared, unwanted press coverage would continue. The trouble on Irish Cup final day only served to confirm the negative stereotypes held by the club's critics. Yet amidst the bleak outlook, there were reasons for optimism. The Board could see enough improvement in the team to offer Bowyer a new contract. League Cup success was a platform to build on, and reaching the Irish Cup final demonstrated that the side was moving in the right direction. The Management Committee believed Bowyer was the man to deliver a League or Irish Cup triumph the following season.

Three years had passed at Linfield without a major piece of silverware, and there was a feeling this would soon be put right.

Chapter 5

# *Fine Margins*

When Jim McFadden rejected Linfield's approach in March 1992, he maintained that it did not appear "viable" for a Catholic from Northern Ireland to join the club. Yet within a matter of months, the seemingly unfeasible became a reality. In early June, press reports linked the Blues with a young utility player from Cliftonville. His name was Chris Cullen. On 9 June, Cullen told the press that being the first NI-born Catholic to play for the Blues in years didn't worry him "at all, not in the slightest". For Cullen, the only thing he wanted to do was "play football". On 3 July, Chris Cullen became a Linfield player. In public, the Blues refused to comment on the political and religious significance of the signing. Club secretary Derek Brooks played down the importance of Cullen's arrival, and stated the 21-year-old was "only another player".[1]

Linfield had endured a difficult six months, and officials were anxious to avoid more controversial headlines. Further scandal would, however, rock the club the day after Cullen's transfer was announced. The *Irish News* exclaimed that as Cullen's signing was confirmed, a "mock threat" made against Father McManus "came to light". By the time the *Irish News* exposed the alleged threat it had been in the public domain for three months. The paper's story referred to material that had appeared in *The Blues Brothers* fanzine: a publication which modelled itself as a Rangers-Chelsea-Linfield magazine. In the offending April 1992 edition, a photograph of McManus appeared with a target on his forehead. This was accompanied by the comment, "Blues sign new Target Man." According to the fanzine editors: "This was meant as a joke, a football pun." However, an outraged McManus did not find the caption amusing. He maintained that he had set out to expose "the... anti-Catholic ethos, sectarian ethos at Windsor Park and... the picture proved the point graphically... it reflects the thinking of fans, which in turn reflects the ethos that is tolerated".[2]

At the end of July, a United States Congressional body weighed in on the latest fanzine controversy. The ad hoc Congressional Committee for Irish Affairs argued that the acceptance of the publication indicated a "condoning" of "anti-Catholic bigotry" in Northern Irish football. The body wrote to IFA secretary David Bowen, stating that the fanzine picture had a "very clear [meaning] – shoot Father McManus". The letter criticised the Association for "shirking its responsibility... by remaining silent" and not condemning the picture. Over 50 Congressmen signed the letter. They asserted that the IFA was wrong to have avoided comment on the contentious subject. Yet on the day that the *Irish News* had highlighted the picture, Derek Brooks pointed out that the fanzine had "nothing to do with Linfield Football Club". Brooks' swift rejection of the publication's legitimacy displayed anything but acceptance of the "joke". There wasn't much more for the IFA to add.[3]

The furore over *The Blues Brothers* fanzine marked the high point of the McManus-led crusade. Whilst the boycott of Coca-Cola remained, and the Irish National Caucus did its best to keep pressure on the club, the ferocity of the campaign died down. Earlier in 1992 a *Belfast Telegraph* editorial spelt out that the best way to answer criticism was for Linfield "to become beyond reproach". So if Chris Cullen could become just another Linfield player and other Catholic players could follow, then the sting of the Caucus' criticism was nullified. Cullen's first interaction with supporters came on the afternoon of 1 August, Linfield's Open Day. This was a chance for fans to meet their idols. Over a two-hour period, supporters mobbed the young player with requests for pictures and autographs. By the end of the afternoon, Cullen quipped: "My hand's sore... At Cliftonville I was only asked for my autograph twice."[4]

Cullen's first game for the Blues arrived on 12 September against Bangor in a Gold Cup tie that finished 1-1. The Downpatrick man was named as a substitute, and came on with 50 minutes gone for the injured Martin McGaughey. *Ireland's Saturday Night* reported that Cullen's arrival "brought a mixed reaction from the Blues supporters with some cheers and some boos, but generally the 'clapometer' was registering on the high side". Cullen had proved that a Catholic could sign, and play, for Linfield. The symbolism of his appearance against Bangor was monumental. Ten months before, Blues boss Eric Bowyer rated the chances of Linfield signing a Catholic as "almost impossible", yet Cullen would indeed become just another Linfield player.[5]

Less than two weeks after Cullen's debut, the Blues took the first silverware of the season, with a win over Ards in the Ulster Cup final. Prior to the game, the papers had focused on how David Jeffrey – who had swapped the blue of Linfield for the red and blue of Ards – would fare against his old team. Yet on the night, it was a man who had moved in the opposite direction that stole the headlines. Former Ards winger Robert Campbell opened the scoring for Linfield on 25 minutes. Campbell then played a part in Linfield's second, to ensure a 2-0 win. Afterwards, a jubilant Bowyer told the press: "I believe we have the ability to make a big impression."[6]

When the League programme kicked off in the early autumn there was, however, little sign of this. The hallmark of the previous three seasons – inconsistency – remained in evidence. With four games played, Linfield had won two, drawn one and lost one. Bowyer's men went into the fifth League match, away to Distillery, under considerable pressure, and the result only piled more misery on the club. A 69th-minute goal from Winkie Armstrong settled the tie in Distillery's favour. *Ireland's Saturday Night* reported that as the Linfield players left the pitch they were "given 'the treatment' by the fans [whilst] board members came under a barrage of verbal criticism". The paper added: "The natives are becoming restless at Windsor."[7]

Little more than 48 hours after the defeat, Eric Bowyer was whisked away from first-team training and summoned to a Management Committee meeting – here he was relieved of his duties. After receiving the news, Bowyer went to the manager's office, where coaches Lindsay McKeown and Billy Rodgers were waiting. He informed them, "I'm away lads", shook their hands, and left Windsor. In the following day's newspapers, Bowyer expressed his disappointment at leaving. But maintained: "I did what I wanted to do, be the manager of Linfield… I would have liked more time and the opportunity to finish the job I started… I'm convinced we're not too far from being a good side." At a club where success was demanded, time was in short supply – and Eric Bowyer knew this. "Since the day and hour" he took the position at Linfield, he knew that his job was in the balance.[8]

The Management Committee acted quickly in naming a replacement. The same night the Board dispensed of Bowyer's services, they appointed Trevor Anderson as caretaker boss. Anderson had enjoyed a distinguished career in English football, playing with Manchester United, Swindon and Peterborough, prior to joining the Blues. He made over 300 appearances for Linfield and scored just shy of 100 goals before retiring in 1987. Five years after finishing his playing career, Anderson returned to the Blues. In January 1992, Eric Bowyer asked him to take up a position as coach of Linfield's youth team – something the lifelong Blueman gladly accepted. Nine months later, when Eric Bowyer departed as manager, Anderson stepped into the breach.[9]

Anderson's first job was to assess the quality of his squad. When he looked around the dressing room he saw "good players who needed a bit of confidence". Over the weeks that followed he went about instilling this, and it paid dividends, as his first four League matches ended in Linfield victories. Seemingly the Management Committee had seen enough – Anderson was handed a contract until the end of the season. On receiving the Board's endorsement, the new manager commented that it was "a great honour to be in charge of such a famous club". He knew, however, that the squad needed strengthening, and resolved to bring in "quality".[10]

A couple of weeks after landing the permanent contract, Anderson followed through with that vow. On 17 December, Linfield swooped for Dundalk-based forward, Dessie Gorman. When the press first got wind of the club's interest, the player's footballing prowess was of secondary importance. The *Belfast Telegraph* labelled the move "sensational" on account of its "ground-breaking" significance. Gorman was a Catholic from the Republic of Ireland, and it was almost 50 years since Linfield had signed a player from South of the border. Davy Walsh of Limerick at the end of the Second World War had been the last Southern player to make the move. Fanfare thus greeted Gorman – the 'Dundalk Hawk' – penning a contract. That said, the political ramifications of the deal were played down by the 28-year-old. In Gorman's first media duty as a Linfield player, he quipped: "What's all the fuss about? ... Linfield's background may be different to other clubs I have played for but football is the same the world over – the fans want to see their team scoring goals and winning games. That's why I'm here."[11]

Like Gorman, Trevor Anderson was keen to downplay the non-footballing aspects of the deal. The manager was only concerned with the forward's ability on the pitch, maintaining that he "wasn't there to sort out the politics of Northern Ireland... All I was interested in was good players." Anderson had every faith in his new striker, and told the press, "He'll do the business for us." Two days after the deal went through, Gorman sparkled on debut in a 4-0 rout of Ballyclare Comrades. Although he did not get on the scoresheet, he assisted by winning a penalty, and impressed himself on the game. The win over Ballyclare began a fruitful Christmas and New Year period.[12]

By February, Trevor Anderson had guided Linfield to the top of the Irish League. The arrival of Gorman had invigorated the team, but established players were also finding their feet. Lee Doherty was enjoying a purple patch, and regularly contributing goals from midfield. In total, 'the Doc' weighed in with a tally of 14 goals that 1992/93 season. As the Blues surged to the top of the tree, goals flowed from all over the team, whilst at the back the defence was rock solid. Statistics showed that at the time the Blues had the best defensive record of any team in a top-flight FIFA-recognised league.[13]

Trevor Anderson had instituted one significant change in the defence, which reaped considerable reward. The new manager moved Noel Bailie to the sweeper position, and the decision proved an instant success. Bailie had previously filled in at the back under Bowyer, but this was only as cover for injuries. When Anderson took charge, he told the 22-year-old, "Your best position is sweeper." This was music to Bailie's ears as he had enjoyed playing there as a youth. He moved from the midfield to centre-back, and flourished. Over the next two decades, the cultured player made the position his own.[14]

In early 1993, Trevor Anderson continued to ring the changes, making three signings to shore up the resurgence in form. The first was midfielder Martin Bayly, who arrived in January from League of Ireland side, Home Farm. He was thus Linfield's second recruit from south of the border in a matter of weeks. he signed until the end of the season. Upon learning of Bayly's move, the INC noted that this took the number of Catholic players at Linfield to three. A 1993 publication (*The MacBride Principles*) penned by McManus, implied that the Caucus-led campaign had brought change at the club. This was not the case. The pressure brought to bear from outside may have hastened developments. But it was Eric Bowyer's 'opening up' to *One Team in Ulster* that set in motion the changes that came.[15]

Two more seasoned professionals joined Bayly in signing short-term contracts until the end of the 1992/93 campaign. In late March, Scottish striker Graham Harvey and Liverpool-born defender Geoff Twentyman agreed deals. Both had vast experience of professional football. Harvey had played with Hibernian, Dundee and Airdrieonians, whilst Twentyman had represented Preston North End and Bristol Rovers. Prior to the pair's signing the Blues had maintained their impressive League form, but Anderson felt that more experience was needed to see the team over the line. Upon arrival, both made significant contributions. In Harvey's first game, the Scotsman notched a hat-trick in a 5-2 win over Larne, whilst Twentyman drew upon his experience and know-how to settle nerves as the finish line approached.[16]

The additions to the squad and the other changes Anderson implemented proved to be masterstrokes. With one game remaining, the new manager guided the Blues to the Gibson Cup. On 17 April, title rivals Crusaders and Portadown both slipped up with a draw and a defeat respectively. This enabled Linfield to (all but mathematically) win the title at the Oval, home of cross-town adversaries Glentoran. The Glens had led the Blues 1-0 at half-time through a Stephen Douglas goal, before Glenn Hunter grabbed an equaliser. Substitute Ritchie Johnston then scored the winner to give Linfield the title. At the end of the game, Anderson – bedecked in an ankle-length all-weather coat – ran on to the pitch to congratulate his players. The *News Letter* likened his sprint across the pitch to that of a "a caped crusader", though in the euphoria of the occasion Anderson didn't care if he "looked like Batman galloping across the ground".[17]

Captain Alan Dornan had worried that "we'd never return to the title [considering it had] been four long years" since the last League triumph. Yet Linfield's wait was nothing compared to the lean spell that was soon to end in the northwest of England. A couple of weeks after the Irish League finished, the inaugural English Premier League was won by Manchester United – a team that had waited 26 years for a League title. In the ecstasy of success, United supporters toasted the impact of a mid-season signing. The mercurial talents of Eric Cantona – who had famously crossed the Pennines from major rivals, Leeds – helped inspire the Manchester side's triumph. Like Gorman at Linfield, Cantona's signing attracted huge media interest because of factors bigger than the game of football. But also like Gorman's transfer, it proved a stroke of genius.[18]

Gorman relished the big stage at Windsor. He enjoyed playing in front of sizeable crowds and the limelight that went with it. 'The Hawk's' move had brought considerable attention, yet for Gorman it made playing for the Blues "the easiest job in the world". He did not give any interviews that reflected on the political aspects of his move; instead he referred any questions of this nature to Trevor Anderson. This meant that all he had to do "was play football… and the football I found very easy, so I enjoyed it". The confidence that Gorman displayed inspired others, and played a major role in the club's success.[19]

Winning the Gibson Cup brought a twofold reward for Trevor Anderson. Firstly, the Linfield Board granted him a new two-year contract. Then secondly, the success presented Anderson with the honour of leading the club in Europe. Four years had passed since the Blues had last played in such competition (and six since Windsor had hosted a game). As champions, Linfield returned to the European Cup, but the club entered a competition undergoing an overhaul. It had rebranded as the 'Champions League', and the restyled competition reflected a changing Europe. Since Linfield had last played in the European Cup, the political map of Europe had altered significantly. The 1989 tournament had taken the Blues to the Soviet Union, which by 1993 no longer existed. Fifteen new countries emerged out of the former USSR, whilst elsewhere across Eastern Europe new nation states arose after the fall of communism. As new countries came into existence, UEFA's membership expanded. In the 1989 European Cup, 32 teams had taken part; in 1993, 42 teams competed. As the number of teams in the tournament rose, a preliminary round was introduced.[20]

During the 1993/94 European Cup preliminary, 20 teams would enter, and Linfield were among them. The Irish League's lowly UEFA ranking of 29th ensured that the club had to negotiate this qualifier. When the European draw was made in mid-July, Linfield were paired with Dinamo Tbilisi of Georgia, and club officials could not hide their disappointment at the outcome. Chairman David Campbell lamented the "long and costly journey to what I believe to be the furthest point in the European football area!" The new state located in the Caucasus region, was about 3,000 miles from Belfast. Arrangements for the game thus proved a logistical nightmare.[21]

The quick turnaround between the draw and game did little to help. Instead of playing a first-round game in September, the Blues were entering the competition in the middle of August. The first leg of the tie was scheduled for 18 August in Tbilisi. A week prior to this, the Foreign Office advised the Linfield party not to venture anywhere unattended, as they were travelling to a state that had emerged amidst conflict. Between 1989 and 1993, the region was beset by three wars, including a civil war for power in Tbilisi. During this time 13,000 lives were lost, while 200,000 people were 'ethnically cleansed'. The turmoil in Georgia was rarely covered in the British media. However, a matter of days before Linfield travelled, the press reported on the gunning down of a US CIA agent at Tbilisi's airport. Against the worrying backdrop of violence and the Foreign Office advice, Linfield travelled to the Georgian capital on 16 August.[22]

Three fans and League of Ireland side Shelbourne accompanied the team party on a flight out of Dublin. Shels had Cup Winners' Cup duty in Ukraine, and it made sense for both clubs to share the travel expense. The Dublin side would journey as far as Lviv where they had a game later that week with Karpaty Lviv, but as the plane approached Lviv airport it started to experience difficulties. Problems were detected with the wheels and the aircraft was forced to circle in the sky for 15 minutes. When the plane eventually touched down (on a second attempt) it was stressful for all on board, particularly as fire engines had lined the runway as the plane landed. Management Committee member Ivan Foster described the ordeal as "terrifying with the plane juddering both violently and erratically". Midfielder Lee Doherty admitted to the *News Letter* that he had "never been so frightened in all [his] life".[23]

Two and a half hours were needed to repair the wheel damage before the plane could take off for the final three-hour leg of the flight. All told, the journey from Dublin to Tbilisi took over 17 hours! This was far from ideal preparation for what was a tough assignment. When the travel-weary team disembarked in the Georgian capital, they were struck by the city's poverty. Yet the hardship within the city stood in stark contrast to the Metechi Palace Hotel where the team stayed. Ivan Foster described the hotel as "the essence of opulence". Foster also pointed out that, "Armed men of the diplomatic corps guarded the hotel, night and day, walking round and round the perimeter carrying anything from sub-machine to hand guns!" The imposing security served to re-emphasise the Foreign Office advice, and made for an intimidating welcome.[24]

The task awaiting the players on the pitch was as daunting as the introduction to Tbilisi. The Georgians were odds-on favourites for the tie. The Blues played in a league with a higher UEFA ranking, but this was only on account of the Georgians' recent admission to UEFA. Dinamo had quality players and considerable European pedigree. The club had won the 1981 Cup Winners' Cup, as representatives of the Soviet Union. There was also the not-so-small matter of 50,000 fans packing into Dinamo Stadium on the night of the match. Such was the significance of Tbilisi representing an independent Georgia in the Champions League, that nearly every diplomat in the new state attended the game.[25]

When Linfield lined up for the match, the team included two major summer signings. The first was midfielder Gary Peebles, who joined from Partick Thistle. The second was Garry Haylock, a striker who signed from Shelbourne for an Irish League record fee. Huddersfield-born Haylock's price tag was £35,000, but manager Trevor Anderson knew a major financial outlay was needed. Linfield had let go of striker Stephen Baxter, who had scored 102 goals in 221 appearances, and also Martin McGaughey. 'Buckets' had amassed a staggering 313 goals in 485 games for the Blues, and did not want to leave. However, his 1992/93 season was decimated by injury, and Anderson informed the striker that his Linfield career was over. After leaving, McGaughey paid tribute to the manager, saying: "Linfield have got themselves a great manager in Trevor. He doesn't let sentiment get in the way of difficult decisions and that's the sign of a man who will always put the club first." Anderson had worked wonders during his first half-season in charge – and he needed to produce more of the same in Tbilisi.[26]

Dinamo dominated the game from kick-off, and it was no surprise when the home side took an eighth-minute lead through Shota Arveladze. After that the Blues made it to half-time without conceding again. Trevor Anderson's game plan had been to soak up pressure and hit the Georgians on the break. Shortly after the start of the second half, the manager's tactics bore fruit. On 56 minutes, striker Ritchie Johnston put the ball in the Tbilisi net, silencing the 50,000-strong stadium. For the next 10 minutes the Blues held the Georgians at bay, but then succumbed to a Tbilisi second on 66 minutes. The match finished 2-1 in Dinamo's favour, with one man almost single-handedly keeping the scoreline respectable. Linfield's goalkeeper Wes Lamont had the game of his life, pulling off world-class save after save. In the *Belfast Telegraph*, John Laverty commented that there was not "enough space" to recount all Lamont's fine goalkeeping. A passport official in Tbilisi airport went further still. As the team passed through departures en route to their awaiting plane, the official hailed Lamont as "the greatest goalkeeper in the world".[27]

European football returned to Windsor Park (after an absence of six years) on the evening of 1 September. Six thousand Bluemen flocked to 'the Shrine' to see if Linfield could overturn a Dinamo side the press had lauded. Those in attendance were on the lookout for one Dinamo player in particular – the 'number 10', Georgi Kinkladze. After the game in Tbilisi, *Ireland's Saturday Night* said: "The boy has everything – vision, pace, terrific skill and shooting power." At Windsor, he did not disappoint. The *Belfast Telegraph* reported that the "teenage genius" was in "buzzing" form. The diminutive playmaker would later go on to enhance his growing reputation. In 1995 he signed for Manchester City and enjoyed cult status at Maine Road. Arveladze, who opened the scoring in the first game, similarly enjoyed a distinguished career outside of Georgia. He went on to play nearly 100 games for both Ajax Amsterdam and Glasgow Rangers.[28]

Dinamo's squad for both of the encounters with Linfield was thus laced with talent – but as a team, the Georgians did not replicate their performance from the first leg at Windsor. In Belfast, things were much more evenly matched. Neither goal was breached in the first half, but 50 seconds after the start of the second, Dinamo took the lead. Again, Shota Arveladze broke the deadlock. Linfield pushed to get back into the game, and on 71 minutes new-boy Haylock scored with a header from an Alan Dornan cross. The Blues pressed for a further goal to take the tie to extra time, but it just wouldn't come. Linfield were out of Europe and hadn't even reached the first round.[29]

A couple of days after the game, Trevor Anderson received some intriguing news whilst at his City Hospital day job. Anderson had popped out of the office for a visit to the dentist, and when he came back, colleagues informed him that Linfield were still in the Champions League. News had filtered through that prior to the first leg, a Dinamo sponsor had allegedly paid a bribe to the referee and linesmen. Turkish referee, a Mr Toroghu, had taken the bribe (as evidence), then presented it to UEFA in Geneva. Upon learning this, UEFA expelled Tbilisi and brought Linfield back into the competition. Dinamo would contest Toroghu's allegations and instructed lawyers to appeal the decision. Tbilisi claimed that the money given to the referee and his officials was for expenses. Yet after a six-hour meeting in Zurich, UEFA dismissed the Dinamo appeal. The governing body rejected their version of events, stating that rules had been breached as expenses could not be presented without documentation. Jonathan Wilson, an authority on Eastern European football, explained that the scandal caused little surprise in the newly independent state, as "corruption had become a way of life [and] nobody seemed particularly concerned".[30]

Regardless of the circumstances, Linfield had progressed past a round in Europe for the first time since knocking out Shamrock Rovers in the first round of the 1984/85 European Cup. Almost a decade on, the Blues were making it through the Champions League preliminary, and their reward was a matchup with FC Copenhagen of Denmark. One week after UEFA had rejected Dinamo's appeal, the Blues took on Copenhagen at Windsor, and all who attended witnessed a special night. On 16 September, Linfield produced one of the club's finest performances on the European stage. With 38 minutes gone, Linfield took the lead through Garry Haylock. Then just before the end of the half, that lead was doubled. John McConnell powered a header from a Stephen Beatty free-kick into the Copenhagen net to give the Blues a 2-0 half-time lead. Ritchie Johnston then completed the scoring in the 62nd minute to give the Blues a comprehensive 3-0 victory.[31]

The whole team was lauded for the performance. The press credited Haylock with having his best all-round game since joining, whilst Peebles and Doherty in the midfield were described as "masterful". At the back, Noel Bailie was referred to as "simply brilliant". After the game, Trevor Anderson admitted to being "up in the clouds like everyone else", while chairman David Campbell asked cheekily, "Where's the final being staged?" Copenhagen's manager, Benny Johansen, understandably had different emotions. He admitted that the defeat to Linfield was the "worst" experience of his career. Johansen's Copenhagen had previously triumphed 6-2 over Bayern Munich en route to a UEFA Cup quarter-final. Therefore slumping to defeat by a part-time Irish League side did not sit easily with the Danish club's reputation and expectations. Indeed, Copenhagen had only recently been founded after a merger of two sides – and the new club's specific aim was competing on the European stage. Their resources were much greater than Linfield's and the upset was huge. Thus an embarrassed – but calm – Johansen vowed that he would get things right for the second leg. His plan of attack was to sit down, listen to some music and work out where it all went wrong.[32]

Trevor Anderson was a veteran campaigner, and knew the tie was only at half-time. Linfield still had to negotiate the return game in Denmark. Going into the return fixture on 29 September, preparations were rocked by the loss of two key players. Both Ritchie Johnston and club captain Alan Dornan were sidelined by knee injuries. The team would miss Johnston's presence up front and Dornan's leadership at the back. Anderson knew that being without the pair was a huge disadvantage, but hoped that the Blues had enough to see off the Danes. If Linfield could do so, this would be an incredible achievement – in the early 1990s, it was becoming even harder for clubs from 'smaller' leagues to succeed in Europe. As Chris Lightbown of the *Sunday Times* noted: "UEFA like part-timers such as Linfield to be off-stage by the time the big boys come out to play."[33]

Lightbown travelled to Copenhagen, and was struck by the rapport between players and supporters. Nine-hundred or so Bluemen made the journey to Denmark, a sizeable number of whom found their way to the team hotel in the city centre. Lightbown explained that there "had been an attempt to keep the team's location a secret from the fans, to give the players as much rest as possible, but that was a forlorn exercise in a club where the captain is on first-name terms with easily 10% of the crowd". Indeed, the downtown Copenhagen hotel was almost a 'Little Belfast', where "players, directors and fans milled around the lobby as if they were friends and neighbours, which in many cases they [were]".[34]

The Danish press had, unsurprisingly, savaged the Copenhagen players and management after the first leg. Club owner Harald Nielsen had even waited at the airport to give manager Benny Johansen a dressing down after his return from Belfast. It was thus a determined Johansen that stressed, "We are still in the tie." Furthermore, an editorial in the club programme asserted: "Linfield CAN be defeated and we can beat them." If they were to do so, the Danes needed a strong start; unfortunately, what they needed, they got. Not long after kick-off in the return leg, the home side took the lead. This was doubled before half-time, but after that the Blues weathered the storm. With 90 minutes played, Copenhagen led 2-0, which meant that Linfield would go through as 3-2 aggregate winners.[35]

Then in the 95th minute, controversy struck. Lee Doherty conceded

a questionable free-kick just outside the Linfield box. Copenhagen's Lars Hojer stepped up to take the set piece and smashed it past a despairing Wes Lamont. This took the game into extra time. John Laverty of the *Belfast Telegraph* was incensed by both the amount of added time played and the decision to award the set piece. The journalist did not hold back in his assessment of Austrian referee, Roman Steindl, writing: "Never have I witnessed a display as appalling as this one." Assistant manager Lindsay McKeown was so outraged that he confronted Steindl before extra time began. In disgust, McKeown implied that the ref had cheated. McKeown then threw money down in front of Steindl, saying, "You'll be getting a lot more where that came from!" The outburst landed the Blues assistant a red card, forcing him to watch the rest of the game from the stands. UEFA later punished McKeown's actions by banning him from European competition for two years.[36]

Copenhagen had entered extra time with momentum, and in the first half the home side scored a fourth to take an aggregate lead in the tie. Kim Mikkelsen beat the Linfield defence and an advancing Lamont. This was the final – and decisive – goal in the tie. Linfield's players just couldn't find the net on the night. Copenhagen had edged the two games 4-3, and the defeat was hard to take. David Campbell admitted: "I have been chairman of Linfield for 15 years and never felt so bad and annoyed.... Even the Copenhagen officials admitted afterwards they were very, very lucky."[37]

Symptomatic of this luck, the Danes drew AC Milan in the second round. Milan were one of the top teams in Europe at the time, and went on to win the Champions League that season. In an all-conquering Rossoneri team the likes of Baresi, Costacurta, Maldini, Boban, Simone and Papin all starred. Seeing players of this calibre grace Windsor was the stuff of dreams, but it had come tantalisingly close to being a reality. Linfield had narrowly missed out on this occasion; whether a chance like this would present itself again was highly questionable. UEFA was implementing initiatives like the preliminary rounds, which increasingly meant that teams from leagues with low rankings had little chance of playing sides of Milan's stature. European football's governing body was stripping away the rewards attached to winning a domestic league title. As Chris Lightbown of the *Sunday Times* argued, UEFA did not want the likes of Linfield stealing the big boys' limelight.[38]

After the fine performances against Tbilisi and Copenhagen, expectations were high for the local season. These appeared vindicated by the turn of the year. Though only halfway through the season, two trophies were already in the bag. In August, the Blues had earned share of the Charity Shield after a 1-1 draw with Bangor. Then just before Christmas, Linfield won their first ever Budweiser Cup, with a 3-0 win over Ards. The goals on the night had come from Lee Doherty, Garry Haylock and recent signing Raymond Campbell, who had joined in a controversial move from cross-city rivals Glentoran. The winger from Downpatrick indicated he wanted a move away from the Oval in June, and a transfer saga had dragged throughout the summer. Campbell eventually joined in September for £33,500, a figure set by a tribunal after the two clubs could not agree on valuation. Ray Campbell was not cheap, but he didn't take long in establishing himself with the Windsor crowd. Inspiring a 2-0 Boxing Day defeat of his former club went a long way to making him a favourite.[39]

Early in the New Year the club again dug deep to secure another signing. Pat Fenlon joined from Shelbourne in mid-January 1994, for a fee of around £20,000. Trevor Anderson was delighted at the capture, describing his new player as "the best midfielder down South". Anderson and the Linfield Board realised that big money was needed if the club was to meet expectations. Under Eric Bowyer, Linfield had not forked out large sums; consequently, the Blues fell behind the likes of Glenavon, Glentoran and Portadown. Success had returned with the 1992/93 League title, and the Linfield hierarchy was eager to see this remain. In the eight months after that victory, the Blues spent approximately £100,000 on Haylock, Peebles, Campbell and Fenlon. The management and Board were showing their intent to maintain Linfield's status as the number one Irish League club.[40]

Linfield's players were matching this intent on the pitch. The strong first half of the season was built upon in the business end of the campaign, as interest was sustained in the League, Irish Cup and League Cup. This made for a hectic end of season. In April, Linfield's part-time players took to the pitch on nine occasions, including an eight-day period when they faced four matches! The fixture congestion resulted from a lengthy backlog of games and came at the end of the month. From 23-30 April, Linfield players had to contend with three League games and a League Cup final. If they could win all four games, the League and the League Cup would reside at Windsor. Then – and only then – could the players turn their thoughts to an Irish Cup final on 7 May.

The Blues travelled to Portadown on 23 April for a crunch game with the League leaders. According to the *Belfast Telegraph*, this was the biggest Irish League game in years. A win would keep Anderson's men in the chase, whilst the Ports would just about clinch the title with three points. Ten thousand fans crammed into Shamrock Park and they witnessed a Linfield victory. A Portadown banner at the game hailed the home side's midfielder Tony Gorman as 'Stormin Gorman'. However, it was Linfield's star by the same surname who stole the headlines. Dessie put the Blues ahead on three minutes. Then the Dundalk Hawk doubled his tally and Linfield's lead on 20 minutes, by steering a Raymond Campbell cross into the net. There were no further goals as Linfield stayed in the hunt and earned a first win at Shamrock Park since December 1988.[41]

Three days later, on Tuesday 26 April, the club won its third piece of silverware that season. A 2-0 victory over Coleraine secured the League Cup, but the players had little opportunity for celebration. Trevor Anderson was preaching the old adage of 'one game at a time', and the next was 48 hours later in Newry – a postponed fixture from early January. Prior to travelling, the Blues sat in third place, a point behind Portadown and Glenavon. If Linfield could beat Newry, the club would move two points clear of the mid-Ulster sides, thus stealing the advantage going into the final League game. Trevor Anderson arranged for the players to be off work on the day of the game to help them prepare. The manager knew that weary limbs needed rest and recuperation. Despite this, Linfield's players could not find the win. The Blues went ahead after 27 minutes through Pat Fenlon, but just before half-time a Ciaran O'Kane header drew the South Down side level. No more goals followed and Trevor Anderson rued at full time, "We didn't function – never played at all."[42]

The draw left Linfield level with Portadown and Glenavon going into the League's final round of matches. All three clubs had 67 points, though Portadown had by far the best goal difference. Glenavon's was second best, which meant Linfield occupied third position. The Blues simply had to win their last game against Glentoran to have any chance of lifting the Gibson Cup. In this most intriguing end to a season, first-placed Portadown would travel to second-placed Glenavon at the same time as Linfield faced the Glens. Fans of all three title-challenging clubs worked through the various permutations ahead of 3pm on the Saturday, and so did Trevor Anderson. The Linfield manager took the Friday off work and considered how best to organise his players going into the season finale. When he got to the dressing room on Saturday 30 April, he told his team: "We're going to win this, because Portadown and Glenavon will play a draw."[43]

On a day of high drama, Glenavon were the first to edge ahead. With eight minutes on the clock at Mourneview, Raymond McCoy put the Lurgan Blues 1-0 up. No more goals were scored at Mourneview in the first half, whilst in Belfast neither Linfield nor Glentoran could break the deadlock. This meant that as the second halves got underway, Glenavon sat top, Linfield second, and the Ports in third. The Lurgan side soon strengthened its grip on the title, with a second goal through Stephen McBride. Back in Belfast, Linfield supporters – aware of events at Mourneview – knew their team had to break the stalemate against Glentoran. Linfield did just that with 20 minutes remaining in the game. A mistake in the Glentoran defence presented an opportunity for Pat Fenlon, who went past keeper Alan Paterson and scored. The Dubliner sent Windsor wild; then not long after, he played a hand in Linfield's second. Fenlon passed to Dessie Gorman who turned, shot and made it 2-0.[44]

Just as Gorman strengthened Linfield's lead, events in Lurgan took a twist. Portadown's Sandy Fraser pulled a goal back to reduce Glenavon's advantage. As the drama was unfolding, the Gibson Cup sat in a car between Belfast and Lurgan. The trophy was in the company of Irish League president Morton McKnight, and secretary Harry Wallace. With Glenavon holding the advantage, the pair hedged their bets and sat closer to Lurgan at the Moira roundabout. Then with six minutes left at Mourneview, Portadown grabbed an equaliser – Fraser scoring again. The Gibson Cup now appeared destined for Windsor, and the Irish League top brass left Moira bound for Belfast.[45]

Shortly after Fraser equalised in Lurgan, the game at Windsor was brought to a close by referee Norman Cowie. Linfield had won 2-0, and could now only hope that neither mid-Ulster club found a winning goal. The wait for all connected with Linfield was agonising, as there was still some time to go at Mourneview – five minutes all told. Players and supporters gathered around radios hoping no further goals would come in Lurgan. The memories of Copenhagen were fresh, and all knew how quickly victory could be snatched away. Both Portadown and Glenavon came close, but neither team could get the winner – meaning the Blues won the title by two points. A day of tension had gone down to the wire, and resulted in Linfield's second Gibson Cup triumph in two years. *Ireland's Saturday Night* maintained that the crowd's "victory roar" was so loud it "must have been heard even at Mourneview!" In the same paper, Malcolm Brodie put the day's excitement into perspective. He wrote: "Never do I remember anything quite like this in more than 40 years covering Irish League football."[46]

After the title was presented, assistant manager Lindsay McKeown joked, "The next game cannot come quickly enough." The Blues had just endured an exhausting week and a nail-biting climax, but an Irish Cup decider with Bangor still awaited the following Saturday. Twelve years had elapsed since Linfield's last Irish Cup triumph, and there was a resolve that the drought would end. Ahead of the game, Noel Bailie told the *News Letter*: "It's time the Irish Cup came back to Windsor Park… it's time to make amends."[47]

Bailie and his teammates were good to those words. Linfield controlled the final and emerged 2-0 victors. Gary Peebles broke the deadlock with a glancing header from a Stephen Beatty corner. Then Pat Fenlon scored a second. At the other end of the pitch, goalkeeper Wes Lamont enjoyed a comfortable day at the office. The only worry for him came afterwards. During the celebrations, the keeper dropped his winners' medal. Fortunately, a photographer found the medal on the pitch and reunited Lamont with his well-earned prize.[48]

One player, though, was only too happy to part with his medal. Lee Doherty presented his memento of the victory to his dad. The Doc's father, Alex, had missed out on cup glory 36 years previously, with Ballymena. Alex Doherty was set to play in the North Antrim side's win over Linfield in the 1958 cup final, only for a family death to rule him out. Thirty-six years later, Lee was able to give his father an Irish Cup medal and say: "Daddy, I've been looking for that for you for so long." The Doc had been with Linfield throughout the lean years of Irish Cup failure. He was therefore delighted to finally be part of a Linfield team that brought the cup back to Windsor. He had come on as a second-half substitute in the final, making what turned out to be his last appearance in a Linfield shirt. In the close season, Doherty moved to Glenavon. The Blues had lost a quality and experienced player in Lee Doherty. Still, there was every expectation that Linfield would go on to dominate the local game again. The squad that had just won the Double was strong. Captain Alan Dornan explained that there was a good balance: "It was a quality side; we had no fear," whilst Trevor Anderson would state: "I think we haven't seen the best of the current team."[49]

Chapter 6

# *More of an Ordeal than an Adventure*

During the 1990s the bigger clubs were unquestionably getting their way on the European stage. The changes to competitions such as the Champions League – which the likes of Linfield had borne the brunt of – would continue to be rung as the decade wore on. Money was talking, and it would be fair to say that the squeeze was being put on the minnows. Ironically this was coming at a time when the Irish League was actually moving to a more streamlined competition.

Significant business was undertaken at the 1994 Irish League AGM. On the evening of 27 May, a two-tier league with promotion and relegation was confirmed for the 1995/96 season. After years of withstanding change, 'the powers that be' were finally dragging local football into modernity. The system was utilised across Europe, and the Irish League had long been considered an anomaly in not employing it. In Britain, the English game had used promotion and relegation since the late nineteenth century, whilst top-level Scottish football introduced it in 1921/22. For years, the Blues had championed the system, arguing that increased competition and an improvement in standards would result. However, the club struggled to garner support. Critics felt that promotion and relegation was not feasible in Northern Ireland. Arguments centred on fears that an inadequate number of teams existed to maintain a functional pyramid league structure. The size of the Province was always highlighted as an issue, yet this had never stopped places such as the Isle of Man and the Faroe Islands employing promotion and relegation within their domestic leagues.[1]

It was thus a relief for the club when the Irish League finally adopted the system in the mid-1990s. Its introduction meant that the 16-team Irish League would split in two. The top eight teams in the aggregate table would form the Premier League, and the bottom eight the First Division. Promotion and relegation between the two new leagues would then operate from 1995/96. This meant the 1994/95 season was crucial in determining which teams entered the new leagues. Each side's points tally from the upcoming season would be added to the 1993/94 total to give an aggregate score. There was thus much more than usual riding on the 1994/95 Irish League season.[2]

In England's top flight, the outcome of 1994/95 also carried greater weight than in a standard season. At the end of that campaign, the Premier League would decrease in size from 22 to 20 clubs. Four teams faced relegation (instead of the normal three), and only two promotion places (instead of three) were on offer for the First Division. The reduced number of elite positions meant more money and more power for the established 'powerhouses' of English football. This was in keeping with the motivations behind the 1992 Premier League breakaway from the Football League. As James Walvin explained in *The People's Game*: "The restructuring [of England's top tier] was driven by commercial interests; by a small band of elite clubs anxious to confirm their position and enhance their wealth." The control of these elite clubs would only tighten with the reduction of available positions. For teams that struggled at the wrong end of the Premier League, the 1994/95 season carried extra stress.[3]

Southampton was one of the teams feeling the pressure going into this vital season. The Saints had struggled in the first two Premier League campaigns. In both seasons the club had finished 18th, narrowly missing relegation. The South Coast side was therefore hoping that its fortunes would improve in 1994/95. As part of the Saints' preparations for the important upcoming season, a visit to Windsor for a friendly with Linfield was included. This was the first meeting between the Blues and a top-flight English club in the Premier League era. On 30 July, Southampton lined up at Windsor with a strong team. Included were the likes of English internationals Matt Le Tissier and Dave Beasant. Yet it was the Belfast part-timers who emerged victorious with a 2-1 scoreline. Goals from Garry Haylock settled the tie in Linfield's favour. His first came on six minutes, then on 70 minutes he grabbed his second from the penalty spot. After his brace there were chants of "Haylock for England!" *Ireland's Saturday Night* acknowledged that, "Pre-season friendlies can be deceptive", but Linfield's performance against "Premier opposition" gave "every indication" that the Blues would again be "the main challenging force in Irish League football".[4]

The win against Southampton was also ideal preparation for a European campaign that started in mid-August. Linfield had qualified by virtue of the previous season's League triumph. However, the Blues would not partake in the 1994/95 Champions League. In an outrageous move, UEFA undermined the prestige of winning a domestic league, and only 24 teams were afforded the honour of entering the premier European club competition that season. Linfield, along with a host of other league winners, were not even placed in a qualifying round. Instead they had to make do with the UEFA Cup – a poor relation of the Champions League. To soften the blow, UEFA paid out approximately £100,000 to the snubbed league winners. European football's governing body was demonstrating that it was not concerned by merit: money was the prime motivator.[5]

When UEFA revamped the European Cup as the Champions League, group stages became a component of the competition. The exact format of the stages varied, but usually a couple of rounds were held to decide which teams made the groups. UEFA was stacking the deck in favour of teams from stronger leagues. Group stages guaranteed regular glamorous games between the likes of Madrid, Milan and Manchester United. The move from a straight knockout European Cup to a Champions League was all about ensuring UEFA had a consistently strong product. Big games meant big money in television revenue. This would centralise power and capital in the hands of a small elite band of clubs that UEFA wanted to market. On the flip side, a team like Linfield now had next to no chance of landing a payday after drawing one of the 'big boys' in an open draw. The composition of the 1994/95 Champions League showed just how far UEFA was prepared to go to ensure the 'right sort' of champions played in Europe's premier club competition. As John Laverty put it in *Ireland's Saturday Night*: "UEFA have no time any more for the smaller clubs."[6]

There were obvious parallels between the Premier League's impact on English football and what UEFA was doing to European club football. In England, the top clubs were putting the squeeze on 'smaller' sides, whilst across Europe UEFA was facilitating a similar process. This meant that Northern Irish sides would fall even further behind. It was ironic that just as the local game was introducing promotion and relegation to improve internal competition, UEFA was creating a 'closed shop' for Europe's elite. Part-time Irish League clubs were never going to challenge for the Champions League. Nevertheless, champions like Linfield should have had the chance to compete in the competition.

Trevor Anderson was naturally disheartened by the Champions League snub. Yet he tried to see the positives, telling the press: "We would have preferred to be in the European Cup. But who knows what team we will draw in the UEFA Cup." Anderson and all connected with Linfield were hoping for a 'big name' – and the UEFA Cup would deliver. Unfortunately, 'big' in this case referred to the number of letters in the opponent's name rather than the team's stature. Icelandic side Fimleikafélag Hafnarfjarðar stood between the Blues and the first round of the UEFA Cup. Very little was known about Hafnarfjarðar, but there was an expectation that Linfield would progress. Indeed, Anderson gave his team "a fighting chance" of making it to the first round. He wasn't counting on an ill-disciplined first leg away from home. Linfield went down 1-0, with Raymond Campbell and Garry Haylock both sent off on the night. The *Belfast Telegraph* described the performance in Iceland "as one of the poorest... by a Blues team in European competition... It was embarrassing". [7]

Going into that first leg, Linfield's players were rusty and couldn't keep up with the Icelanders, who competed in a summer league. However, back in Belfast there was marked improvement, as the Blues defeated Hafnarfjarðar 3-1. Goals from Stephen Beatty, Dessie Gorman and Gary Peebles swept the Icelandic challenge aside. The home leg was Linfield's sixth competitive game of the season and it told. For the first time in 10 years, Linfield's exploits on the pitch had taken the team through a round in Europe. Off-field issues had taken the club past Tbilisi the previous year, but this time it was on merit. Linfield's reward for making it past Hafnarfjarðar was a first-round tie with Danish side Odense. As soon as the draw was made, thoughts turned to the last visit to Denmark and the agonising defeat to Copenhagen.

Trevor Anderson informed his players that they would "have to be at [their] best" to get past Odense, as he rated them much higher than Copenhagen. In the first leg Linfield had the home advantage, and just as Anderson had predicted, the Danes came out strong. However, by half-time Linfield had managed to stave off Odense. Then just as the second half was getting underway, Linfield succumbed to a setback. The unfortunate Noel Bailie diverted an effort from Jens Thorup past stranded goalkeeper Wes Lamont. As the second half wore on, Odense went in search of a second, but Bailie and his defensive partner John McConnell kept the Danes at bay. As the game drew to a close, Linfield looked as likely as Odense to score, and with four minutes left on the clock snatched an equaliser. An Odense defender struggled to clear his lines and Gary Peebles pounced. The midfielder got the ball to substitute Mark Anderson, who from a difficult angle placed it past keeper Lars Hogh. The next day's *Belfast Telegraph* extolled that, "Mark Anderson's principal claim to fame [prior to his equalising goal] was that he happened to be the Blues manager's nephew." Suddenly he was lauded as the man who gave Linfield a chance to progress, "by scoring a goal uncle Trevor would have been proud of".[8]

Odense held the advantage on away goals, meaning Linfield would have to go to Denmark and either win or achieve a high-scoring draw to progress. Upon arrival in Odense, Trevor Anderson had to make a big call on team selection. UEFA had a rule that capped the number of foreign players a team could play in European competition. Only three players from outside a country could take to the field for any side. This was problematic for British teams, as England, Scotland, Wales and Northern Ireland were regarded as separate entities – despite all home-nation players holding the same passport! Linfield's first-choice team had an Englishman in Garry Haylock, a Scotsman in Gary Peebles and two players from the Republic, Dessie Gorman and Pat Fenlon. One of the above would thus have to sit the fixture out. Trevor Anderson called the rule "stupid", and pointed out that "big teams including AC Milan and Manchester United want it changed... so hopefully something will happen soon". Just over a year later the "big teams" got their way. In December 1995, the European Court of Justice ruled the practice of capping players from European Union countries illegal. However, in late September 1994, when the Blues took to the field in Denmark, Pat Fenlon would be the unfortunate player to miss out.[9]

Minus the inspirational Fenlon, Linfield played the reverse leg on 27 September. For those who lined up it was a wretched evening, as the Danes won 5-0. Linfield's UEFA Cup campaign was over in the most ignominious of circumstances. Afterwards a disappointed Anderson reflected: "To be honest it was men against boys." Linfield could not cope with the Odense players, and for Anderson, "the difference between part-time and full-time players was clear". The Danish side could boast no household-name players, but they had a professionalism that part-time footballers could not match. Odense were a strong, functional team without frills. Drawing a side of this nature was not something to be relished. In the home leg, only 3,500 supporters had attended. European football was definitely losing its glamour.[10]

The UEFA Cup campaign of 1994/95 brought the rapidly evolving face of European football into sharp focus, and it was clear that such competitions were becoming more of an ordeal than an adventure. Sides like Linfield appeared destined to remain at the bottom of the pecking order with no real chance of taking on the giants. Preliminary rounds and defeats by competent but uninspiring opponents appeared to be the future for Irish League involvement in Europe. UEFA's membership expansion had presented an opportunity to protect elite interests, and the governing body grabbed it. For teams like Linfield, the developments were frustrating, but there had been an air of inevitability.

What was not expected was a disappointing 1994/95 Irish League campaign. At the outset of the season, Alan Dornan told the press: "I think the team is a wee bit special." He was echoing the sentiments of his manager, who had said at the end of the previous season that the best of this Linfield team was still to come. However, these predictions never came good. Disappointing results punctuated the entire League campaign, leaving Linfield to finish in eighth place – over 20 points behind winners Crusaders. The accumulated table of that and the previous season, which decided the make-up of the Premier League, had the Blues in fourth, but this was scant consolation. *Look at Linfield* described "Our League form this season [as], quite bluntly... very disappointing."[11]

Cup form, though, was much stronger. A February County Antrim Shield success (the first for 11 years) was followed by a run to the Irish Cup final. On 6 May, the players had the opportunity to turn around an otherwise disappointing campaign at the Oval, with Carrick Rangers providing the opposition. The build-up to the final was dominated by references to the previous time both clubs had met in an Irish Cup decider. In 1976, 'B' Division Carrick had pulled off one of the greatest upsets in the competition's history. A double from Gary Prenter secured a 2-1 victory for the junior outfit, and ensured significant losses for the bookies. The Blues manager at the time, a young Roy Coyle, was crushed by the defeat. Nineteen years later he told *Ireland's Saturday Night* that a Linfield win "would help ease the disappointment of '76". On the morning of the final, Blues midfielder Raymond Campbell told the *News Letter* he was "tired hearing about" the famous upset.[12]

Mercifully for Campbell, his Linfield team would not have to live with the ignominy of such a defeat, as the Blues recorded back-to-back cup success for the first time since 1963. Garry Haylock was the hero on the day, scoring twice in a 3-1 win. The big striker was awarded man-of-the-match as the press praised his performance. John Laverty commented in *Ireland's Saturday Night* that Haylock's display married class and effort. The *News Letter* contended that the Oval had witnessed "perhaps one of his 'finest hours'" as Linfield escaped a grip of mediocrity". The East Belfast stadium had also just observed Haylock's final act in the club's colours. In two seasons, Garry Haylock netted just shy of 80 goals for the Blues; he was therefore a highly sought-after player.[13]

Before the cup final, rumours had linked the Yorkshireman with a move to Middlesborough, and after the game Haylock joked, "Wouldn't it be something to get a call from Bryan Robson?" That season Robson had led Boro into the Premier League, but Garry Haylock was not bound for Teesside and the bright lights of England's top flight. Instead he was headed for mid-Ulster. In early January, Portadown manager Ronnie McFall had informed the press of his club's interest in Haylock. Five months later, McFall landed his target. On 15 June the *Belfast Telegraph* reported that the Englishman's move to mid-Ulster made him the highest-paid footballer in Irish League history. Linfield had tried to hold on to the star player (who was at the end of his contract), but the club's terms fell short of Haylock's demands. Chairman David Campbell fumed: "I've never dealt with a more mercenary player."[14]

Haylock refuted the charge that he was mercenary, explaining that the move "wasn't just a question of money... the truth is I felt I needed a new challenge and Portadown offered me that." However, he also stated: "I'm a professional footballer – it's all I do... I have to get the best deal for myself... Portadown granted me certain conditions and clauses that Linfield weren't prepared to offer and admittedly that helped make up my mind." Haylock made no secret of the fact that he played football to make a living. In a September 1993 edition of *Ireland's Saturday Night*, the striker had joked that when he finished playing he wanted to lie back and count his earnings. Two years later, the same paper reflected on the shock within the local game after Haylock had "voluntarily left the club for a 'smaller' Irish League outfit... angry, confused [Blues] fans... are now realising... what cold professionalism means."[15]

*Ireland's Saturday Night* had a point. Though supporters in the early 1990s had also witnessed the club miss out on players when other sides were prepared to pay bigger wages. Haylock's move fitted into an already established pattern in the League – and indeed, with wider trends in the European game. UEFA's innovation of the Champions League was driven by profit, and Linfield had fallen foul of it. The club was well aware that money talked. Although the Irish League was not flush with finances, clubs were mimicking what they saw happening elsewhere. Players could literally cash in on this. When Garry Haylock left the Blues, he did so as a professional, with no emotional attachment. He was offered a better deal at Portadown, and he took it.[16]

The Yorkshireman signed for the Ports in mid-June. Yet it took the best part of half a year to settle the amount he would cost. In the intervening months, relations between the Blues and Ports became strained. Linfield's Management Committee maintained that the club had offered Haylock a new contract after his deal had expired. They insisted the terms were put to the player within the required 31-day time period to trigger a transfer tribunal – the mechanism used to resolve disputes between clubs unable to agree a fee for an out-of-contract player. Portadown, however, disputed this. The controversy centred on a discrepancy between Haylock's contract with Linfield and his League registration. The Blues claimed that the date on his contract entitled Linfield to a fee, but the Ports argued that the date on his registration made him a free agent.[17]

Off the pitch, the wrangling between the two sides (and the Irish League) would stretch into November. Yet the League Cup brought the teams together much earlier in the 1995/96 season. On 29 August,

Linfield's players travelled to Shamrock Park for a winner-takes-all cup tie. They did so unaccompanied by the club's Management Committee. The dispute had poisoned relations between the clubs to the point that Linfield's Board stayed away from the fixture. Supporters were split on whether to travel. Those who did dished out abuse for Haylock, and to the delight of the travelling support, the striker failed to get on the scoresheet. Indeed, no goals were registered on the night and the game went to penalties. When Haylock stepped up to the mark, the Linfield fans relished the Yorkshireman failing to find the net. However, that joy was short-lived – as the Ports emerged victorious 5-4 in the shoot-out. Ironically it was another former Linfield player who scored the decisive penalty. Gary Peebles (who the Blues had allowed to leave in the summer) converted his kick and decided the tie.[18]

Shortly after the defeat, the Blues served writs on the Irish League and Portadown. The League had rejected Linfield's claim that Haylock's contract details entitled the club to a transfer tribunal. The Management Committee thus felt that the legal route was the only way to obtain a fee. Arguments played out over the next three months, and during this time Linfield returned to Shamrock Park. On 28 October, League commitments brought the two quarrelling clubs back together on the pitch. Again the Board refused to attend in an official capacity, and again Portadown triumphed. Off the field, Linfield were having more success against the Ports than on it. By the time the second Shamrock Park fixture came about, the Blues' legal team had successfully argued a fee was due. Over the weeks that followed, negotiations established the exact figure Portadown would pay. Then on 16 November, the *Belfast Telegraph* informed its readership that Haylock was "no longer Irish football's most famous free transfer". The paper reported that Portadown would pay Linfield about £35,000 for his services. Linfield had valued the player at around £70-80,000, so the figure was well short of what the Blues had hoped for. Nonetheless, the club had ensured compensation for Haylock's departure.[19]

To bring the saga to a conclusion, Linfield held a Special General Meeting on Wednesday 22 November. That evening the club vice-chairman Peter Lunn regaled members with the details of the striker's move to Portadown. It was the second time in a matter of days, that Mr Lunn had held council at Windsor, with a large number of supporters. The first time was impromptu. At around 5pm on the previous

Saturday, Mr Lunn had, according to the *News Letter*, "tried to placate [an] angry horde" that gathered behind the South Stand. A 3-0 home defeat to Glenavon sparked a protest as supporters voiced their frustrations to the Board. Just like the previous campaign, results in 1995/96 were indifferent and tensions had built.[20]

The season had kicked off with the by-now traditional early European start, followed by the customary swift exit. After lifting the 1994/95 Irish Cup, the Blues entered the Cup Winners' Cup. In the qualifying round, they were pitted against Shakhtar Donetsk of the Ukraine. This meant another long journey to face an unglamorous – but much stronger – opponent. Chairman David Campbell estimated that fulfilling the away leg of the tie would cost Linfield £50,000. He based the figure on "the cost of the aircraft, payment for loss of players' wages, hotel accommodation and other incidentals". UEFA would compensate the club £40,000 next July, but that still left a £10,000 shortfall. A healthy home gate was required just to break even on the European adventure. Unfortunately, that did not materialise. The first leg was played in Donetsk and Linfield were comfortably defeated 4-1. The return game was only a formality, and Windsor would not be packed.[21]

Those who attended the game in Belfast witnessed a strong defensive performance from Linfield, but ultimately a Shakhtar win. The Ukrainians scored an 86th-minute sickener to complete a 5-1 aggregate victory. Over the two legs the gulf in class was apparent. Linfield's part-time players simply could not cope with the Ukrainians, and Pat Fenlon maintained: "We were a long way away… from full-time outfits who had a lot at their disposal." The game in Donetsk was the first of the season and Linfield found that hard to cope with. According to Fenlon it was "very, very difficult" to get up to speed against professionals. Even when Linfield had matched the Ukrainians for much of the return leg, the full-timers always had more up their sleeves. Fenlon pointed out that eventually the difference between teams would show after 70-75 minutes or so, and "they would hurt you".[22]

The disappointing domestic form that followed was hard for Linfield's support to stomach. The club had invested in its squad ahead of 1995/96, and supporters hoped the side would challenge for honours. In June, the Blues brought in defender Stuart McLean and midfielder Alan Ewing from Coleraine for a combined fee of £45,000.

Then in August, two strikers were signed. Paul Millar arrived from Cardiff for a fee of around £30,000, and Darren Erskine from Ards for £35,000. The chequebook came out yet again in late October when midfielder Alan Byrne arrived from Shelbourne, but the team were struggling. Performances were indifferent, and by the autumn, results were becoming a worry. November began with a 4-0 pasting at home to the Glens. A couple of weeks later came the loss by Glenavon that sparked protests. This was followed by two defeats to Crusaders in a matter of days. The first knocked the Blues out of the County Antrim Shield, the second was a 3-0 drubbing at Seaview in the League.[23]

By the start of December, Linfield were 13 points behind League leaders Portadown. Too much ground was already conceded, and the club's chances of winning the inaugural Premier League were all but gone. Linfield could not put together a run of good results. Just when the team appeared headed in the right direction, the inconsistency returned. Amidst the frustration, Linfield recorded a memorable 3-0 Boxing Day victory over Glentoran at the Oval. Two goals from Alan Ewing and one from Ian McCoosh secured the victory, but the game was remembered more for the conditions it was played in than for the result. Heavy snowfall covered the pitch, which made it nearly impossible for players to maintain their balance. Spectators found the elements just as tough. Keeping warm was a challenge, but so was watching the match. For the entire second half, supporters had to follow a game played on a white surface with a white ball. An orange ball was used in the first half, but it split in two places. Glentoran did not have a replacement, so – emblematic of the lack of professionalism that has bedevilled the local game – the match was played out in a farce.[24]

The victory over Glentoran demonstrated that Linfield had the capacity to pull off big results. However, when it really mattered, they came up short. Defeat to Crusaders in the quarter-final of the Irish Cup highlighted this. On 9 March 1996, Linfield travelled to Seaview for a match that would make or break the season. By then, League success was ruled out, and the Irish Cup presented the campaign's only opportunity for silverware. On the day, Crusaders dominated proceedings and won 2-0. An insipid Linfield performance had received its just reward. At the time, Irish Cup rules prevented teams in the quarter-final stages and onwards, from displaying a sponsor on their shirts. Clubs therefore had to commission kits without advertising to fulfil these fixtures. In the run-up to the Seaview game, the Blues' specially designed strip was stolen, and Linfield ended up playing in a kit without a badge. *Ireland's Saturday Night* considered this "appropriate" because the performance did not "resemble a Blues team".[25]

Linfield stumbled to a fifth-place finish in the inaugural (eight-team) Premier League. The club programme considered the lowly position and the absence of trophies simply "not good enough". *Look at Linfield* guaranteed that change would come before the start of the following season. New players would come in, but there was also a significant alteration to the coaching set-up. In mid-April, the Blues parted company with Lindsay McKeown – Trevor Anderson's second-in-command. Former club captain David Jeffrey would replace McKeown, coming in as assistant manager. Jeffrey was back at Windsor after an absence of four years. In 1992 he left to play for Ards, before joining Larne in 1995. At both clubs, he served his apprenticeship as a coach, and at Larne he became the club's assistant manager under Shay Hamill. When Jeffrey returned to Linfield in 1996 he could not hide his delight, telling the press on arrival, "There's no doubt where my loyalties lie."[26]

After Jeffrey's return, Anderson made significant changes to the playing staff. Fringe players like Robert Campbell, Philip Knell and Mark Anderson were all shown the door, whilst captain Alan Dornan was given a free transfer. Wes Lamont and Pat Fenlon, who were both at the end of their contracts, also said their goodbyes. Then coming in were strikers Stephen McBride from Glenavon and Richie Barker from Sheffield Wednesday, as well as midfielder Tony Gorman from Coleraine. McBride cost almost £20,000 and the other two upwards of £30,000. Linfield had again spent big, and there was an expectation that success would follow. *Look at Linfield* asserted that after "two lean years, [the Blues] must be up there challenging for every trophy". Going into 1996/97 Anderson's side was under immense pressure.[27]

Preparations for that crucial season included a gala friendly at Windsor. In August, Liverpool visited Belfast for the second year running. Twelve months beforehand, the Merseyside club had triumphed 1-0 with a goal from Ian Rush. In the return a year later, the teams drew 2-2, though Liverpool were lucky to snatch the draw. With minutes to go the Blues looked on course for a famous victory, but the referee awarded a controversial penalty. John Barnes sent in a cross from the left that Noel Bailie attempted to clear. Unfortunately for Bailie he was adjudged to have handled it, and Robbie Fowler equalised from 12 yards with one minute left on the clock.[28]

Games against Premier League giants like Liverpool were financially lucrative. Gate receipts from the match in early August came in at over £62,000. Yet the game also served as the perfect way to mark a significant milestone for the club. The evening of 2 August 1996 was the last time fans packed the standing terraces of Windsor's Spion Kop. It was fitting that Liverpool, famed for its Anfield Kop, brought the curtain down on Windsor's terrace. Though it was somewhat ironic that a Manchester United fan, Ian McCoosh, scored Linfield's second against the Reds. His strike was the last goal scored in front of a packed Kop before work would begin to make the stand all-seating.[29]

McCoosh's connection with the refurbishment did not end there. His father Walter worked for contractors Gregg Patterson, who were completing the steelwork on the new stand. When finished it would hold 4,000, and the former title of Kop Stand would be kept. This brought Windsor's seating capacity to 15,000, which was significant for

Northern Ireland internationals. World Cup qualification games had required all-seater stadiums since 1992; the new Kop was therefore much-needed. Though it must be noted that unlike construction taking place at football grounds across the UK, there were no inclusion of corporate facilities in the new stand. It was great that Windsor was moving ahead as an all-seater stadium, but the lack of corporate provision was indicative of wider Irish League stagnation.[30]

If the progress made off the pitch was to a degree limited, progress on the pitch during early 1996/97 was much more assured. In mid-November Linfield won a first piece of silverware for 18 months, with

victory over Glenavon in the Gold Cup final. The club's League form was also showing signs of improvement. As 1996 drew to a close, Linfield resided in third place and the media were positive about the direction the club was headed in. That said, the high expectation levels meant that the Blues needed success immediately, and inside the club all was not well. Assistant manager David Jeffrey recalled that "the pressure leading up to and over Christmas was intense... it was a horrible period". By the start of 1997, the strain on Trevor Anderson had built to an unbearable level. In a move that rocked the local game, Anderson left Linfield and headed for Newry Town as director of football. His decision to leave came less than 24 hours before a League game away to Portadown on 4 January. Former manager Roy Coyle and Steven Beacom of the *Belfast Telegraph* described the sudden move "as the biggest Irish League story in 30 years".[31]

Five years in the hot seat was enough for Trevor Anderson: "I'd done my time and wanted a new challenge." He "wanted to get away" and the Newry job appealed. Newry languished in the First Division, but had an ambitious chairman in Joe Rice. Anderson could go to Newry and enjoy football again, something he was not doing at Linfield. The job "was affecting me, it was affecting my health – and it was affecting my family... The time was right for going."[32]

Dessie Gorman felt that other Irish League clubs had caught up with Anderson's methods and ultimately had beaten him at his own game. Gorman believed that Anderson was enterprising in utilising the Southern market: "Trevor was a wee bit ahead in going looking for the likes of myself, the Haylocks and the rest. Then the other clubs started to do that as well... Portadown and Crusaders both copped on and had great success with it." Pat Fenlon pointed to other issues at the Park: "We had a lot of big personalities in the team and maybe in hindsight they probably got a little bit big, rather than just concentrating on getting results and winning games, and it dropped off a little bit in that regard." Noel Bailie recalled that the loss of Haylock was crucial and the signings that came in after "just didn't work out".[33]

Bailie had assumed the responsibility of club captain after Alan Dornan left the club. Becoming captain was an honour the player described as "a special privilege". During the 1996 pre-season, Trevor Anderson had pulled the sweeper aside one night and given him the armband. Anderson felt that Bailie was "made" for captaincy: "He was playing at the back so he could see everything, but it was more than that. He was a natural leader and a special player." Although Anderson departed half a year after selecting the sweeper for captain, his choice left an important legacy. In Bailie, Linfield had a strong and reliable leader on the pitch.[34]

Noel Bailie was shocked when he heard Trevor Anderson had left. The captain only learned of the news when he boarded the team coach for the away game with Portadown on 4 January. Assistant manager David Jeffrey was placed in charge of team affairs for the trip to Shamrock Park, which Bailie wholeheartedly endorsed. Prior to the game, the skipper convened a meeting of the players and they gave their backing to Jeffrey. Bailie told the *News Letter*, "We would be extremely happy if Davy becomes our manager... [he] was a leader on the field and hopefully he will be our leader off it."[35]

Bailie and his teammates would get their wish, with Jeffrey appointed permanent manager after two games in the caretaker role. For the former club captain, it was a "huge honour". He told *Look at Linfield*: "Playing for Linfield was a privilege, managing the Club is the ultimate... This is a once-in-a-lifetime opportunity [and] I intend to make the most of it." Jeffrey brought in Brian McLaughlin (the pair had played together at Larne) and both went about reshaping the club.

McLaughlin was vitally important according to Jeffrey, as he brought an outsider perspective to the club. Brian McLaughlin was not steeped in Linfield Football Club, and Jeffrey valued the insights of someone without previous ties to the Blues.[36]

One of the first major decisions that the new manager took was to release Dessie Gorman. David Jeffrey observed that Trevor Anderson's

transfer policy had begun to "unwork itself". Anderson had reaped great success by bringing in players from outside Northern Ireland in the early part of his reign, but this was not the case in the later years. Jeffrey maintained that the influx of big-money signings from outside had created a "schism" in the dressing room. According to Jeffrey, the local players (who worked amongst fans) were "getting it in the ear every week". This was not the case for players coming in from elsewhere. The likes of Stuart McLean from Scotland, Richie Barker from England and Alan Byrne from the Republic travelled home after games and were not exposed to the criticisms. The new manager wanted to address this, and letting go of Gorman heralded a change in direction. Jeffrey stamped his authority by releasing a player synonymous with the Anderson regime.[37]

David Jeffrey had inherited a side sitting in third place in the Irish League. However with all the upheaval, there was little expectation that the club would challenge for the title that 1996/97 season. Essentially the season was a "gimme" for Jeffrey, and the team finished in fifth place. The new manager needed time and an opportunity to impose his philosophy on the club. That said, he would have to do so without heavy financial backing. A *Look at Linfield* editorial that appeared shortly after Jeffrey took charge, gave an indication that the new manager would not have large sums of money to enter the transfer market. Instead, the club hoped to rebuild with "a progressive youth policy".[38]

Having spent big during the mid-1990s, Linfield was now in financial trouble – though the Board did not want to admit just how serious this trouble was.

Chapter 7

# *Uncool Britannia*

As the 1990s wore on, the peace process allowed for a transformation of Northern Irish society. Opportunities that had for years been stifled were now opening up. In November 1998, Linfield would make a cross-town journey to Cliftonville – for almost three decades, that short trip had been an impossibility. Indeed, there was an overarching optimism and a positivity about this era that was allowing for significant social change. It was however unfortunate that this positivity, so prevalent throughout the Province, was not always apparent in the local game. In many ways the Irish League only seemed to be drifting further and further away from top-level football.

UEFA's commercialisation of European football had effectively ended the possibility of competitive matches against top-class opposition – though friendlies still provided Linfield with the opportunity to play against the big names. In the mid-1990s the Blues enjoyed hosting one particular English giant on a regular basis. Liverpool made the trip to Belfast each year from 1995 until 1997. In 1996, the Reds had helped Linfield say goodbye to the old Kop terracing. Then in 1997, the Merseyside club returned for the first game played in front of the new all-seater West Stand. The match took place on 26 July and witnessed a special performance from a soon-to-be superstar. Michael Owen, a 17-year-old prodigy, arrived in Belfast with quite a reputation. Earlier that year the *Guardian* reported that Owen had "been variously described as the next Kenny Dalglish, the next Ian Rush, and even the next Robbie Fowler".[1]

The striker's performance against the Blues appeared to justify the considerable hype. In the closing minutes, Owen turned the game on its head. Linfield had taken a surprise lead and looked on course for a famous victory. Then the future international took centre stage. In the 77th minute, the young striker beat the offside trap and at lightning

95

speed raced towards the Kop-end goal. He took sight of Linfield keeper Bobby Geddes and placed the ball past him. Owen's goal was the very first scored in front of the new Kop Stand. Seven minutes later he grabbed a second in front of it. This time Owen highlighted his poacher's instinct by finishing from two yards out in a crowded goal-mouth. His strikes earned Liverpool a 2-1 victory.

All who witnessed the young forward's performance were struck by how good he was. Steven Beacom of the *Belfast Telegraph* marvelled, "master Owen is a good one alright, a very good one in fact and if he applies himself will undoubtedly become a great one". A year later, 18-year-old Owen was confirming his pedigree on the global stage, scoring *that* goal against Argentina in France '98; his slaloming run and strong finish is still considered one of the most spectacular goals ever scored by an English player at a World Cup. In its aftermath, the international media lauded the player for his pace and skill – just like all who had been lucky enough to see him in action at Windsor in late July '97.[2]

A month and a half after the Kop was treated to Owen et al., the new stand was again packed for Linfield's first trophy success under David Jeffrey. On 10 September, the Blues faced the Glens in the League Cup final held at Windsor. The game was far from a classic. Both defences were strong throughout, and only one goal was scored in 90 minutes of football. Ironically, it was defender Jeff Spiers who grabbed it. As half-time approached, the big man rose to meet a Stephen Beatty corner and sent the ball into the Glentoran net. Spiers, who was not accustomed to getting on the scoresheet, revelled in his goal. Afterwards he exclaimed, "This one is very special because it won the match. It was sweet." Jeffrey was similarly delighted. He enjoyed his first piece of silverware as manager, but pointed out that it was "only the start".[3]

The lack of goals in the League Cup final highlighted a major deficiency at the outset of the new manager's first full season in charge. Early on in the campaign, Jeffrey sighed, "We just can't put the ball in the net... Frankly we've not had a goal scorer since Garry Haylock and before that Martin McGaughey." To address the issue, the young manager moved at the end of September to add some firepower to his side. He brought in a striker by the name of David Larmour. The centre-forward was 20 years old, and had previously played with Liverpool and Doncaster. Larmour maintained on arrival that "playing for Linfield is something I've always wanted to do… they were the only Irish League team for me". Later that autumn, Jeffrey moved for another attacking player. On 26 November, Lee Feeney, a highly sought -after young talent from Ards, signed terms at Windsor.[4]

Both players settled in well, producing goals and good form, but Jeffrey felt that something else was needed. The manager wanted an experienced Irish League striker with a proven track record. Finding an available player who fitted that description was difficult – and so was sourcing the capital to complete any potential deal. Two separate issues had financially crippled the  club by the late 1990s. Firstly, the upkeep of Windsor Park as an international stadium, to FIFA and UEFA regulations, was costly in the extreme. Secondly, the Blues had spent big in the pursuit of success during the mid-1990s.

Linfield could do little about the money needed to maintain Windsor; however, the outlay on players was another matter. In September 1992, Linfield's Finance Committee had expressed "concern with the seriousness of the Club's financial position", yet this had not stopped big spending. When the Blues paid £35,000 for the services of Garry Haylock in June 1993, the club breached its £100,000 overdraft limit. Linfield's substantial spending then continued over the years that followed, and the financial position of the club deteriorated. All told, over £300,000 was spent on players in the four and a half years after the Finance Committee had expressed "concern". By March 1997, the bank was warning that efforts to address the club's debts were needed.[5]

Jeffrey knew that financially the club was "on its knees", but in early December 1997 it appeared there was an opportunity to sign one of the League's top strikers. Press speculation linked Glenavon's Glenn 'Spike'

Ferguson with a move to Windsor, and Jeffrey was keen to capitalise. The manager understood that acquiring Ferguson required a large fee, but he was confident it would pay dividends. Ferguson was 28 years old, and the Blues boss felt that if he could get three good years out of the striker, spending big was justified. Paper talk over a deal rumbled on into the New Year. This indicated to other clubs that Glenavon were contemplating parting with the player. Notably Glentoran also showed an interest in Ferguson's services. By mid-January 1998, it was apparent that Glenn Ferguson would be leaving Glenavon and he had a choice to make. He was either headed for Windsor Park or the Oval.[6]

Ferguson's family were Linfield supporters, and he knew that chances to sign for the Blues did not come around often. He was therefore minded to move to Windsor, but out of courtesy spoke to the managers of both clubs. Roy Coyle had recently taken over at the Glens and it was his job to sell the Oval to the striker. After the Glentoran

boss had made his pitch, Ferguson came back with a question. He asked Coyle to imagine he was still Linfield manager, and in that instance how would he sell the Blues? Coyle responded by saying, "I'd ask you to come sign for the biggest club in the country." That was exactly what Ferguson resolved to do. After the player had decided he was Windsor-bound, it was then up to Linfield and Glenavon to work out how much he would cost. Ferguson's strike rate was clinical, and understandably the Lurgan Blues wanted big money for their asset. In just over 200 games for the mid-Ulster side, Ferguson had netted 99 goals. Glenavon thus decided that an Irish League record of £55,000 was appropriate, and the Blues agreed to the terms. Linfield chairman Billy McCoubrey (who was into his second season in the position) explained: "Perhaps it cost us a bit more than we wanted to pay but circumstances dictated this – supply and demand."[7]

Given the Blues' debt-ridden position, the deal was only made possible by an interest-free loan from a group of fans. In a move Billy McCoubrey hailed as epitomising "what being true Bluemen is all about", the Linfield European Supporters Club put up £35,000 of the needed cash. Chairman of the club, Jackie Hewitt, told the *News Letter* that the three-year-old body was set up "to support Linfield in Europe – to travel overseas and support the boys… Unfortunately we have not managed to get into Europe during that time, so we have a few quid in savings." Jeffrey, McCoubrey and the entire Linfield hierarchy were humbled and grateful for the help rendered. Yet remarkably, it was the second occasion that season when fans had dipped into their pockets to help out. In September 1997 another group, the Linfield Supporters Association, had stumped up £5,000 to help sign Ards defender William Murphy. The club was in dire financial straits, but there was a resolve to ensure that it would compete for honours. A month after Ferguson signed, that was realised.[8]

On 17 February, Linfield picked up a second piece of silverware for the season. That evening, the Blues faced Crusaders in the County Antrim Shield final at the Oval. Neither team could find the net during 90 minutes, but in extra time David Larmour struck to give the Blues a 1-0 win. After the game, Larmour's manager hailed the striker as "special", though he was not keen to dwell on the success. Jeffrey had just won his second Linfield trophy, but he was planning on bringing a lot more honours to Windsor Park. The former club captain told the *Belfast Telegraph* that it was "brilliant for me to have won my second trophy as a manager but I want to win even more… Roy Coyle won 31 trophies here and I believe when you are in charge of Linfield that is what you must aim for."[9]

Three weeks after the Shield triumph, Coyle was again in Jeffrey's thoughts. This time Linfield's young manager was pitting his wits against his old boss in a decisive League fixture. The Blues and Glens both sat adrift of table-topping Cliftonville, and both needed three points to maintain title challenges. The match was staged at Windsor, and was Coyle's first game at the stadium in charge of the Glens. Roy Coyle was a man accustomed to the big occasion, and relished returning to his old stomping ground with Glentoran. He told the press: "It won't annoy me going back, no matter what reception I get." The former Linfield boss was well versed in the fixture and knew what to expect. For recent Linfield signing Glenn Ferguson it was a new experience, and the striker similarly couldn't wait for kick-off. Ferguson had played in plenty of mid-Ulster derbies, but since arriving at Windsor he had been told that Linfield vs Glentoran was "the real Big Two". The Irish League's record signing was thus keen to see what all the fuss was about.[10]

When Ferguson took to the field he revelled in the occasion, and his performance inspired a 3-0 victory. Afterwards *Ireland's Saturday Night* hailed the forward as "superb", which was hard to argue against. Ferguson had scored twice and set up the other goal. Yet the match was not remembered for his individual brilliance. Instead, ugly scenes on the pitch and in the stands overshadowed the derby win. In a game that witnessed a 19-player brawl, the Glens had three players red-carded; whilst off the field there was near anarchy. At half-time an individual from the Linfield end forced his way into the Glentoran dressing room and attempted to assault Roy Coyle. Then in the second half there was fighting on the terraces, as Glentoran fans in the North Stand's lower deck ripped up seats and hurled them at RUC officers. In the chaos, referee Frank McDonald halted the game for six minutes. The stoppage brought brief respite from the disturbances, allowing the game to finish, but trouble flared again after the final whistle. Outside the stadium, hooligan elements from both sets of supporters clashed with each other and the police. One RUC officer suffered a broken leg, and another a serious eye injury. All told, 20 policemen and numerous civilians were injured.[11]

The scenes inside and outside Windsor did little for the reputation of Linfield or the Irish League in general. Malcolm Brodie sighed, "For decades those of my generation have seen it all before – often much worse." Yet he also detected that by the late 1990s there was less tolerance of such scenes. Brodie explained that by then, "Society felt enough was enough." He had discerned a cultural shift, linked to changing perceptions of football on the mainland. According to Irvine

Welsh, "a conventional wisdom" took hold, which maintained that, "When the '90s kicked in... football violence had all but vanished." Truth be told, this was far from the case. Football-related trouble had "become more specialised [involving a] dedicated hard-core of participants". It had not gone away. Regardless of that reality, the perception held that the game had cleaned up its act.[12]

As well as supposedly having its house in order, football on the mainland was fashionable. The beautiful game was riding on the crest of a wave, and was an essential component of the mid-1990s 'Cool Britannia'. This cultural reawakening portrayed the United Kingdom as chic, celebrating its music, arts, cuisine and sport. The *Guardian*'s Michael Cox explained that New Labour had "swept to power on the coattails" of Cool Britannia, and had done so with "a clear attempt to embrace the game". In opposition, Tony Blair famously played head tennis with Kevin Keegan at the 1995 Labour Party Conference. Blair had also professed a love for Newcastle United in a bid to assert his credentials. While the media were quick to question and lampoon his bona fides as a fan, Blair's bid to cast himself as a supporter indicated the cultural currency that the game possessed.[13]

It seemed everyone had an interest in football – well, in the English Premier League anyway. Huge sums of television money had flowed into the League, making its members very rich. This allowed clubs to spend big and attract world-renowned stars like Bergkamp, Klinsmann and Zola. The Premier League had revolutionised England's top flight, and the glamour attached to it went into overdrive. The transformation of English football since the dark days of Heysel, Bradford and Hillsborough could not have been starker. Unfortunately the game in Northern Ireland had not experienced such a boom.

Competing with a product like the English Premier League was impossible for the local game. The Irish League's quality lagged well behind, and critics were only too keen to stress this. Having an apparent hooligan problem only gave detractors another stick to beat local football with. Three weeks after the Glentoran riot, the IFA punished both clubs. Linfield received a £1,000 fine, and Glentoran £2,500. The extra £1,500 imposed on the East Belfast side accounted for the considerable damage caused by supporters to Windsor's North Stand. On top of this, hefty restrictions were also placed on the next meeting between the two sides – an Irish Cup semi-final scheduled for early

April. The game was to take place at Windsor, but only 6,000 fans would be allowed to attend. Furthermore, kick-off was set for 11am.[14]

It was estimated that the reduced crowd would cost each club approximately £20,000. Both teams were thus hit harder by the semi-final sanctions than by the levied fines. When Belfast's Big Two met at the unusually early time on 4 April, there was no repeat of the crowd trouble. There was also no repeat of a comfortable win for the Blues. This time, Glentoran ran out 2-1 victors. The tie showed that although Linfield had improved during Jeffrey's first full season in charge, his team were not quite the finished article.[15]

In the race for the title, Linfield again fell short. Marty Quinn's Cliftonville proved too good and tied up the League with a game to spare. The Blues had pushed the Reds right up to that point, but in the end had to settle for second place. Finishing runners-up had at least brought the club back into European football – the Blues would enter the qualifying rounds for the 1998/99 UEFA Cup. This was significant, as Linfield had gone three years without entering UEFA competition. Much-needed finances would follow, and Linfield would again sample the prestige attached to playing in Europe.

Unfortunately, during the club's three-year European absence, UEFA had again adversely tampered with the format of the various competitions. When Linfield played Shakhtar Donetsk in the 1995 Cup Winners' Cup, the first game took place in mid-August. By 1998 the qualifying rounds were stretching into July. The start of European competition had moved into the Irish League off-season. European football had thus become even tougher, with yet another barrier placed between local sides and the big clubs. Just getting up to full fitness for the games was a challenge. Pre-season could start earlier, but having players match-fit was another thing. A couple of friendlies here and there would hardly see a team ready for the European stage.[16]

The draw for the first UEFA Cup qualifying round paired Linfield with Omonoia Nicosia, a full-time Cypriot outfit. The Blues would travel out there on 22 July, before hosting Nicosia a week later. Prior to the first leg, Linfield had only one friendly under its belt, and on top of this, the players would have to cope with the Mediterranean heat. The full-timers started the game as favourites and, as expected, were comfortable winners. A 5-1 scoreline ensured that the tie was over even before Nicosia travelled to Belfast. Glenn Ferguson (who had grabbed a consolation in the 77th minute) admitted afterwards that Linfield found the going tough. The temperature hit 28°C, and Ferguson explained that "by the second half we found it hard to keep running".[17]

In a highly entertaining second leg, Linfield brought back a bit of respectability by running out 5-3 winners. Nicosia had led 3-1 early on, but a remarkable fight back saw the Blues earn victory. The scoreline was not enough to progress to the next round, but it was nevertheless an impressive result. In the following day's press, a delighted David Jeffrey exclaimed, "my players did... the local game proud". He was right to heap praise on his team. The Blues had comprehensively beaten a professional side. Yet there was also a harsh reality. Linfield's European campaign had ended two days before the start of August. UEFA Cup commitments were over, and the 1998/99 Irish League season was still two weeks away.[18]

For Jeffrey and his players, the start of that season could not come quickly enough. Although the club was operating on a severely reduced budget, there was a feeling that Linfield could win the title. At the end of the previous campaign, defender Tommy McDonald told the *Belfast Telegraph* that in 1998/99 the Blues could "go for the big one". The Gibson Cup had not resided at Windsor since 1994, and there was determination amongst the squad to end that drought. This four-year stretch was the longest the club had gone without a League title since the Second World War. Success was thus considered paramount, but the significance of the campaign went further than rectifying an unwanted sequence. During the season, Linfield would make a return to one Irish League ground after a 28-year absence. The Blues had not played a game at Solitude, the home of Cliftonville, since April 1970. Security considerations throughout the Troubles had precluded the club making the journey. Given Solitude's location in a nationalist area of North Belfast, the RUC had maintained that it was unable to guarantee public order. However in 1998, the authorities decided that the time had come for the Blues to return.[19]

The year 1998 heralded a changed social and political landscape in Northern Ireland. That April, the Belfast Agreement was signed. Then in May, the document was endorsed at the polls. The Agreement was a notable milestone in the 1990s peace process, which was to pave the way for 'normalisation' of life in the Province. For years, the Troubles had impinged on nearly all aspects of Northern Irish society. Everyday activities, like fulfilling football fixtures, were hostage to the associated violence. But the political settlement thrashed out in early 1998 was a game-changer. For the first time in 28 years the RUC was prepared to allow the Blues to visit Cliftonville. On 20 June, *Ireland's Saturday Night* reported that, "when the fixture calendar for season 1998-99 was finalised… one line said Cliftonville vs Linfield, November 21. Notably the words Windsor Park were not in brackets."[20]

During Linfield's 28-year Solitude absence, nearly all Cliftonville's 'home' games against the Blues were staged at Windsor. This was something that the Reds hierarchy was appreciative of in the darkest days of the Troubles. In 1987, Cliftonville vice-chairman Jim Boyce put on record his club's "deep debt of gratitude to Linfield over the last 15 years for putting Windsor at our disposal". The arrangement was, though, an understandable gripe for the Reds and a source of embarrassment for Linfield. By default, the Blues had home advantage every time the sides met. As long as conflict raged, there had been no chance of Linfield playing at the North Belfast ground. An emergent peace process had opened up the possibility of a return. However, it would take some time before this came to fruition.[21]

By the mid-1990s, the mood music in the Province was relatively optimistic. A framework for peace was outlined with the December 1993 Downing Street Declaration. Then over the 12 months that followed, paramilitary ceasefires were issued. Against this backdrop calls were made for Linfield to return to Solitude. A Cliftonville fans' organisation, 'Home for a Change', was established at the time to campaign on the matter. During the 1993/94 season the body organised a boycott to highlight its case. In late March 1994, the North Belfast side's 'home' fixture against the Blues was almost completely devoid of Cliftonville support. *Ireland's Saturday Night* counted just 32 spectators in the Kop, which housed the Reds fans. Cliftonville's Board had not approved of the boycott. Yet the club hierarchy expressed a willingness to work with all relevant parties to bring the Blues back to the North Belfast ground.[22]

The position outlined by the Reds Board was exactly the same as that of Linfield's Management Committee. A couple of weeks after the protest, Blues chairman David Campbell informed the press that his club would "cooperate 100 per cent with… efforts to get the game back to Solitude". A frustrated Campbell added, "We have received so much bad publicity down the years about... our away matches against Cliftonville being staged at Windsor [but] we have played the thing straight down the middle and complied with the instructions of the security forces." As far as Campbell and his Board were concerned, enough was enough. Vexed by the criticisms, the Management Committee took matters into its own hands. In April 1994, Linfield informed the Irish League that in future Windsor would no longer be available to stage Cliftonville 'home' games.[23]

The Blues had forced the matter. Yet the RUC was unwilling to facilitate. In late May Ronnie Flanagan, the force's Assistant Chief Constable, stated: "I am not in a position in the present climate... to recommend Cliftonville's home fixture with Linfield be hosted at Solitude." According to Flanagan, the problem lay in "getting supporters safely to and from the venue". Furthermore, the Assistant Chief Constable explained that "overwhelming public opposition" would preclude Linfield travelling to the North Belfast ground for "the foreseeable future". The RUC's ruling was frustrating, but both clubs had to abide by it. Backed into a corner, Linfield's Management Committee reversed its stance at the start of the 1994/95 campaign. Cliftonville would be able to use Windsor Park for future 'home' fixtures, though there was a caveat. The Blues Board requested that "over the period of the current season [the Irish League] actively sought an alternative" venue.[24]

Finding a 'Plan B' during the 1994/95 season proved unattainable. So the Irish League decided that it would take the matter up with the RUC. A League delegation would petition the force to try to change the authorities' mind-set. If the plea was unsuccessful, the adverse publicity over Linfield's extra 'home' fixtures was only going to intensify. 1995/96 was the first season of the Premier League, and it brought a reduction in the number of teams competing in the top flight. This dramatically changed the campaign's fixture list. Instead of teams facing each other twice (home and away), teams would now meet four times (twice home and twice away). Linfield would thus have two extra games at Windsor Park each season.[25]

On 7 July 1995, the Irish League brought the case before the police. At the time, Belfast was fraught with political tension. Rioting had erupted in nationalist areas during the previous month after Private Lee Clegg was released from jail. Clegg was one of eight paratroopers who in September 1990 had fired at a stolen car in West Belfast – two teenagers in that car were shot dead. Three years later, Clegg was convicted of murder and given a life sentence. However in 1995, new evidence challenging his conviction came to light. Taking this into account, Secretary of State Patrick Mayhew released Clegg on licence. Mayhew's decision proved highly controversial and ignited civil unrest on the streets.[26]

The following month (and just a couple of days after the Irish League's appeal to the RUC), there was further strife across the Province. This occurred after Portadown Orangemen were prevented from completing their annual Drumcree parade on Sunday 9 July. An illegal protest blocked off part of the route, and the security forces kept the Orangemen at Drumcree Church. A standoff between the police and marchers ensued for three days. It only ended after a compromise deal was struck and the marchers finished their parade route. Anthropologist Dominic Bryan maintained that during the standoff it looked as if "parades and street demonstrations would lead to civil disturbances serious enough to bring about renewed armed conflict". Amidst the unrest the RUC was not prepared to sanction Linfield's Solitude return.[27]

Crises like the dispute at Drumcree demonstrated the fragility of the peace process. Yet as the 1990s wore on, the Province inched closer to political settlement – and the calls for Cliftonville to host the Blues got louder. In January 1996, the *Belfast Telegraph*'s John Laverty complained that "the security forces are running out of excuses for perpetuating the Solitude ban... We can trust paramilitaries not to take our lives... But seemingly we still can't trust two sets of football fans to behave on a Saturday afternoon."[28]

Two years later, in the aftermath of the Belfast Agreement's publication, Laverty repeated his call. On 21 April 1998, he exclaimed: "it's high time now that this anachronistic scenario was banished to the dustbin of history!" A telephone poll conducted by his paper agreed – 93 per cent of those who responded said it was time for Linfield to return. Laverty's 1998 comments had partially reflected on Cliftonville's League triumph. He observed that the Reds "were not slow to point out that their success was achieved despite having to play all four matches against Linfield at Windsor". Seemingly the snipes over the Blues' extra 'home' games had reached crescendo. This led the Management

Committee to act. After taking stock of the views expressed at the 1998 AGM, they again informed Cliftonville that Windsor was no longer available for Reds 'home' games. Unlike in 1994, the club would not have to backtrack. In November 1998, the Blues would return to Solitude – the authorities had finally deemed the time right.[29]

The RUC's willingness to facilitate the fixture was demonstrative of a post-Agreement resolve to 'normalise' life in the Province. The political settlement had offered a way out of conflict, and there was a wish to capitalise on its momentum. However the peace was very fragile. Indeed, the summer of 1998 was particularly tense. That year's Drumcree dispute (by then an annual standoff) had resulted in rioting across the Province. Then in August, the Real IRA exploded a 500lb car bomb in Omagh. The blast ripped through a crowded Saturday afternoon street, killing 29 people. A return to the dark days of the Troubles appeared a distinct reality, yet there was a resolve to ensure that this did not happen. That autumn brought renewed political activity; this included the first ever direct contact between the leaders of Ulster unionism and Sinn Féin. In September, David Trimble and Gerry Adams met behind closed doors. According to political commentators David McKittrick and David McVea, "the fact that [both] spoke but did not shake hands pointedly [indicated] that while new relationships were emerging they were accompanied by neither friendship nor trust". It was amidst this cautious atmosphere that Linfield travelled to Solitude.[30]

Not surprisingly, security around the fixture was tight. Kick-off was set for 11am and the crowd capacity was capped at 1,500. Linfield's allocation was limited to one-third of the total (500), and restrictions were placed on who could attend. Only members and season-ticket holders were allowed to travel. On top of this, the authorities decreed that all Blues fans had to be escorted to Solitude by bus. As Ronnie Flanagan had outlined in 1994, police fears over the fixture lay in getting Linfield fans to the ground. This stemmed from the Blues' last visit to Solitude in April 1970, when trouble had erupted in the area around the ground after Linfield's Irish Cup final win over Ballymena. Determined there would be no repeat 28 years later, the RUC stipulated that all Linfield fans were bussed with a police escort to and from the game.[31]

Early on the morning of 21 November, Linfield supporters congregated at Windsor to board the escorted buses to Solitude. In total, just 325 fans made the trip; this figure was considerably shy of the club's allocation. Unhappy about the arrangements, a large number had decided to give the game a miss. Those who travelled enjoyed a swift journey across town. Writing in the following week's *Look at Linfield*, supporter Stuart Gilmore explained: "The route had obviously been

planned impeccably as every junction on the way was sealed off by RUC motorbikes, and we sailed through red lights with ease." When the buses arrived at the North Belfast ground they were met by a large media contingent. Linfield's return to Solitude was a big news story, with the events off the field every bit as important as those on it. Thankfully any fears of trouble soon subsided. A heavy police presence ensured that all passed off peacefully. Gilmore's *Look at Linfield* article maintained that the "only 'fright' of the day" lay in not getting a programme, as fans swamped the Reds' programme seller with orders.[32]

Ahead of the game, Cliftonville's chairman Hugh McCartan had assured all connected with the Blues of a "very warm welcome from everyone at Solitude", and one banner in the Reds support spelt this out. It read 'Céad Míle Fáilte LINFIELD' – Irish for 'A Hundred Thousand Welcomes LINFIELD'. Symbolism like this was a big part of the day. Cliftonville's players applauded the Blues onto the pitch. Then both teams kicked footballs into the opposing side's supporters. When the game began, Linfield started brightly – Reds keeper Paul Reece had to perform heroics just to keep things scoreless by half-time. Reece, however, could do nothing on 52 minutes when William Murphy put the Blues ahead. Cliftonville's defence failed to clear a Stephen Beatty corner, and Murphy smashed the ball home from eight yards. Murphy's joy though would soon turned to anguish – less than 10 minutes after scoring, he received his marching orders following an altercation with Reds player Michael Collins. It didn't take long for Cliftonville to capitalise on their one-man advantage – Tim McCann equalised on 63 minutes. But as no more goals followed, the historic fixture finished one apiece.[33]

Afterwards, David Jeffrey maintained: "I think the occasion overshadowed everything… Football was the winner today." Cliftonville manager Marty Quinn wholeheartedly agreed, and was quick to praise both sets of fans for creating "a terrific atmosphere". This was something highlighted by the media. That said, *Ireland's Saturday Night* made reference to "a few not unexpected sectarian chants". Other publications similarly picked up on this. Writing in the following Monday's edition of the *Irish News*, Kenny Archer noted that the "party songs were aired of course", though he added, "they lacked a real edge". In the *Belfast Telegraph*, Steven Beacom mused that, "while there are more easy listening terrace songs around, that sort of banter will never cease no matter the state of the peace process in this country… Can you imagine a Celtic vs Rangers match without the sectarian songs?" Setting aside any controversy over certain chants, the general consensus on Linfield's return to Solitude was positive. To borrow the words of *Irish News* journalist Liz Trainor, the match would "be seen as an important step towards normality and the latest reflection of the peace process". For Trainor, the successful fulfilment of the fixture demonstrated that Northern Ireland was "moving forward" after the Troubles.[34]

Putting aside the social and political significance of the game, the draw represented two points dropped in the quest for a League title. At the start of the 1998/99 season, the Blues had hoped to go one better than the previous campaign's second place. Yet unfortunately that did not come to fruition. Linfield never reached the level of consistency needed to lift a Gibson Cup, and had to settle for another runners-up place. This time Roy Coyle's Glentoran won the title at a canter, with eight points separating the Big Two at the season's end. The emphatic nature of Glentoran's triumph led pundits to speculate that the East Belfast side would dominate local football for the foreseeable future. *Belfast Telegraph* columnist Tommy Cassidy maintained: "Coyle's men can rule the game for years."[35]

Inevitably, the projections of long-term Glentoran supremacy led to questions over Jeffrey's future. In late April, the press was awash with articles casting doubt on the manager's position. Indeed, his position was even discussed by the Board at the final League game of the season. Ultimately nothing would come of this. However, there was an understanding that Jeffrey simply had to deliver a League title the following season. Linfield had gone five years without a Gibson Cup, and this was something that the club's demanding fans were finding hard to stomach.[36]

Next season was crucial. The turn of the Millennium would either be win the League or bust for Jeffrey.

Chapter 8

# *Triumphs Over Adversity*

Going into Jeffrey's third full season in charge (1999/2000), the expectation heaped on the manager and his players was immense. Captain Noel Bailie recalled, "you could fairly feel it... you felt the pressure from everybody, fans, coaching staff, other players, ex-players and commentators". Bailie and his teammates knew that another near miss would not be good enough. Linfield simply had to lift the Gibson Cup. As the club programme put it, "this has to be our year for the Championship... failure should not be a considered option".[1]

Spending big in pursuit of that Championship was not an option either. Despite the savings made over the previous few seasons, Linfield's financial situation had not improved. Windsor's upkeep was still a huge drain on resources; thus splashing out on transfer fees to strengthen the squad was out of the question. The sale of Lee Feeney during the previous campaign was illustrative of just how unhealthy the Blues' economic position had become. Prized asset Feeney had joined Glasgow Rangers for £100,000, yet none of this figure was available to sign a replacement. Unable to pay out big sums, Jeffrey strengthened his squad by bringing in free agents. Midfielders Stuart Callaghan and Norman Kelly both signed terms after impressing in pre-season friendlies. The midfield pair would go on to become first-team regulars, vindicating Jeffrey's judgement. The same went for Scottish goalkeeper Paul Mathers, who signed in early August. Going into his third full season in charge, Jeffrey was displaying an ability to pick up quality players on the cheap.[2]

On a shoestring budget, Jeffrey had assembled a strong squad – one that looked capable of mounting a serious League challenge. However at the very outset of 1999/00, the team was dealt a severe blow. Injury ruled Glenn Ferguson, the Blues' main striker, out of the first half of the campaign. Ferguson was Linfield's top marksman. His presence and goals would be dearly missed. Without him, the Blues' two other strikers, David Larmour and Chris Morgan, would have to carry the team's goal-scoring burden. Morgan had arrived the previous summer from Crusaders. Whilst neither possessed the experience of Ferguson, both were hungry for success and eager to prove they had what it took to spearhead Linfield's forward line.[3]

In Ferguson's absence, Larmour and Morgan more than stepped up to the mark. Both coped with the pressure heaped on their shoulders, and both netted regularly. Early on in the campaign, Linfield emerged as the top goal-scoring side in the League, and David Jeffrey was quick to hail the pair. The Blues manager praised his strikers for netting consistently, but also paid tribute to "the rest of the team" who Morgan and Larmour were feeding off. Linfield were strong all over the pitch, and by October sat top of the Irish League. Midfielder Jamie Marks attributed the impressive start to playing open, attractive football. Marks maintained that "on the big Windsor Park pitch… it [was] difficult for the opponents to close us down".[4]

Over the autumn, the Blues' position at the top of the table was strengthened with an impressive run of results. By the end of November, the club had opened up an 11-point gap on second-placed Glenavon. Linfield were winning consistently and were doing so with a swagger. This was something that the press lauded Jeffrey's players for. After a Halloween victory over Glentoran, Steven Beacom of the *Belfast Telegraph* described Linfield as "magnificent". He maintained that although the "score was 2-0… the difference between the teams was so much more… In every department, the Blues were better than their bitter rivals." In the same edition of the paper, columnist Tommy Cassidy added that things would soon get even better for Linfield. He commented, "when Glenn Ferguson returns it can only add to the team… A lovely thought for manager Jeffrey isn't it." For the other teams in the League, it was ominous.[5]

When Ferguson returned to the first team, the Blues went from strength to strength. By early January 2000, the gap between Linfield and their nearest challenger stood at a staggering 19 points! It appeared that no Irish League side could live with Linfield. On 8 January, second-placed Coleraine had visited Windsor hoping to put a dent in the Blues juggernaut, but as *Ireland's Saturday Night* stated: "There [was] simply no stopping this incredible Linfield side… like so many before them, [Coleraine] left the international arena with nothing." The Blues saw off the Bannsiders 3-0, with two goals coming from Jamie Marks and one from David Larmour. For Marks it was a day when everything appeared to go his way. After a successful afternoon on the pitch, the midfielder picked up £200 worth of winnings in the club's weekly draw. Luck had smiled on Marks when he won Linfield's draw, but played no part in the Blues' impressive run. Jeffrey's side was a well-oiled machine and was reaping its just reward.[6]

All at the club were revelling in the team's form – none more so than stalwart Stephen Beatty. The midfielder was enjoying a well-earned testimonial year at the time, and drawing upon his vast experience, rated this Blues team as the best he had played in. Beatty reflected: "I have been a part of some good Linfield teams but none compare with this one… The professionalism is frightening and our focus is without doubt as good as I can ever recall." The resolve that Beatty spoke of drove him and his teammates to equal a post-war Irish League record. On 26 February the Blues defeated Distillery 1-0 at Windsor. This gave Jeffrey's side a 39th consecutive home League game without loss. The feat matched the exploits of the Linfield side from the mid-1950s that had also gone unbeaten in 39 home League games. Almost 50 years later, the club was replicating this little piece of history. Incredibly, Linfield had not lost a League game staged at Windsor since 10 January 1998.[7]

After the record-equalling display the Blues boss was understandably thrilled. A proud Jeffrey informed the press that, "To date our campaign has been more than satisfactory." Linfield's majestic form had placed the Gibson Cup within touching distance. Nine games remained after the win over Distillery, and only seven points were needed to secure League glory. However, just as the Irish League top brass were getting ready to hitch blue ribbons to the trophy, Linfield hit a sticky patch. At the start of March, the Blues suffered a 3-0 defeat to Glenavon at Mourneview. This was followed a couple of weeks later by Glentoran ending the Blues' 39-game unbeaten run at home. A 2-1 loss reminded the Windsor faithful what it felt like to experience a home defeat in the League. The two defeats in quick succession were certainly unwelcome, but no real cause for alarm. Linfield's imperious form until that point had ensured that no other team stood any chance of catching them. Victory away to Ballymena in the next game got the title challenge back on track, and reduced the points needed to lift the Gibson Cup to just four.[8]

On Tuesday 28 March the title was all but secured with a decisive 3-2 victory away to Cliftonville. That evening, the Blues visited Solitude for a rearranged fixture. The game was notable for more than just its significance in terms of the Gibson Cup's destination. It was also the first time that Linfield had played an evening fixture at the North Belfast ground since the RUC had permitted the Blues to travel there in 1998. Originally the game was scheduled for Saturday 15 January, but a frozen pitch forced its postponement. When no alternative Saturday could be found to host the fixture, the police had to facilitate Linfield travelling there on a weekday evening. The stipulations for the match were far from routine. Kick-off was set for 6:30pm to allow the game to finish in reasonable light, and supporters were again bussed in. Nevertheless, just being able to host the tie in the evening was a step forward for both clubs and for the Irish League.[9]

The game itself proved far from plain sailing. Cliftonville dominated the first half and deservedly went in 2-0 at the break. At half-time, Jeffrey re-jigged his team and switched from a 4-4-2 formation to 4-3-3. The move turned the game on its head, and not long after the restart Ferguson made it 2-1. After that it was all one-way traffic in Linfield's favour. The equaliser came from William Murphy, with the big defender steering the ball toward the goal from a Stuart Callaghan corner. Then Chris Morgan, the extra striker that Jeffrey had brought on, scored the winning goal. Callaghan again played a vital role in the all-important third. The midfielder crossed from the right for Ferguson, who headed back across the area, and Morgan was there to glance the ball into the Cliftonville net.[10]

Morgan's effort had effectively sealed the Blues' first League title in six years. The following day's *Belfast Telegraph* proclaimed: "Linfield will be the first side to be crowned Champions in the new Millennium." The club sat 15 points clear of second place with only five games left to play. Mathematically the Blues could still be caught on goal difference, but that was highly unlikely. Linfield's 'goals scored' and 'conceded' columns were vastly superior to those of Glentoran – the only club that could match the Blues' points tally. One more point would put the title beyond any doubt. Anything but a loss in the club's next game away to Coleraine would see the Gibson Cup back at Windsor.[11]

Droves of Blues fans made their way to the North Coast on 1 April, hoping to see Linfield clinch the title. Such were their numbers that the 3pm kick-off was delayed nine minutes to allow everyone to pack inside the Showgrounds. When proceedings finally got underway, Linfield's support was noisy and created what *Ireland's Saturday Night* described as "a cracking atmosphere". Unfortunately the events on the pitch did not match those off it. No goals were scored in the first half, then after the break Coleraine netted twice. Unlike at Solitude a few days earlier, the Blues would not stage a dramatic comeback. This time Linfield could only manage one goal in reply. However, the huge blue contingent did not travel home disappointed. Events 60 miles away ensured that the title was Windsor-bound. At Ballyskeagh, Glentoran succumbed to a 1-0 defeat at the hands of relegation-threatened Lisburn Distillery. This ended the East Belfast side's title challenge and put the destination of the Gibson Cup beyond doubt. Ironically, the Whites' winning goal came via Graeme Arthur, a former Linfield ball boy. When news of his 87th-minute strike filtered through to the Coleraine Showgrounds, the party got underway in the stands.[12]

At 4:57pm the final whistle sounded, unleashing unbridled joy amongst Linfield's playing staff. Defender William Murphy found it "hard to take it all in". The centre-back explained: "We have strived for the title all season and after finishing second two years running and experiencing the pain of that to enjoy this moment is just incredible – the best feeling ever." For defender John Easton, the euphoria of it all was just as sweet. Easton had spent his whole career at the Blues and was a fans' favourite. Having played through the Gibson Cup drought, he understood just how much the triumph meant to supporters. Basking in the glory, Easton informed reporters: "It's a great feeling to be champions again."[13]

Winning Linfield's first Gibson Cup since 1994 (and the first since the formation of the Premier League) was an impressive achievement. It was also a befitting accolade for a strong Irish League outfit. At the back, experienced goalkeeper Paul Mathers was a cool head and an assured performer. In front of him was a formidable defence. At the heart of the team was the resolute partnership of captain Noel Bailie and William Murphy. Both were top-drawer defenders in their prime. Bailie's reading of the game was second to none in the Irish League, whilst Murphy's physicality was the perfect foil. At right-back, two players battled it out to make the first XI. Tommy McDonald and Stephen Collier fought for the slot and demonstrated a healthy competition for a place in the squad. On the other side, John Easton had established himself as a no-nonsense, tough-tackling left-back that gave his all. Supporters lauded him in song when they exclaimed,

"You'll never beat John Easton!" The back four was solid and, according to Glenn Ferguson, gave confidence to the rest of the team: "You're set up when you've got four guys like that."[14]

In midfield there was the right mix of tenacity and flair. Dictating play was Stephen Beatty, a player David Jeffrey described as a "powerhouse in the middle of the park". For most of his Linfield career Beatty had played out on the left, but when he moved into a central role his game went to another level. Adding bite alongside him was either Jamie Marks or Norman Kelly. Their role was to sit and offer protection to the defence, letting the likes of Tony Gorman and Stuart Callaghan take the game to the opposition. Both Callaghan and Gorman contributed with goals from midfield. However, their primary remit was to create chances, and they did so with aplomb. Linfield were the season's highest-scoring Irish League team with 67 goals.[15]

The forward line of Glenn Ferguson, David Larmour and Chris Morgan shared the attacking burden between them, and all three weighed in with vital contributions throughout the season. As Jeffrey preferred playing with two up top, usually one of the strikers missed out on a starting place. Yet no matter what combination the manager went with, the prospect of facing Linfield was daunting.

Near the end of the 1999/00 campaign, one more piece of silverware was added to the Windsor trophy cabinet. On 18 April the Blues took Coleraine apart in the final of the Coca-Cola Cup. That night Linfield put four past the Bannsiders at the Oval. On the surface all at the club appeared rosy. Linfield were by far and away the best team in the country. However, behind the scenes the money problems remained. Earlier in the season, the Finance Committee decreed that the players' wage bill would be cut by £100,000. Worryingly, the Committee indicated in May that even with these savings, "the Club could not service [its] current debts". The financial difficulties made it impossible to keep the title-winning squad together. Cutting costs was essential, even if this meant the sale of first-team players.[16]

Influential midfielder Stuart Callaghan was one who fell foul of the club's plight. He was released not long after the season's conclusion. Callaghan lived in Scotland and was flown in to play. Offloading his services thus saved transport costs on top of a wage. A disappointed Callaghan accepted that "finances dictate... with me travelling over for games I suppose I was the obvious one to leave". Squad players Trevor

McMullan, Philip Rogan, John McGrath, Ryan Semple and long-time club servant Ian McCoosh all followed the Scot out the door. Given the circumstances, there was limited scope for bringing players in. David Jeffrey had to accept missing out on key transfer targets because Linfield could not afford to break its wage structure.[17]

Anyone who signed at this time was not coming for the money. Instead, they joined because they wanted to represent Linfield. Gavin Arthur of Glenavon was one player who fitted into this category. When he agreed terms in May, David Jeffrey hailed him as the replacement for Stuart Callaghan. His new manager also stated: "What really pleased me is Gavin's desire to play for Linfield." Another who arrived was youngster Garth Scates. He joined from Blackburn Rovers on a one-year deal, and upon his arrival Jeffrey stressed that the move was "possible because of... the generosity of a group of supporters clubs." The transfer dealings at the start of the millennium indicated one thing – Linfield was near broke.[18]

Having no money ensured that maintaining a high domestic standard was a challenge. It also made the difficult assignment of competing in Europe all the more arduous. Most teams that reached UEFA competition were professional, even those in the qualifying rounds. A penniless part-time club was therefore always likely to struggle against such outfits. Yet in the summer of 2000, Linfield would have to try. As title winners, the Blues entered the Champions League first qualifying round, drawing FC Haka of Finland. Taking on what was a professional side was made even tougher by the date of the tie's first leg, 12 July. This was one month before the start of the Irish League, but right in the middle of the Finnish season. The timing of the tie very much suited Haka. The Finns went into it in peak fitness, whereas Jeffrey admitted that Linfield had no warm-up game under their belt. It was thus easy to understand why *Ireland's Saturday Night* labelled the "early start" a "dubious reward for winning the Gibson Cup".[19]

If the mood music coming out of Ulster was downbeat, there was much more positivity from Scandinavia. As UEFA had drawn the first two rounds at the same time, both the Blues and Haka knew Inter Bratislava awaited the winner. Feeling assured of success, the Finns had sorted their itinerary for Slovakia, even before a ball was kicked in the first-round tie! However, when Haka and Linfield met, the Finnish club's supreme confidence appeared ill-founded. In the first leg, played at Haka's Tehtaan kenttä stadium, the home team only just shaded affairs. Haka midfielder David Wilson scored the game's solitary goal, but otherwise the Finns flattered to deceive. The *Belfast Telegraph* reported that, "FC Haka were nowhere near as good as many thought they would be." Experienced campaigner John Easton reflected, "They are certainly not the best side I've played against in Europe."[20]

Windsor hosted the second leg a week later on 19 July. Aided by home advantage, the Blues took the game to the Finns and received an early reward. Twenty minutes were on the clock when Chris Morgan was brought down in the area. The referee gave the penalty, and Glenn Ferguson put the Blues 1-0 ahead on the night. Ferguson then doubled the lead in the second half. On 74 minutes, the forward headed home a Stephen Beatty cross. The two strikes gave the Blues the upper hand in the tie and it appeared that Jeffrey would be leading his men to Bratislava.

There was though, a late sting in the tail. With only three minutes left, Haka's Kai Nyyssonen carried the ball towards Linfield's goal. Norman Kelly had tracked his run and put in a tackle. Yet instead of taking the ball, Kelly caught Nyyssonen. The Finnish player went down, and Icelandic referee Egill Mar Makusson pointed to the spot. Television replays showed that the infringement came outside the box, but all that mattered was the referee's call. The Finns had the chance to reduce the deficit on the night and take the tie on away goals. Péter Kovács, Haka's tall Hungarian striker, stepped up, scored past Paul Mathers and silenced Windsor.[21]

Once again, Linfield had crashed out of Europe in gut-wrenching fashion. For Norman Kelly the defeat was particularly hard to take. The midfielder told the press: "I've never felt so bad after a match... I thought [the foul] was outside the box and now knowing that was the case, it doesn't make me feel any better." John Easton sighed: "It wasn't quite as bad as the way we lost in Copenhagen but it was up there with it... we were hit by a killer blow." Although disappointment was the overriding emotion, David Jeffrey was filled with pride for his players. The manager stated: "The boys were a credit to themselves and the Irish League. I know a lot of hurdles are placed in the way... and for us to nearly jump them all and get through makes me feel very proud."[22]

When competing in Europe, League of Ireland sides faced similar challenges to Irish League teams. Yet in that Champions League campaign, Shelbourne successfully negotiated the first qualifying round. Shels dispatched FK Sloga Jugomagnat of Macedonia, before being knocked out by Rosenborg in the second round. Both Linfield and Shelbourne were part-time clubs fulfilling fixtures well outside their domestic seasons. The Dublin outfit, however, had one big advantage. The Football Association of Ireland (FAI) gave Shelbourne a grant to help prepare for the early start.

The FAI's assistance showed that in some of the countries negatively impacted by UEFA's transformation of European competition, steps were being taken to adapt. In Northern Ireland there were no such positive moves. The IFA displayed no inclination to offer financial support for teams competing in Europe. Support for local sides could have facilitated training camps – helping part-time players get up to speed with opposition teams. Yet it appeared that the governing body of football in the Province was unconcerned about the progress of Irish League sides in Europe.[23]

Linfield had to wait almost a month after the Champions League exit before starting the domestic campaign. In that time, Windsor Park hosted a string of glamorous fixtures. The first came on 22 July between the Blues of Belfast and Manchester. Memories of the famous Cup Winners' Cup tie between the two sides were evoked in the run-up to the game. This time, however, it was not a close-fought affair. City proved too good for the Belfast Blues and recorded a 4-0 victory. The huge gap between the Irish Premiership and England's Premier League (Man City had just been promoted there) was apparent on the day.[24]

Another famous name was in town a week and a half after the City game. On 2 August, the Blues took on Portugal's Benfica. Just like with Manchester City, there was footballing history between Benfica and Linfield. In the first round of the 1983/84 European Cup, the Portuguese side had defeated the Blues 6-2 on aggregate. Both of Linfield's goals in the tie had come in Belfast as part of a 3-2 defeat. Almost 20 years later, the two sides replicated that Windsor scoreline. Benfica had raced into a 3-0 lead with only 25 minutes on the clock, but then the Blues fought back. On 27 minutes, Tommy McDonald crossed for David Larmour to score from close range. Larmour then grabbed a second on 49 minutes, after good work in the build-up from Chris Morgan and Gavin Arthur. There was certainly no shame in going down by the odd goal against a team like Benfica.[25]

The Portuguese club's Belfast commitments did not end with the 3-2 victory over Linfield. Benfica were in town for the 'Carlsberg Belfast Challenge'. This was a four-team tournament, which comprised the Blues, Benfica, Glentoran and Liverpool. Twelve months earlier, Belfast's Big Two had battled it out in the same competition with Feyenoord and Liverpool. On that occasion, the Merseyside Reds had left Belfast with the trophy after beating Linfield in the first game then Feyenoord in the final.

Sports promoter Noel Lemon was the driving force behind the tournament. He was the man who had previously organised the Blues' North American tours and brought World Cup winners Argentina to Windsor. With the Belfast Challenge, Lemon had once again injected glamour into Linfield's commitments. There was, however, an inbuilt mechanism in the competition to ensure no Irish League involvement in the final. The two touring teams were assured of their places in the showpiece before the first round even kicked-off. As was explained in the magazine *When Saturday Comes*: "Nobody was prepared to tolerate a repeat of the fiasco in Dublin a few years [previously] when Derry City accidentally beat Celtic to reach the final" of a similar competition.[26]

Twenty-four hours after Linfield played Benfica, cross-city rivals Glentoran hosted Liverpool at the Oval. On the night, the Reds ran out 4-0 winners, which meant everything had gone according to plan for the organisers. The most successful club teams from England and Portugal could play out the final knowing they both deserved to be there. The decider would take place at Windsor on 5 August. Just beforehand, Linfield played Glentoran in a battle for third place in the competition, though it also doubled up as the Charity Shield – a meeting between the previous season's League and Irish Cup winners. Title-holders Linfield took the lead on 40 minutes. Tony Gorman sent in a free-kick from the left, which Glenn Ferguson met with his head. Glentoran keeper Alan Gough managed to keep the effort out, but failed to hold on to the ball. This allowed Ferguson to sweep the rebound into the net.[27]

Farce then ensued a matter of seconds after the goal. With only 40 minutes on the clock, referee John Ferry blew his whistle for half-time. Confused fans wondered whether Ferry had mistimed proceedings, yet it turned out he was following the wishes of the competition organisers. The Charity Shield was only scheduled to last 80 minutes. It began at 2pm, and would be followed at 4pm by Benfica vs Liverpool. This second tie was being screened live on television, thus Linfield vs Glentoran was shortened to ensure the 'big' game started on time for the cameras.

The local sides only found out minutes before their match kicked off that they were involved in a condensed affair. Glentoran manager Roy Coyle explained that, "The referee came up to me just moments before the match and said it was going to last 80 minutes… it was a disgrace," and Steven Beacom of the *Belfast Telegraph* agreed. The journalist maintained that "telling them to play 10 minutes less was a bit of an insult". Chris Morgan would add a second after the break to secure a 2-0 win, but the game had become an absurdity.[28]

Come four o'clock, Channel 5's cameras beamed the Liverpool vs Benfica game across the UK. Those who tuned in saw the two sides play out a 2-2 draw. With no extra time or penalties on the day, Liverpool won the tournament by virtue of scoring more goals in the first round. At the end of the game viewers watched as Liverpool lifted the Belfast Challenge trophy. They had also just witnessed something that would become much less frequent. From that point on, big-name British and European sides stopped travelling on a regular basis to Belfast for friendlies. Glasgow Rangers proved a notable exception to this rule, but in the main, the days of glamorous friendlies were over.

*When Saturday Comes* pointed out that the Belfast Challenge allowed Liverpool to re-establish "contact with their Irish fans", as well as presenting the club with the opportunity to sell "a few more replica kits". That financial aspect of pre-season was becoming more and more important. Increasingly, friendlies were as much about money-making as they were about improving match-fitness. Clubs like Liverpool understood that they could earn serious amounts from fulfilling these fixtures – match fees, television rights and the sale of merchandise all added up. Unfortunately for Linfield, there was only so much to be made by coming to Belfast, while other destinations were becoming more lucrative and appealing.[29]

Interest in football was expanding in North America as well as the Far East, and 'big' teams were thus keen to exploit these markets. Considering that Liverpool alone could count 60 million supporters in China, it was little wonder that touring Asia became popular with English Premier League sides. The Premiership even went as far as establishing its own biennial Asia Trophy in 2003. Worldwide promotion of a club's 'brand' became an essential part of pre-seasons, and friendlies against Irish League sides could offer little to further this aim. The days of the likes of Ards hosting Manchester City and Bangor bringing Sheffield Wednesday to the Province – as had happened in the 1990s – appeared to have ended.[30]

Losing out on regularly holding crowd-pulling friendlies would hit the Blues and other local sides hard. Games against teams like Liverpool had been an important revenue stream. Linfield had netted nearly £100,000 from the two years of hosting the Belfast Challenge. Without this money coming in, the club would simply have to cut its cloth accordingly. However, strict budgeting was nothing new at the Blues. Ever since David Jeffrey became manager, the club had been slashing spending. Given these testing circumstances, he had worked wonders in putting together a title-winning side. Jeffrey had established a winning mentality in his players, and they took that into the following season. Linfield hit the ground running in 2000/01 – such was the club's impressive form, by mid-autumn *Ireland's Saturday Night* was convinced that consecutive titles were on the cards. The 11 November edition asked, "IS IT EVEN A RACE, LADS?" The bookies were in full agreement with that assessment. At the end of November, Eastwoods stopped taking bets on the Blues retaining the Gibson Cup.[31]

Jeffrey put his team's high-flying position down to the "phenomenal work rate" of his players, something that was very much in evidence at the 2000 Big Two Boxing Day game. In the traditional festive showdown, Linfield took the Glens apart. The Blues went ahead on 13 minutes through Russell Kelly. Then 10 minutes later it was 2-0, after Gavin Arthur smashed a free-kick home from 25 yards – though Arthur himself claims it was 30 yards. No more goals followed, but the Blues controlled proceedings. In the aftermath, the press gushed over Linfield's performance. The *Belfast Telegraph* exclaimed: "[The Blues] are outstanding – true champions and are getting used to that title."[32]

Linfield's strong early-season form was taken into the second half of the campaign. In late January, the County Antrim Shield was added to the trophy cabinet, and by mid-February, 21 points separated the Blues from second-placed Glenavon. It was thus only a matter of when – not if – Linfield would retain the Gibson Cup. Yet tying up that title proved more difficult than expected. On 24 February the Blues went into a game with Omagh, knowing that two wins would finish the job. The first of these would not come that day. Instead, a resilient performance from the Tyrone men ensured that Linfield had to make do with a point. Then the following week's game away to Glentoran was called off on the advice of Health & Safety, due to refurbishment work on one of the stands at the Oval. Fans and players reacted with frustration to the cancellation. However, both had to get used to a lack of football.[33]

For a couple of weeks at the start of March, no competitive matches were sanctioned in the Province. An outbreak of foot-and-mouth disease had plunged agriculture across Great Britain and Northern Ireland into crisis. The disease, which afflicted livestock, was first spotted in Essex on 19 February. Soon afterwards, other cases were confirmed throughout the UK, and a number of measures were implemented to combat its further spread. An immediate ban was placed on the export of British meat and livestock; this was followed by the mass slaughter of pigs and cattle. As well as the regulations placed on farming, there were limitations attached to everyday activities. Travel was restricted and sporting fixtures were cancelled. On 2 March, the day when the disease was first detected in Northern Ireland, all Irish League games were suspended.[34]

Fortunately the postponement of matches was short-lived, and restrictions were eased by the middle of March. Yet by then Linfield had missed nearly three weeks of football, and it appeared the disruption had affected the players. When the League resumed, defeats to Newry and Portadown followed. Instead of wrapping up the title in emphatic fashion, the Blues stuttered toward the line – the Gibson Cup was not secured until 21 April. That Saturday afternoon in lashing rain, the Blues put three past Coleraine at Windsor. The Bannsiders had taken the lead on 38 minutes, threatening to spoil a Championship party, but Linfield's response was swift. Less than a minute later, Tony Gorman had equalised. Soon afterwards (and just before half-time), Jamie Marks made it 2-1. Then in the second half a superb team move, finished by Chris Morgan, ensured the three points – and the title.[35]

Linfield had become the first Irish League side to retain the Gibson Cup in the Premiership era, and manager David Jeffrey was the first to pay tribute to his players. With the title secured, he told the press how happy he was with his team's efforts: "They maintained a fantastically high level of performance throughout the season and now they have got their just reward." Jeffrey was right to extol the virtues of his players, but *his* role in the success was vital. He had assembled an immense side that knew how to win, and did so with flair. Achieving this against the backdrop of Linfield's crippling financial plight was no small feat. Jeffrey had shown great acumen and demonstrated an ability to stretch a limited budget. He had also proved adept at getting the most out of his men. As captain of the side, Noel Bailie maintained: "We had good players, but you've got to know what you are doing and you've got to know what way you want to play. The manager and his coaching staff knew what they were doing."[36]

Chapter 9

# *Doubling Down*

Near the end of the 2000/01 campaign, Linfield's Team Committee met with the playing squad to put forward a host of cost-cutting measures. Unsurprisingly, both parties failed to settle on every detail. However, a broad consensus between the two was reached. Afterwards, the committee reported to the Board that: "The players had agreed to 90 per cent of what they had been asked to accept including the abolition of signing-on fees and bonus payments for individual matches." This approval of payment reduction was only one episode in Linfield's long list of saving initiatives. Ominously, significantly more savings were needed.[1]

In late May 2001, the club's bank stressed that urgent "debt reduction" was required. Linfield's overdraft had increased to £450,000 and the bank was adamant that it had to be addressed. This was not easy, especially when the club appeared to be a victim of its own success. Winning the title had ensured passage to the Champions League, but the 'reward' appeared more of a bind. Much to the chagrin of club officials, the first qualifying round for the competition paired the Blues with Georgia's Torpedo Kutaisi. Chairman Billy McCoubrey could not hide his disappointment after the tie was confirmed. He told the press that, "these tournaments in Europe are a disaster... We seem to be repeatedly handed draws that mean long travel and high costs." The Blues would receive over £91,000 prize money for qualifying, but this was not paid out until almost a year later. The 2001/02 season thus began with the club forced to incur further debt.[2]

Fulfilling the second leg, away in Kutaisi, cost a staggering £28,000. For a club struggling to make ends meet this was a huge outlay, and it only allowed the Blues to bring the bare minimum of a playing squad. A frustrated David Jeffrey explained that Linfield would take just 16 players to Georgia: "I would have liked to have brought a full panel of 18 or 20, but finances dictated numbers." The small travelling party stood in stark contrast to the large numbers Kutaisi brought to Belfast. This was due to a major advantage that the Georgian side had on Linfield. Government funding subsidised Kutaisi's travel. It also sponsored a four-week training camp prior to the first leg at Windsor on 11 July. That game ended in a scoreless draw. The return fixture in Georgia was thus effectively a straight shoot-out between the two sides.[3]

On 16 July, Linfield's costly Georgian adventure began with a long-haul flight to Tbilisi. This was followed by a four-hour coach journey which struck fear into all on board. The *Belfast Telegraph* compared the driver to "Michael Schumacher, only without the German's control", whilst *Ireland's Saturday Night* queried whether he was "impersonating Sandra Bullock in the film Speed". After racing through the countryside the coach arrived in Kutaisi at 10am on 17 July. This was 6am back home, and hardly the best preparation for a match the next day. Considering these arduous travel arrangements, the Georgians were the favourites to progress, and they did so on the evening of 18 July. In an  evenly matched tie, Kutaisi went through 1-0 on aggregate. A left-footed free-kick from Mikheil Ashvetia sealed the win and the Blues' fate. Linfield's involvement in European football had once again ended at the first hurdle.[4]

After the defeat, the return to Belfast proved just as stressful as the journey to Kutaisi. This owed to a blocked section of the road en route to Tbilisi's airport. Thunderstorms had created landslides, which spilled debris onto the thoroughfare and impeded travel. Almost an hour was lost as a path was fashioned to enable Linfield's coach to pass. Steven Beacom joked in *Ireland's Saturday Night* this was the only thing that delayed the party's driver. From start to finish, the trip was an ordeal. Alex Mills of the *News Letter* summed up Linfield's "travelling arrangements" as "horrendous". Glenn Ferguson maintained that "in years to come all the players will look back and say it was a nightmare".

Taking all this into consideration the £28,000 needed to cover the trip seemed extortionate. Yet it was the sort of money needed to finance taking a squad to the far reaches of Eastern Europe.[5]

Billy McCoubrey explained that Linfield's costs had been kept "down to a minimum". Bringing a party of 16 players to Georgia was evidence of that. However, having to scrimp on travel only made European competition even less appealing. For this reason, McCoubrey advocated that "UEFA started zoning the early rounds on a geographical basis". Club secretary Derek Brooks added that the IFA could do more to help local sides with expenses. Brooks appealed for roundtable discussions on the issue. This unfortunately did not happen. Instead, by way of response, the Association issued an underwhelming statement. In it the body drew attention to the UEFA prize money on offer. The statement detailed that Linfield received over £91,000 for participation in the 2000/01 Champions League – adding that it "warmly [welcomed the] on-going support from UEFA and [confirmed] that similar amounts of grant [would] be paid, in June 2002".[6]

The monetary reward for making it to the Champions League was unquestionably significant. Even if it took almost a year to come through, £91,000 was worth waiting for. That said, further progression would have meant greater remuneration. In theory, competing in the first qualifying round presented Linfield with a good chance of achieving this. The Kutaisi tie certainly lent credence to that thought. Not much separated the two sides on the pitch and the Georgians were lucky to advance. If Linfield had benefitted from a training camp, as Kutaisi had, perhaps the result would have been different. Small margins mattered, and having outside backing to help prepare was a major advantage. Irish League sides were going into European games under their own steam. The unwillingness of the IFA to lend assistance was thus a huge disservice to local football. Additional funding could have yielded greater UEFA rewards, which would have meant more money in Northern Irish football. Ultimately this did not come, ensuring that as other European leagues progressed, the Irish League stagnated and was left further behind.

Suggesting that the IFA aided local sides in European competition was far from a radical call. Common sense dictated that strong foundations improved the chances of progress. A similar logic held that any successful outfit needed investment to maintain dominance. David

Jeffrey was well aware of this. He knew that to continue Linfield's impressive domestic run, his squad had to be kept fresh. Yet given the Blues' mounting debts this was difficult. First wages had to be freed up before anyone could come in. During 2000/01 Stephen Beatty had indicated he would leave for a fresh challenge, so that was one space. Then at the end of the campaign the manager let long-serving defender John Easton go. Early on during the following season, Tommy McDonald was also released. All three players were big personalities who had contributed to Linfield's success over a long period. Those who filled their places would thus have high standards to maintain.[7]

Two major signings arrived at Windsor that summer of 2001. Winger Mark Picking signed from Coleraine, and forward Justin McBride joined from Glentoran. McBride's transfer was one of the stories of the off-season. *Ireland's Saturday Night* called it "an extraordinary development" that sent "shockwaves" through Northern Irish football. Moving from one side of Belfast's Big Two to the other was unusual, though it had been done before. For instance, Johnny Jameson left Linfield for the Glens in 1980, and of course Raymond Campbell had moved in the opposite direction in 1993. Yet according to *Ireland's Saturday Night*, "McBride [was] the biggest name of the lot". He had scored 132 goals in his Glentoran career and was an icon at the club. Therefore, joining rivals Linfield was a big deal. The forward explained that Ards and Coleraine were also interested in him, with those clubs offering more money. But he chose the Blues, as he wanted "to win trophies".[8]

Something must have been in the air around the time that McBride joined the Blues. A couple of days after the shock move, Tottenham's Sol Campbell signed for Arsenal. This startling transfer rocked British football and provoked acrimony amongst Spurs fans. There was no love lost across North London's divide, and Campbell's decision was extremely controversial. In the transfer's aftermath, Tottenham supporters decried Campbell as a "Judas". Despite the furore, the change of clubs proved very successful for the player. Two English Premier League titles and three FA Cups were earned whilst Campbell was at the Gunners. One of those Premier Leagues came in his Arsenal debut season.[9]

Unfortunately, Justin McBride would not replicate this success in his opening campaign with the Blues. His Linfield debut, in the home leg of the Kutaisi Champions League tie, was cut short by injury. After only seven minutes he limped off the pitch with a thigh strain. Then before the player had fully recovered, he was involved in a car accident that kept him out until the late autumn. When McBride returned on 24 November, he stole the show in his first League appearance against Crusaders. The forward inspired a 4-0 victory after coming off the bench to grab a hat-trick. The local press lauded his "dream debut", but the win had come at a high cost.[10]

A cruciate ligament injury had forced David Larmour to make way for McBride, and the afternoon's bad news did not end there. In a freakish occurrence, William Murphy suffered the same injury! Both were integral members of the first team, and both were ruled out for the long term. Losing players of that quality was tough at the best of times. Losing them amidst the disappointing run of results Linfield were experiencing was a heavy blow. The 4-0 victory over Crusaders had come during an indifferent first half of the League campaign. In October, the *Belfast Telegraph* had caricatured "Champions Linfield" as "playing like chumps".[11]

League form did not improve in the second half of the campaign, and disappointingly Linfield would finish in third place. Winners Portadown sat 13 points ahead of Jeffrey's men in the final standings. This was hard to take for fans that had enjoyed two consecutive Gibson Cups. It was not, however, a great surprise. The off-field financial difficulties were beginning to bite. Jeffrey had tried to keep his side fresh, but in doing so with a limited budget had been forced to sacrifice veteran campaigners. When the likes of Easton and McDonald left, their experience went with them. There was also the bad fortune of injuries striking at crucial times. Justin McBride's debut season was ravaged by injury, whilst the fate of Larmour and Murphy deprived the club of two stalwarts. Given these complications, Linfield were unable to attain the consistency needed to win the title.

Although the League performance was underwhelming, on their day Jeffrey's players were still up there with the best in the country. The club's strong showing in the 2001/02 cup competitions demonstrated this. In November Linfield lifted the League Cup, then in the New Year the team marched to the Irish Cup final. Here the Blues faced League winners Portadown. En route to the end-of-season showpiece, Portstewart, Carrick Rangers, Glenavon and Killyleagh were all dispatched. In each of these games a common thread ran throughout – the goals of Chris Morgan. The striker's name had appeared on the scoresheet in every one of the rounds. This was quite the achievement, and everyone connected with the club hoped that Morgan would take his good form into the final. Supporters like six-year-old Matthew Ferguson were anxious to see their hero succeed. Young Matthew was a mascot for the big day, and in the game's build-up his father, Blues forward Glenn, told the *Belfast Telegraph*: "He is a Linfield fanatic and his favourite player is Chris Morgan."[12]

Seven years had passed since Linfield's last Irish Cup success. A 2001 defeat by Glentoran in the final was as close as the club had come in the meantime. It was therefore little surprise when the club's ticket allocation sold out well in advance of the final. On the day, hopeful fans packed out the South and Kop Stands eager to see their team end an unwanted sequence – though proceedings did not start well. On six minutes, the Ports went ahead through Kyle Neill. But less than 10 minutes later, the seemingly irrepressible Chris Morgan had the Blues back in the game. Good work by Tony Gorman set up Morgan, and the forward did the rest by unleashing an unstoppable shot past Portadown goalkeeper Mickey Keenan. On 22 minutes, Morgan scored his second to put Linfield 2-1 ahead. Jamie Marks found the striker at the edge of the box and he placed the ball in the corner of the net. No further goals were scored in what was an entertaining game, meaning that Linfield lifted the trophy. For the first time since 1995, the Irish Cup came back to Windsor.[13]

*Ireland's Saturday Night* asserted that Morgan's Cup final performance was "a magnificent way to finish his magical season", though the day was just as special for Blues boss David Jeffrey. Remarkably, 2002 was Jeffrey's first taste of Irish Cup success. In his playing days, Jeffrey had only experienced Irish Cup disappointment. During his early managerial career, he had similarly suffered. Yet finally, 'Irish Cup winner' could be added to his CV. Linfield's manager told the *Belfast Telegraph* that he would "never forget" the occasion, and admitted that such was his excitement, he had slept with the trophy on the Saturday night.[14]

Jeffrey's elation was understandable considering he had waited 20 years as a player and manager to taste that success. In stark contrast, Linfield's Cup final goalkeeper, Alan Mannus, had earned a winners' medal at the first time of asking. Prior to the decider, the 19-year-old had only made a handful of starts, but his manager had no fear in including him in the first XI. It was a call that bore fruit. The young keeper was more than assured in dealing with the Ports' strike force. Taking into account the mid-Ulster side's record in front of goal, the keeper's performance was impressive. Portadown had topped the 2001/02 scoring charts and keeping them at bay was no small feat. The player's showing indicated that he had a bright future in football.

The teenager had progressed from the Linfield Swifts, and the exciting prospect for supporters was that others were on the brink of making that jump. Three days after the Irish Cup win, a talented Swifts team (which Mannus played in) also lifted silverware. For the first time in 30 years, the Intermediate Cup was brought back to Windsor. A 1-0 victory over Donegal Celtic secured the trophy. Portuguese midfielder Miguel Chines settled the tie with a sublime free-kick. The win, however, was about more than just a piece of individual brilliance. The Swifts had a solid spine with players like Mannus at the back, Michael Gault in the midfield and Peter Thompson up front. It would only be a matter of time before these names would all feature in the first team.[15]

Peter Thompson had to wait a while for his break, but during 2002/03 Michael Gault followed the lead of Alan Mannus. In the second half of the campaign, Gault made a name for himself as a no-nonsense player who did not shirk a challenge. The midfielder (like Mannus) was still a teenager when he made it into Linfield's starting line-up. Pulling on the Blue shirt at such a young age did not, however, faze him. Gault explained: "I was just happy to go out, play football and do something that I loved." Strong performances for the Swifts had propelled the teenager into Jeffrey's first-team plans, and Gault soon proved his worth. That said, there was also an element of necessity pushing the Blues boss to consider the merits of players from the Swifts. After the 2002 Cup final, Linfield's playing staff had once again been trimmed and the first-team squad was threadbare.[16]

Cost-cutting measures ensured that Tony Gorman, Norman Kelly and Gavin Arthur all left in the summer of 2002. Thus the midfield that had driven the club to title glory at the start of the Millennium was by that time decimated. On top of this, the Blues still had to contend with the long-term injuries suffered by Larmour and Murphy. Effectively Jeffrey had five gaps to fill in his squad, but he only had the money to plug two of them. When it came to refashioning the team ahead of the 2002/03 campaign, Jeffrey chose to cover the voids left by the injured pair. Defender Hugh Dickson was signed, and up front saw the return of Lee Feeney from Glasgow Rangers. Things had not worked out for Feeney in Scotland, and unfortunately did not go as planned back at the Blues either. The supremely talented player struggled to hold down a starting place and endured a troubled season – in April, his contract was cancelled by mutual consent.[17]

Lee Feeney's tumultuous time back at the Blues was analogous to Linfield's bleak 2002/03 campaign. From the start to the end of the season, the club appeared in disarray. A 5-1 aggregate defeat to Stabaek of Norway dumped the Blues out of the UEFA Cup, and domestically things were just as bad. By November, David Jeffrey had conceded there was no chance of winning the title. Then in late winter came the season's low point. On 13 March, Linfield crashed out of the Irish Cup away to Omagh Town. A 90th-minute winner scored by Omagh striker Andy Crawford settled the tie – and effectively ended Linfield's campaign. The defeat confirmed that no trophies would reside at Windsor that season. On the night the Blues had enjoyed the bulk of possession, but could not make it count. A victorious Omagh manager, Roy McCreadie, admitted afterwards that, "The best team with the best players lost." This was little consolation for David Jeffrey, who sighed, "It has been a disappointing year… [We must] assess and reflect."[18]

There was little to shout about when reviewing the campaign. The few positives included a friendly win over the Kenyan national side, and the emergence of young talent like Gault. However, Jeffrey's comments after the Omagh defeat captured the overriding sense of dismay that supporters felt. As *Look at Linfield* put it, this had been "the worst [campaign] for the club in more than a decade". The League finished on 29 April with the Blues sitting in a lowly fourth place. Three days later on 2 May, club members assembled for their AGM. What transpired at the meeting was, according to Malcolm Brodie, "unprecedented in the history of the club". Chairman Billy McCoubrey, who was standing for re-election to the Management Committee, failed in his bid and had to leave the Board.[19]

Billy McCoubrey had served 22 years on the Management Committee, seven of them as chairman. So naturally he was "disappointed" to have to leave the post. He told the following day's *Ireland's Saturday Night* that he had wanted to stand down "with Linfield in a better position in every respect but, alas, that was not to be". His tenure as chairman was without question one of the most trying in the club's history. The funds were not there to chase success, and McCoubrey had steered a wise financial course. Yet expectation levels at the Blues had never changed, and at the 2003 AGM, Linfield members indicated that they wanted a change of tack. A couple of weeks after the meeting, Linfield's Board decided that David Crawford would fill the position of chairman. Crawford – like McCoubrey – had vast experience on the Board, having served 35 years on it. Upon stepping up to the role, the new chairman acknowledged the financial difficulties that beset the club, but maintained: "We simply cannot have another nightmare scenario like the one we have just passed through." Linfield had to bring back success, and do so forthwith.[20]

If the club was to prosper on the pitch, money had to be spent in the summer of 2003. That was clear for all to see, but Linfield's financial position was still perilous. In fact, it was so bad that in April the club had availed of a £30,000 interest-free loan (provided by one of the club's Trustees) to help with cash-flow problems. Then in May, Linfield's bank informed the Management Committee that if debts continued to rise, the club "would be required to sell Midgley Park to meet the overdraft". Midgley was the club's training ground and the home of Linfield Swifts. Situated between the Kop and the Boucher Road, the venue was named after former club chairman, Harry Midgley MP. The land had been in Linfield's possession since the 1950s and was a valuable asset.[21]

There was no question that Midgley was of great worth to Linfield. However, what was also clear was that the club's other major asset, Windsor Park, was in many ways a burden. As the home of Northern Ireland the stadium had to be kept up to the required FIFA and UEFA specifications. Maintaining these standards needed money, and lots of it. The 14 May edition of the *Belfast Telegraph* explained that, "the huge financial strain of operating Windsor Park as the international stadium" had helped to create Linfield's "crippling overdraft". The heavy expenditure on players during the mid-1990s had of course also contributed to the bleak financial position. That had ended prior to the turn of the Millennium, but it was the required costs of running Windsor international stadium that was now debilitating the club.[22]

Every time that Northern Ireland staged an international at Windsor, the IFA was contracted to give the Blues 15 per cent of the money earned. This covered rental costs, but was something that other clubs decried as an unfair advantage to Linfield. During the 1990s and early 2000s, this was simply not the case. The money was nowhere near enough to meet the huge expenses needed to keep Windsor at the required standard.

At the time, it was rare for Northern Ireland attendances to reach anywhere near 10,000, and the television revenue from games was small. Yet, year upon year very costly improvements were demanded for dressing rooms, medical rooms, drug testing, delegates' facilities, press and media areas, TV studios, pitches and pitch lighting, control rooms, first aid rooms, VIP seating and so on. No one could deny that these changes were other than a good thing but to effect them with the 15 per cent rental contribution and at the same time maintain and operate the large stadium was an impossibility. Linfield appeared trapped. Unless something changed, it looked like the club would flounder in debt for the foreseeable future.[23]

The potential of a forced sale of Midgley indicated just how critical the club's position had become. It also had the effect of focusing minds. Backed into a corner, the Management Committee took a gamble – and decided that the club would seriously invest in the team, in the hope that the title could be won. A Gibson Cup meant prize money, and also the financial rewards associated with entry into the qualifying rounds of the Champions League. In late July 2003, the Management Committee added an additional £20,000 to the team budget. Effectively they had doubled down on winning the League and reaping the rewards that went with it. In the short term, the club was increasing borrowing to achieve success, hoping that this would help pay off part of its debts.[24]

Linfield was not returning to the expenditure of the mid-1990s, but would again be competitive in the transfer market. Given the Blues' plight, this was a high-risk strategy. If the gamble did not come off, an even more uncertain future awaited. The Management Committee was well aware of just how high the stakes were. A similar strategy on the mainland had crippled one of England's biggest clubs.

In March 2003, Leeds chairman Peter Ridsdale had left his post, with the Yorkshire outfit in disarray. Under his stewardship United had taken out huge loans to sign players. It was anticipated that finances from Champions League qualification would allow United to pay the loans back, but this spectacularly backfired. The signing of Rio Ferdinand from West Ham epitomised the failure of the policy. Ferdinand arrived in November 2000 for a fee of £18.5 million, yet Leeds finished that season outside the Champions League spots. In total, United racked up over £100 million in debts. Ridsdale had chased a dream and it turned into a nightmare. A year after he left the club, the side would tumble out of England's Premier League. The sort of money that Leeds had gambled with, was very different to the amounts Linfield would risk, but the principle was similar. Going out and spending big was thus a bold decision.[25]

For the first time in years, more players would join rather than leave the Blues. In late May, Jeffrey released Justin McBride, Russell Kelly, Jamie Marks and Garth Scates. Then over the following months, the Blues boss assembled a squad he (and the Board) hoped could win the Gibson Cup. In total, Jeffrey added seven players to the first-team panel during the summer months. Four were local – defenders Pat Wall and Stephen Douglas, as well as midfielders Aidan O'Kane and Paul McAreavey; the other three were professionals from outside the Province. In a move reminiscent of Roy Coyle's swoop for Coly and Khammal, David Jeffrey brought in Paul Dalglish, Kenny Irons and Phil Charnock. Irons and Charnock were midfielders with vast experience in England's Football League. Charnock had spent most of his career at Crewe Alexandra and Port Vale, whilst Irons had carved out over 500 appearances at Tranmere Rovers and Huddersfield Town. Paul Dalglish on the other hand was a striker in his mid-twenties who had not settled at any side before his move to the Blues. Linfield was Dalglish's seventh senior club since he had made a breakthrough for Newcastle United in 1997.

Of all the transfer activity prior to the new season, the recruitment of Dalglish made the biggest splash. After the deal was confirmed, an excited William Murphy told *Ireland's Saturday Night*: "It is signings like this that really whet the supporters' appetites for the new season." Although Dalglish had earned a reputation as a journeyman, he possessed tremendous ability, having started his career at the top level in England. There was also an aura around his name. Paul was the son of Celtic and Liverpool great, Kenny Dalglish. According to Paul, "having the surname [had] caused problems in the past [therefore] I try and keep my Dad separate from my game". At Linfield he hoped he could do this, and explained he was eager "to play regularly again and start enjoying it". The striker's early form indicated that he would get his wish. Dalglish scored twice in his first competitive game against Larne (played in the group stages of the League Cup) – and in the short term his good form continued, with five goals arriving in the forward's first five appearances.[26]

The impressive start by Dalglish helped Linfield to six wins out of six in the League Cup's group stages. However, when the League began in mid-September, the sequence of victories was abruptly ended. A 2-0 loss away to Coleraine put a dampener on the early promise. This was followed four days later by a home defeat in the League Cup quarter-finals to Crusaders. After the second loss, the press was scathing. The *News Letter* highlighted the "furious verbal barracking [that] Linfield fans" had given their manager, and the *Belfast Telegraph* noted the same. A front-page headline in the latter exclaimed: "CRISIS AT LINFIELD: BLUES BOSS FEELS THE HEAT." Malcolm Brodie wrote that "even at this early stage it could be yet another lean season for Linfield."[27]

Up next was a League fixture against Dungannon Swifts, and club captain Noel Bailie knew it was "crucial". Ahead of the match, he told the local press there was "an extra urgent meaning to this game". In short, the Blues had to win. When the match got underway it was a cagey affair. Going into the final 10 minutes, neither side had broken the deadlock. Then on 83 minutes, left-back Pat McShane smashed home a 20-yard drive. As soon as the ball hit the net, McShane turned and ran 50 yards to the Linfield bench where his boss stood. With euphoric adrenaline cursing through his veins, McShane jumped onto his manager and the pair fell to the ground. The scene was representative of the relief around Windsor. Mark Picking would score a second on 93 minutes to seal the victory. Afterwards, *Ireland's Saturday Night* conceded that whilst the performance was far from being comfortable, "a win [was] a win".[28]

Considering that Linfield had spent big, supporters expected success. The tension around the club was thus easy to understand. According to David Jeffrey, this was the point "when the pressure of being the Linfield manager started to really crank up". A couple of days after the Dungannon win, the stress of it all began to show. On Tuesday 30 September, Jeffrey fell ill whilst travelling to a game between Portadown and Cliftonville. In no time at all, he had undergone an ECG examination and was diagnosed with an irregularity of his heartbeat. Doctors told the manager to take a rest and stay away from the club for a bit. However, all told, Jeffrey ended up missing only three competitive games. These included a 1-1 draw away to Portadown along with wins over Cliftonville and Ards.[29]

At the end of October, Jeffrey returned to the dugout for a 2-0 win over Omagh Town. Days beforehand, Paul Dalglish had left the club, with a Management Committee statement indicating: "it has become apparent that Paul's commitments elsewhere have been increasing and the club were not getting the benefits that had originally been anticipated". Dalglish had failed to settle after a strong start. His experience at Linfield stood in stark contrast to that of the other two players brought in from outside. Kenny Irons and Phil Charnock were revelling in the Irish League, as over the autumn Linfield went from strength to strength.[30]

Charnock's game was high-energy; he operated from box-to-box. Though he was more than just a hard worker; the midfielder had a cultured left foot, which allowed him to impose himself on the opposition. If Charnock was noted for his high-intensity performances, the opposite was the case for Kenny Irons. It would be fair to say that Irons' legs had gone; however, he possessed a tremendous ability on the ball. Irons could control the midfield with his skill in picking out a pass, thus dictating the tempo of a game. The veteran's influence on the team was such that David Jeffrey changed his formation to accommodate the player's lack of pace. Jeffrey recalled that whilst "Kenny could pass the ball and tackle like blazes, he couldn't run".[31]

Both Irons and Charnock were quality players in their own right, but together they really hit it off. According to Charnock, this owed in part to the amount of time the pair spent together. In a typical week, each stayed at home in England from Sunday to Wednesday, then travelled together to Belfast on a Thursday. That evening they attended first-team training, but once that was completed there was time to kill before a Saturday game. Friday was thus quite a relaxed affair, with a fair few games of snooker played against each other. During these sessions the pair built up a rapport and a friendship. When they got out on the pitch, it was little wonder they had such a good understanding of each other's game.[32]

Inspired by the impact of the two players, the Blues carried the good form through the autumn and into the winter. Five straight wins were recorded in December 2003. The fourth of these, a 1-0 victory over Larne, took Linfield to the top of the table; but the fifth, a comfortable Boxing Day 3-1 triumph over Glentoran, was the sweetest. William Murphy put the Blues ahead midway through the first half, before midfielder Stuart King stole the show with two goals. King's first came on the stroke of half-time after he turned the Glentoran defence inside out and shot into the top corner of the net. Then on 66 minutes, he scored his second. This time the midfielder carried the ball 50 yards and finished past Glentoran keeper Elliot Morris. After the game, King rather modestly maintained that he was just happy to play his part on the day. In a candid post-match interview, he also admitted that such was his eagerness ahead of the match: "I couldn't sleep overnight with excitement." King was a Linfield fan, and the thrill of taking on the Blues' Big Two rivals had understandably kept him awake at night.[33]

Stuart King was not the only one at the club experiencing sleepless nights during Christmas 2003. Unbeknownst to many outside of the Board, it appeared that Linfield's financial problems had come to a head. Debts had continued to rise, and the forced sale of Midgley Park looked a distinct possibility. By this time, Linfield's overdraft had crept over £700,000. In fact, so perilous was the position, a Finance Committee meeting on 18 December had discussed the very real fear of "the club being without funds to continue in operation". Just three days before the romp over Glentoran, members of that Committee held crisis talks with management consultancy firm, Pricewaterhouse Coopers. Chairman David Crawford, finance director Richard Johnson and honorary treasurer Paul Weir spent most of that day exploring the club's options. According to Johnson, this was Linfield's lowest point in all the years of financial uncertainty.[34]

Then just as all appeared lost, the gamble of spending began to pay dividends. The Blues' resurgence on the pitch had brought punters through the gates and as a consequence, much-needed revenue poured into the coffers. Going top then defeating Glentoran piqued the interest of fans and there was a spike in attendances. At the start of January, Linfield entertained Coleraine and Portadown. In both games there was a notable increase in the numbers through the turnstiles, and continued good form saw high numbers sustained until the end of the campaign. This was significant, and though it would not seriously buck the long-term trend of falling attendances, it gave the Board breathing space. The club was far from safe, but the surge in ticket sales did stave off the imminent threat of selling assets to meet mounting debt.[35]

Buying time was vital in the short term, but it also gave hope for long-term stability. Linfield's IFA contract, that was for so long a financial curse, all of a sudden looked much more lucrative. In December 2003 the draw for the 2006 World Cup Qualifiers was made, pitting Northern Ireland against England and Wales. Fixtures against other UK nations, especially England, meant sell-outs at Windsor and increased television money. Linfield's 15 per cent share of monies raised from home internationals would thus become worth much more. Now it was still nearly a year before the qualifiers began and almost two years before the England and Wales games; thus the club's financial position would not change overnight, but the prospects were much brighter.

On the pitch, the good form that provided the club with financial breathing space continued. The Blues won the County Antrim Shield in February, and in pursuit of the Gibson Cup the side seemed unbeatable. Indeed, after the opening day loss to Coleraine, Linfield did not suffer a League defeat during 2003/04. This would ensure that after a two-year

absence, the League title would return to Windsor. Yet even with this remarkable run, the triumph proved far from straightforward. Portadown pushed the Blues right until the end. Going into the last game, Linfield were three points in front of the Ports and held a superior goal difference of four.[36]

Although the advantage lay firmly in Linfield's hands, there was still work to do. In a twist of fate, the end-of-season fixtures for both clubs were exactly the same as when Linfield pipped the mid-Ulster side to the title in 1994. The Blues entertained Glentoran, whilst Portadown travelled to Mourneview for a game against Glenavon. Back in 1994 the

Lurgan side was also in the title race, yet in 2004 this was not the case; in fact, relegation awaited Glenavon after the Portadown game. It was thus clear that although Linfield had the advantage in points and goal difference, Portadown had the easier task on the day. As expected, the Ports had little difficulty in dispatching Glenavon. The Shamrock Park outfit ran out 3-0 winners, maintaining the pressure on the Blues right until the end.

For Linfield, things were not as smooth that afternoon. With just three minutes on the clock, Glentoran took the lead via the penalty spot. However just two minutes later, Linfield were back level. Glentoran keeper Elliot Morris fumbled a Pat McShane cross, and David Larmour was on hand to knock the ball into the net. The two sides went into half-time all square, then shortly after the break the game's decisive moment came. Morris again fumbled, this time from a Michael Gault shot, and Linfield capitalised. The ball broke loose and Mark Picking poked it into the goal. Picking's strike was enough to make certain of Linfield's title triumph – and Windsor Park went wild.[37]

Given the pressures of the season, winning the title was a significant achievement. For supporters, however, all that mattered was that Linfield were back as the number one side in Ulster. The arrival of Charnock and Irons had much to do with the success. Both breathed new life into the club, and both had a marked impact on the team. Unfortunately though, Charnock had only played until January, a cruciate ligament injury ending his season early. Yet in his absence, Linfield more than coped. Kenny Irons continued to put his stamp on games, and other midfielders like Ryan McCann, Michael Gault, Stuart King and Mark Picking all stepped up to the mark.

The Blues also benefitted from having William Murphy and David Larmour fully recovered from their injuries. This allowed Murphy to re-establish his partnership with Noel Bailie. Both players knew each other's game inside out, and were developing a good relationship with keeper Alan Mannus. Up front, Larmour returned to once again complement Ferguson and Morgan. This tried and tested formula continued to put other teams to the sword, and all players chipped in with goals. It must be said that during 2003/04, it was Ferguson's efforts in particular that stood out. On 17 April, in the penultimate League game against Larne, the striker hit his 400th career goal. This quite outstanding statistic demonstrated just how special a player he was, and how valuable he was to the Blues. Linfield had quality all over the park, but it was the exceptional class of players like Ferguson as well as Bailie and Irons that set the side apart.[38]

Winning the Gibson Cup meant that the Blues would reap the reward for the club's double down on transfers. The League prize money added to the Champions League qualification meant well in excess of £100,000 coming into the coffers. Jeffrey and his Board could thus breathe a little easier. That said, Linfield was still operating on a massive overdraft facility. The prize money would put a dent in the debts, but the club remained, for the time being, on a far from sound financial footing.[39]

Until the projected return from Northern Ireland's 2006 World Cup qualifiers came through, Linfield would continue to tread a tightrope in managing resources.

## Chapter 10

# *An Absolute Machine*

Small margins can make – or indeed break – a season. This was something that Linfield fans were very much aware of during the 2004/05 and 2005/06 campaigns. The first of these seasons witnessed Linfield lose out on the Gibson Cup by a whisker. Then in the second, David Jeffrey's side attained legendary status by winning a Clean Sweep. Dominating the League was one thing. Winning every piece of available domestic silverware was something else altogether. The feat required both luck as well as the ability to give that bit extra when needed. It was small margins that allowed for the club's success during the 2005/06 campaign – though the unbridled joy at the end of that season could not have contrasted more with the dismal emotions experienced in April 2005.

Nearly a year to the day after Linfield fans had experienced the exhilaration of winning a Big Two title decider, they endured the heartache of defeat in a winner-takes-all derby match. On 23 April 2005, Glentoran beat the Blues 3-2 at the Oval to effectively clinch the Gibson Cup. Ahead of the game, in the penultimate round of fixtures, the Blues sat on 69 points and the Glens on 68. The win therefore moved Glentoran two points in front of Linfield. In theory, the Blues could still claw the title back on the last day of the campaign. However, everyone who left the Oval that afternoon knew that the League trophy was bound for East Belfast. Glentoran had the momentum, and would not surrender their advantage.[1]

For all connected with Linfield, the outcome was hard to take. Any loss to their bitterest rival was difficult to stomach – but one that handed the Gibson Cup to the Glens was especially tough. The manner of defeat made the outcome all the more galling. Glentoran had twice taken the lead, only for Linfield to equalise each time. Paul McAreavey had made it one apiece, and David Larmour had grabbed the Blues' second with six minutes remaining. As the 90 minutes ended, the two sides were level at 2-2. Then with the game entering injury time, the Glens won a free-kick just inside the Blues' half. The ball was punted long, toward the Linfield box. When it reached the area, Glentoran striker Michael Halliday rose highest, and directed a header at goal. Blues keeper Alan Mannus dived and got his right hand to the ball. Unfortunately though, he could only parry the effort onto the foot of Halliday's strike partner, a certain Chris Morgan. Instinctively, Morgan poked the ball into the net – and sent one half of the ground delirious and the other into despair.[2]

Morgan had joined Glentoran in the summer of 2004, after he had failed to agree new terms at the Blues. Finances at Linfield were still tight and, as David Jeffrey explained, he "had to let someone go in order to bring in new players". When negotiations between the striker and the Blues had failed to reach agreement, Morgan became that "someone". Jeffrey knew that letting the forward go was "a calculated risk". Morgan had scored 14 goals in 26 appearances during his final season with the Blues. The striker still had something to offer, and he demonstrated this throughout the 2004/05 campaign. On more than one occasion, Morgan proved a scourge on the Blues. In November he scored the winning goal in a Big Two League Cup final. Then in December, he earned the Glens a point with an equalising effort in the holiday fixture between the two sides. Though without question, Chris Morgan's biggest contribution came with the goal that pretty much secured the Gibson Cup.[3]

Not long after the game, Glentoran supporters were referring to 23 April 2005 as "Morgan Day". The striker was synonymous with the match, and understandably, Glens fans were keen to laud their hero. However, the game is remembered for more than Chris Morgan putting one over on the Blues to take the title. Some of local football's most serious rioting in years erupted at the match's conclusion. Stewards were unable to prevent incursions onto the playing area, and pandemonium resulted. Riot police eventually brought matters under control, but as the *News Letter* pointed out, they were far from prompt in appearing. The paper reported it took the authorities "up to 10 minutes to arrive". The trouble left dozens of supporters as well as nine police officers injured. It also further damaged the reputation of the Irish League.[4]

The hype going into the game was huge. For the whole week leading up to the showdown, media outlets were awash with previews of the clash. Ulster Television had even commissioned a one-hour highlights programme. Local football was actually receiving the attention that it craved, and needed. Yet instead of focusing on the exciting match that was served up, it was the action after the game that came under the spotlight. Understandably, the press was uncomplimentary about events at the Oval. Steven Beacom of the *Belfast Telegraph* reflected that the "match of the season [had] brought with it the best of Irish League football... and shamefully, the very worst. Sadly, the latter far outweighed the former." In a similar vein, a *News Letter* editorial commented that for 90 minutes, "football was the winner... but in 20 minutes of madness the local game was horribly tarnished".[5]

A week after Morgan's goal and the ensuing riot, the inevitable happened. Glentoran won their final League game and took the title. Frustration, disappointment and despair were just some of the emotions prevalent within the Blues squad. According to Glenn Ferguson, the sequence of events "certainly hit us hard". William Murphy described the end of the campaign as a "blur". Normally the fallout from a disastrous climax to a season would fester during the summer months, but in 2004/05 things were different. After the League's conclusion there was another competition for Linfield's players to throw themselves into. The inaugural all-Ireland Setanta Cup had begun in mid-March and would stretch into mid-May. The club still had two group-stage fixtures to fulfil, and was very much in contention.[6]

Competitive all-Ireland football had returned after a 25-year absence. The last time a cross-border competition was held the Troubles were raging, which made it difficult to hold. In 1980, the Tyler Cup had ceased after disturbances followed the Athlone Town vs Linfield final. That decider was staged over two legs. When disorder flared after the second match, in Athlone, it was felt enough was enough. To quote the *Irish Times*, Linfield's return to Belfast was "accompanied [by] violence", and this "put an end to that competition". Back then, the Troubles still had the best part of two decades to run, and during those years there was little appetite to revive a cross-border tournament.[7]

When the Setanta Cup got underway, seven years had passed since the signing of the Belfast Agreement. The Province was in the main much more stable, which gave confidence that an all-Ireland competition could take place. It should be noted though, that this stability was not coming from the local political parties. When the Setanta Cup got underway, the devolved power-sharing Assembly at Stormont had been suspended for two and a half years. On 4 October 2002, a police investigation into Provisional IRA (PIRA) intelligence-gathering had plunged the administration into crisis. The Police Service of Northern Ireland (PSNI) claimed that the PIRA was operating a spy ring at Stormont. To gather evidence, the police carried out raids on a number of premises, including Sinn Féin's party offices at Parliament Buildings. In light of the enquiry, Northern Ireland's First Minister David Trimble called for Westminster to take action. Trimble demanded that Prime Minister Tony Blair exclude Sinn Féin from the Stormont Executive. Instead of acquiescing to the call, Blair collapsed the Assembly on 14 October.[8]

In Stormont's absence, the Province lurched from one political crisis to another. Just before Christmas 2004, £26.5 million was stolen from the Northern Bank, and the PSNI was quick to blame the PIRA. Irish Taoiseach Bertie Ahern claimed that Sinn Féin's leadership was aware of the robbery's planning. Then a month later, PIRA members were allegedly behind the murder of Belfast man Robert McCartney. According to historian Gordon Gillespie, the bank robbery and the McCartney murder "seemed to remove the prospect of Sinn Féin's role in an Executive for the foreseeable future". This posed a major problem for any return to devolved government at Stormont. Sinn Féin had the second largest number of seats at the suspended Assembly. Thus any administration minus the party would have lacked legitimacy with a significant proportion of the electorate.[9]

The relative stability in Northern Ireland, despite the country being a mess politically, owed in great measure to communities on the ground and their efforts to break down barriers. Local football was to the fore in such efforts. The Blues' 1998 return to Solitude demonstrated that the impossible during the Troubles could take place in a post-conflict society, and importantly, after establishing that the fixture could go ahead, a degree of normality was ushered in. The police would continue escorting Blues fans to the games, but there were no doubts about matches taking place.

On top of the progress made in travelling to the Reds, Linfield actively engaged in building cross-community relations. This was evidenced by the club's involvement in the Dunfield scheme. Dunfield was a project run jointly by the Blues and League of Ireland side Dundalk, which brought together children from Northern Ireland and the Republic. The venture was launched in August 1999, and was facilitated by the charity Co-operation Ireland. To quote from the charity's promotional literature, Dunfield's aim was: "to use football as a vehicle to encourage young people to play and work together in harmony"; this was: "an ideal opportunity to dispel prejudices and avoid barriers being built up before it's too late".[10]

Joining forces with Dundalk was significant because of the history between the Blues and the Southern outfit. In 1979, the two sides had met in an infamous European Cup match. Late that August the first leg of the tie, staged in Dundalk, produced what Malcolm Brodie described as "one of the saddest nights in the history of Linfield and, indeed, of Irish football". According to Brodie, there was "some of the bloodiest fighting ever seen at a major game in Ireland". Approximately 100 people were hurt in the violence, and 30 arrests were made. Twenty years after these sordid events unfolded, the two clubs came together through Dunfield to build rather than shatter relations. The cross-community initiative proved to be a very successful venture, with lasting friendships established. Such was the bond formed between the clubs that in a difficult time for the Blues, the club was able to count on Dundalk for support. When derogatory comments about Linfield appeared in Roy Keane's bestselling 2002 autobiography, one of the sternest rebuttals came from Dundalk circles.[11]

*Keane: The Autobiography* was published a couple of months after the player had acrimoniously left the Republic of Ireland's 2002 World Cup squad. It was a book far removed from the standard sporting memoir that drew together a collection of semi-interesting anecdotal reflections on a career. Instead, the veteran midfielder's work was one of the most talked-about footballing publications in years. An *Observer* review maintained: "football's human hand grenade has given us an extraordinary book… pulling his own pin in print". Among its many controversies was the player's admission that revenge had motivated a 2001 horror tackle on Manchester City midfielder Alf-Inge Håaland. Keane detailed how he "hit [Håaland] hard. The ball was there (I think) … I didn't wait for [referee] Mr Elleray to show the card. I turned and walked to the dressing room." Keane's disclosure would push the

Football Association to act. The FA handed the Irish player a five-game ban and a £150,000 fine.[12]

Keane's comments on the Blues were just as caustic as those about his attack on Håaland – though no punishment ever followed. When describing the Republic of Ireland's November 1993 World Cup qualifier at Windsor, Keane included some supposed 'background information' on the Blues. He wrote: "For the first time in its history Linfield had recently signed a Catholic, a decision that caused great controversy. The player, who was also black, another major problem for Linfield's bigoted supporters, didn't last long. (Nor did the manager who signed him.)" Keane's remarks on Linfield were ill-informed, inaccurate and frankly bizarre.[13]

The black player he was referring to was Tony Coly. Given that Coly had signed five years before the 1993 Republic match at Windsor, it was hardly a recent occurrence. When he joined, it was obviously not "the first time in its history" that Linfield had signed a Catholic. Furthermore, Blues fans had no issue with Coly's ethnic background or where he went to church. In fact (as highlighted in Chapter 2), he was held in the highest esteem by supporters given his integral role in the 1988/89 League triumph. The add-on comments about Coly and his manager Roy Coyle not lasting long were peculiar. Coly left at the end of his one-year loan deal, and Coyle departed close to the conclusion of the following disastrous campaign.[14]

Distressed by Keane's comments, Blues officials considered taking legal action against the player. Yet with the club's perilous financial position in the early 2000s, this never happened. Had they done so, Phil Flynn, the former Dundalk chairman (who helped establish Dunfield), was prepared to give evidence in the Blues' favour. Flynn had "a very high regard for the administrators and the fans at Linfield", and he worried that "all the good work being done by clubs like Linfield and Dundalk could be undermined by what Keane says in the book". The support from Flynn was much appreciated, and it indicated that those with experience of Linfield were prepared to challenge untrue narratives about the Blues. Participating in schemes like Dunfield had fostered good relations, and also demonstrated that many of the misconceptions about the club were nonsense.[15]

Initiatives like Dunfield had been integral in paving the way for an all-Ireland competition to again take place. Yet Linfield's efforts to improve cross-community relations did not end once notice of the Setanta Cup was given in August 2004. The Blues capitalised on the momentum generated by the introduction of the cup to break down yet another barrier. On 22 February 2005 (one month before the Setanta began), Linfield faced Derry City at the Brandywell in a friendly. This was the first time the two sides had met in Londonderry for 36 years. Linfield had not played at Derry's home ground since the outbreak of the Troubles in 1969. Three years later the north-west club would leave the Irish League, and in 1985 joined the Republic's League of Ireland. In the years that followed, the Blues and the Candystripes had only played once, at a November 1998 friendly at Windsor Park. Meeting in Belfast was one thing. Playing a game in the Maiden City was another thing entirely.[16]

Derry's Brandywell stadium was situated beside the city's republican Bogside area. Throughout the Troubles this had been a no-go zone for the security forces; and ever since the side had joined the League of Ireland, games at the stadium operated without a police presence. According to Londonderry-born journalist and political activist Eamonn McCann, "most Catholics" accepted the absence of police "as a sensible means of avoiding bother", whereas "most Protestants" regarded the situation as "a dangerous outrage". In such circumstances it was easy to understand why Linfield travelling to the Brandywell was considered so contentious. Frankly, the idea of the two sides meeting in the Maiden City during the Troubles was far-fetched. So much so, that in a 1991 Derry vs Bohemians match, half-time entertainment had included a short game between one side in Derry colours and one in Linfield shirts. *Ireland's Saturday Night* explained that the "good-humoured" affair took place to raise money for the BBC charity 'Children in Need'. Seemingly the idea that Linfield would play at the Brandywell was the stuff of satire.[17]

Northern Irish attitudes and everyday realities had transformed unrecognisably in the years between 1991 and 2005. However, these changes were not enough to bring the conditions that allowed for the stationing of police at the Brandywell. This meant that the 300 Bluemen who travelled to the game on designated buses, did so (from the Bogside area onwards) without the protection of the PSNI. In the absence of the police, members of Community Restorative Justice (CRJ) and locals acted as stewards inside and outside the ground. CRJ was a body organised by "politically motivated ex-[paramilitary] prisoners" that, to quote University of Ulster academic Fidelma Ashe, provided "an alternative system of community justice". The PSNI's Foyle District Commander, Richard Russell, believed that this was the best way to facilitate supporters getting to the game. He maintained that the "partnership approach with community leaders and various other agencies… particularly in Derry – [was] the way forward".[18]

Despite Russell's faith in this "partnership approach", the arrangements were not fit for purpose. After the game, Linfield fans were subjected to attack as they left the Brandywell. The scenes at the end of the match were, though, very different to those before kick-off. No issues had arisen on the way into the ground, as supporters arrived in good spirits. However, 10 minutes into the game they were silenced by Derry scoring through an Alan Murphy penalty. The home side's lead would last most of the game, but with only six minutes remaining,

Mark Picking grabbed an equaliser. Derry's defence failed to deal with a corner, and Picking was on hand to drill a shot home from 12 yards. His strike was the last piece of major action in the match, which meant the friendly ended one goal apiece. At the game's conclusion, the CRJ operation to transport fans  out of the ground swung into action – and it was then that the inadequacies of the arrangements were exposed.[19]

An indication of the potential for trouble had come during the second half, when a number of fireworks were thrown from outside the Brandywell at the Linfield goalmouth. Those incidents were minor compared to what happened after full time. As the buses packed with supporters left the ground, a hostile mob lay in wait and peppered the vehicles with projectiles. The ambush left one Linfield fan needing treatment for a minor knee wound, and 10 being treated for shock. Given that six of the buses had windows smashed, it was fortunate that no major injuries were sustained. Understandably, in the days that

151

followed, anger was expressed and questions asked about the arrangements in place. The Democratic Unionist Party (DUP) was withering in regard to the security provided, and questioned why the PSNI were half a mile away from the Brandywell when the attack took place.[20]

Clearly the stewarding of the friendly was inadequate, and the criticism levelled against the arrangements was fully justified. Yet just staging the match was an impressive achievement. Newspapers from across the political spectrum paid tribute to both clubs for fulfilling the fixture. Writing in the *Irish News,* Michael O'Donnell maintained that by holding the game, "Diplomacy was the real winner at Brandywell." The *Londonderry Sentinel* advocated that Derry City and Linfield should not "let the mindless idiots win". The paper carried quotes from First Londonderry Linfield Bluestar Supporters Club chairman, Trevor Roulston, who declared that Derry had "nothing to apologise for. They are a wonderful club, with wonderful supporters... We have to get this game on again – whether it's at Windsor or the Brandywell... for the good of football, we shouldn't leave it too long... We don't want to leave it for another 36 years because of 12 or 15 idiots."[21]

The resolve shown by the likes of Trevor Roulston indicated that even in difficult circumstances there was a determination to take bold steps and make new initiatives a success. It was in this spirit that Linfield entered into the inaugural Setanta Cup. Six teams had qualified for the competition, and they were split into two groups of three. Linfield were joined in their section by Belfast rivals Glentoran and League of Ireland Cup winners, Longford Town. As already noted, the Blues had two group games left to play after the traumatic end of the domestic campaign. In Linfield's first two matches, the team had suffered a defeat away to Longford, then a victory at home to Glentoran. The club was therefore very much in contention going into the final two games, but knew that victories were a must.

Ten days separated Linfield's final League game and its third Setanta group game – a home tie against Longford. Considering the manner in which the club had surrendered the title, Jeffrey knew that his players needed a lift. He therefore set about instilling a sense of belief in his team, and showered them with encouragement. His efforts would pay dividends. At Windsor, Linfield dispatched Longford 1-0. Then, away to Glentoran in the final group fixture, Jeffrey's players recorded an impressive 4-2 victory. Having won three out of its four Setanta group games, the club had reached the competition's first ever final, where it would face Dublin side Shelbourne.[22]

In the mid-2000s, Shelbourne were the powerhouse of Irish football. Between the start of the decade and 2006, the club won five league titles. Even more impressive were the side's European exploits. During the summer of 2004, the Dublin outfit had gone close to making the group stages of the Champions League. Shels had successfully negotiated the first two qualifying rounds, only to fall at the final hurdle against Spain's Deportivo La Coruña. In the third qualifying round, the Dublin side had held the Spaniards 0-0 at home before suffering a 3-0 loss in La Coruña. Getting that close to the group stages was some achievement for an Irish side, and it owed to a couple of factors. For starters, there was the League of Ireland's move to a summer season in 2003. This greatly helped Southern teams as it meant that they were fully fit and able to compete when the qualifying rounds got underway. Then there was the major advantage of financial backing. The 'Celtic Tiger' (the Republic's economic boom) could still be heard roaring, and Shelbourne was the football club most associated with this high-spending culture.[23]

Heavy expenditure had allowed Shels to assemble a strong squad. The ranks of their side boasted a Cameroonian international, Joseph Ndo, as well as a number of current and future Irish internationals. These included Glen Crowe, Jason Byrne and Wes Hoolahan (who would go on to star with Norwich in England's Premier League). Shelbourne had players of considerable ability, and the club had them training on a full-time basis. This alliance of professionalism and proven quality set Shels apart from any other team on the island. Going into the inaugural Setanta Cup final, the Dublin side was thus the firm favourite. The timing of the fixture, three months into the League of Ireland campaign and a couple of weeks past the Irish League's conclusion, only added weight to Shels' "favourites" tag – as did Setanta's decision to play the final at the Dublin side's home ground, Tolka Park.[24]

Ahead of the decider, David Jeffrey was under no illusions about the size of the task in front of his players. In the lead-up to the game on 21 May, he told the *Belfast Telegraph*: "We will be massive underdogs… Shelbourne are the best team in Ireland… they have a squad… the envy of every club north and south of the border." Jeffrey's words helped ease the load on his squad, and as they travelled down to Dublin there was a jovial atmosphere within the group. On the team bus, Michael Gault joked with a couple of his teammates, "Who knows, they might beat us five or six here." The pressure was off, but amidst the relaxed feeling there was a resolve to atone for the loss of the League title; there was also a confidence in the team's ability that the pre-match banter belied. After all, the Blues had come incredibly close to successive Gibson Cups.[25]

Linfield had proven quality within its ranks. Seasoned campaigners like Glenn Ferguson, Noel Bailie and William Murphy could mix it with the best, whilst youngsters like Michael Gault and Alan Mannus had matured into valuable first-team members. During the 2004/05 campaign, Gault had formed an excellent relationship with Paul McAreavey in the midfield. McAreavey had joined Linfield during the previous season, but had only established himself in 2004/05. Injuries and poor form had blighted the player's first year and a half at the club. However, from Christmas 2004 onwards, McAreavey was a revelation. His chance to shine had come after other midfielders had fallen by the wayside. Phil Charnock had returned for another campaign with the Blues, but unfortunately was plagued by injury. Then there was Fitzroy Simpson, who endured a woeful time at Linfield. Simpson, a Jamaican international with World Cup and English Premier League experience, had joined in July 2004, but by Christmas was made available to other clubs. With Charnock injured and Simpson wholly underwhelming, Paul McAreavey was given the chance to make a central-midfield berth his own – and he grabbed it.[26]

The 2004/05 season also witnessed the emergence of the prodigiously talented Peter Thompson. In a manner similar to that in which Paul McAreavey had nailed down his position in the midfield, the young forward became a first-team regular. After Chris Morgan left for Glentoran, his replacement, Andy Crawford, had failed to make the grade. There were thus three strikers – Ferguson, Larmour and Thompson – competing for the central-forward roles. The young striker revelled in the competition and staked his claim. Thompson's breakthrough came at the start of the campaign, and he immediately became a regular name on the scoresheet. In 45 domestic appearances that season he hit an impressive 25 goals. This included scoring twice against Crusaders in the final of the County Antrim Shield. His strikes earned the forward his first piece of silverware with the club, and notably Linfield its 40th Shield victory. Peter Thompson possessed a clinical finishing instinct which was the perfect complement to Glenn Ferguson's all-round game. With Spike the master craftsman and Thompson the apprentice, the pair dovetailed to form a deadly partnership.[27]

Over the 2004/05 campaign, Irish League defences had come to fear the duo, and on the night of 21 May, Shelbourne found out what all the fuss was about. In the 27th minute of the Setanta Cup final, Ferguson broke the deadlock to put Linfield 1-0 up. Aidan O'Kane sent in a cross from the left and Spike scored with a volley. Ten minutes later, he combined with Thompson to double the lead. Ferguson flicked the ball

on, and the young forward was on hand to finish. Incredibly, going into half-time Linfield were 2-0 ahead. Considering that Shelbourne were expected to win with ease, Jeffrey and his team knew the second 45 minutes would be tough. The Dublin side would have to come out all guns blazing, though try as they did, Shels' players could not break through. At the heart of Linfield's defence, the Bailie-Murphy partnership had one of its finest outings. The *Belfast Telegraph* lauded both, maintaining that Bailie, who had played over 800 games, remained "as good as ever", whilst Murphy was described as "a colossus".

Seemingly it was a night when the old hands particularly stood out. The paper added that at 35, Glenn Ferguson was getting "better and better" with age. Back in 1998 when David Jeffrey bought Spike, the Blues boss thought that three good years would justify his record price tag. Yet noting all that Ferguson had contributed in the years that had followed, £55,000 had begun to look like a bargain.[28]

After Linfield's players got their hands on the trophy, the celebrations ran long into the night. The Blues had just won the first all-Ireland competition in 25 years, and understandably there was much to savour. For the 1,500-plus fans that journeyed to the Republic's capital, the emotions were especially sweet. As David Jeffrey put it, they had hoped for "a good day and respectability". What they got was one of the greatest nights in the club's history. The travelling support had, though, witnessed more than a remarkable triumph: this was only the start of something very special. Over the 12 months that followed, Linfield swept aside all challengers in the local game. No one could have foretold what was about to transpire. However, the Setanta win had given Jeffrey an inkling that something out of the ordinary was brewing. Amidst the post-final revelry, the Blues boss took a step back and thought: "This team is a machine… an absolute machine."[29]

This "machine" that Jeffrey spoke of laid down a marker at the start of the 2005/06 campaign. In late July, the Blues progressed past the opening round of a European competition for the first time in 11 years. Back in the 1994/95 UEFA Cup, the club had made it past Icelandic opposition. In the 2005 version of the competition, the Blues would see off Latvian side FK Ventspils. As soon as the draw for the first qualifying round was made, there was a belief that Linfield could get through. Going into the tie, David Jeffrey told the media: "The confidence we gained from winning the Setanta Cup has given us a real edge… FK Ventspils are a good side but I believe my players can do it this time." Jeffrey's faith was repaid in full as his team progressed on the away-goals rule. A 1-0 win at Windsor was followed by a 2-1 loss in Latvia. This meant that although the Blues endured a defeat in the second game, the players experienced the exhilaration of winning a round in Europe.[30]

In between the games with Ventspils, Linfield entertained Glasgow Rangers in a pre-season warm-up at Windsor. Since 2002, friendlies between the two sides had been a regular occurrence, which demonstrated the close bond between the clubs. Rangers had won each time since then, and in 2005 things were no different. In front of a 15,000-strong crowd, the Gers won 2-0 on the afternoon of 16 July. Yet notably the friendship between the Belfast and Glasgow Blues extended beyond a 90-minute friendly. Prior to Linfield's first leg against Ventspils, Rangers sent two videotapes of the Latvians in action to aid the Blues' preparations. The footage was gratefully received at Windsor. Then ahead of the second qualifying round, the gesture was repeated.[31]

Linfield were drawn to play Halmstad of Sweden, and once again the Glasgow side sent a tape of the Blues' opponents. Halmstad were a step up from Ventspils, but in the first match, played out in Scandinavia, the Blues looked to have the measure of the Swedes. In a 1-1 draw, Linfield secured a vital away goal. Coming into the Windsor leg on 25 August, Blues fans were dreaming that for the first time since 1993 their team could extend a European run into September. Unfortunately that was not to be the case, as Linfield went down 4-2. It was the same old story of a full-time outfit proving too strong in Europe. On the night, Linfield's defending was poor; indeed, David Jeffrey was "flabbergasted by the first-half performance". That said, Halmstad's professional class had shone through – with the Swedes clinically dispatching the Blues.[32]

Prior to the 4-2 defeat, the UEFA Cup run had been a tremendous success. Linfield had shown that they could progress past a round, and reaffirmed that the club had the wherewithal to travel away to a full-time side and get a result. The European games also gave an indication of the impact that a couple of the club's recent signings would have on the upcoming domestic campaign. Tim Mouncey, who had signed in January from Distillery, scored the winner in the home game against Ventspils. Then in the 1-1 draw away to Halmstad, summer signing Oran Kearney grabbed the Blues' goal. Mouncey played on the right of midfield and Kearney on the left. Both would be regulars in the side, and both added greatly to the Gault-McAreavey partnership in the centre of the park. Jim Ervin sat behind Mouncey at right-back, and on the other side of the defence was Pat McShane. Like Kearney and Mouncey, the two full-backs were integral cogs of Linfield's all-conquering 2005/06 side.

Wherever one looked across the pitch there was real strength in the Blues first XI. Whether it was on the flanks or in the spine of Mannus, Bailie-Murphy, Gault-McAreavey and Ferguson-Thompson, Linfield were, as Jeffrey had put it, an "absolute machine". It was thus little surprise that the side started the 2005/06 campaign in irrepressible form. Opponents were brushed aside with a swagger. By Boxing Day, the Blues had racked up an incredible 100 goals in 29 starts, only conceding on 22 occasions.[33]

Fans enjoyed watching their side put all-comers to the sword, but it was – as always – especially gratifying to watch their team see off the Glens. In December 2005 this happened on two occasions. The first win over Glentoran came in the League Cup final. On 10 December, a Glenn Ferguson hat-trick inspired the Blues to a 3-0 victory, and earned the club the season's opening piece of silverware. Then came the traditional Christmas fixture and further joy for supporters. In a one-sided affair, Linfield dismantled the Glens 4-1. Afterwards, Linfield skipper Noel Bailie maintained that on the day, the Blues had exhibited "some of the best football we have ever played… Right from the word go we dominated them." As 2005 drew to a close, the Blues had a trophy in the bag and an amazing record of 14 wins out of 15 League starts. By the end of the year, it was evident that the club was on the verge of something special.[34]

Linfield's imperious form would stretch well into the months that followed. Throughout the winter Jeffrey's men went unbeaten in the League and also maintained their winning ways in the cup competitions. On 7 February 2006, the players lifted the County Antrim Shield – their second trophy of the season. In the final, the Blues met Ballymena and endured a tough, though ultimately successful evening. An underperforming Linfield would have to battle for the win. The Braidmen had taken a 33rd-minute lead, but just after the break, Ballymena old-boy Oran Kearney levelled for Linfield. Then as the game appeared destined for extra time, Glenn Ferguson headed home his 36th goal of the season. Ferguson was enjoying a remarkable season and his goal-getting was far from done. In mid-March, Spike's 40th of the campaign – another header – secured Linfield's third piece of silverware. On a cold March afternoon, Ferguson scored the only goal in a win over Armagh City that clinched the Gibson Cup.[35]

Eleven months after "Morgan Day", the Blues had wrestled the League trophy back to Windsor. However, reclaiming the Gibson Cup did not spark wild celebrations amongst the team. They were still in the Irish Cup and on course for a Clean Sweep of trophies. If the Blues could manage to lift the cup, the 2005/06 squad would be etched into club folklore.

This thought was clearly something on the players' minds. The Monday after the League-clinching win, Noel Bailie told the *News Letter*: "Every Supporters' Club dinner I go to, I always end up talking to people about the two seven trophies teams… They are, and always will be legends at Linfield and who wouldn't want to be in the same bracket… I would be lying if I said I wasn't thinking about it." By 2006 there were no longer seven trophies to play for. League restructuring and loss of sponsorship had brought about a much more manageable

season. Thus whilst the Blues could not lift seven trophies, bringing home the four available pieces of domestic silverware would put Jeffrey's men in the illustrious company of the 1921/22 and 1961/62 sides.[36]

An Irish Cup semi-final victory over Bangor on 1 April placed the Blues into a showdown decider with Glentoran on 6 May. This took place more than six weeks after the League had been sewn up. Yet there was no chance that Linfield's players would coast into the final. The squad knew it was close to achieving something truly remarkable, and was not ready to let it slip. On the day, the team demonstrated why Linfield's 2005/06 vintage was so good. Michael Halliday had given the Glens a first-half lead, but in injury time before the break, the Blues hit back. Paul McAreavey laid on a chance for Peter Thompson, who slotted home from six yards for his 47th goal of the campaign. Then in the second half, Thompson doubled Linfield's tally – and in doing so landed Linfield the club's third Clean Sweep. Once again, it was McAreavey who supplied the ammunition. The midfielder sent a left-footed free-kick into the box, and Thompson won the header to send the ball past keeper Elliot Morris. When referee Michael Ross blew the full-time whistle, Linfield had possession of the League, the Irish Cup, the League Cup and the County Antrim Shield.[37]

The *Belfast Telegraph*'s Steven Beacom was in no doubt about the magnitude of Linfield's achievement. Two days after the Blues had completed the Clean Sweep, he wrote: "It would be fair to say [this side] are the best Irish League team since 1962 when the Linfield players of that era did a clean sweep of seven trophies... if the current batch [of players] weren't thought of as great, they should be now... They have the medals and trophies to prove it." A number of factors had coalesced during the 2005/06 season to mark that Linfield team out for greatness. For starters, the hurt of "Morgan Day" had spurred Jeffrey's men on throughout the entire campaign. As Noel Bailie put it, "We didn't want those feelings again." Then there was the belief that came with winning the inaugural Setanta Cup. Going to the home of a professional side and bringing silverware back to Belfast gave the Blues great confidence. When the 2005/06 campaign began with an impressive showing in the UEFA Cup, this self-belief was only strengthened.[38]

Jeffrey's men had also benefitted from an extra night of training each week. Throughout the 2005/06 season, the Blues trained on three evenings instead of two. This allowed the squad to work on different aspects of the game in more detail, and also to improve fitness levels. The manager's wish to better his side had brought about the additional training – and it reaped results. Yet one should not lose sight of the quality that had been assembled at the club. When Mouncey and Kearney joined ahead of 2005/06, they improved what was already an incredibly strong squad. As William Murphy put it: "David had brought in the right players and they gelled." The Blues boss had managed to combine hard graft with talent in his squad, and it produced one of the great Linfield sides. Jeffrey himself stressed the importance of hard work in setting this side apart. According to the Blues boss: "Everyone [bought] into the same ideal… wanting to be the best."[39]

The extra preparation, the confidence within the squad, the determination and the siege mentality all played their part in landing the Clean Sweep. Though as club captain Noel Bailie pointed out, "Big achievements are built on small margins." One off-day in any of the cup competitions would have derailed the Clean Sweep challenge. However, Linfield had that tiny fraction more to give when things were not going the club's way. The County Antrim Shield win over Ballymena was the prime example of this. The Blues' performance on the night was far from impressive, but the team had the know-how to win, even when not playing well. It was this resolve, determination and bit of luck that set that side out as truly great.[40]

Only a very special team could have achieved all that the Blues had during the 2005/06 campaign.

## Chapter 11

# *Escape from the Maze*

Linfield's remarkable 12 months, that started with the May 2005 Setanta Cup win and ended in the completion of a Clean Sweep, brought about much more than well-deserved acclaim. The success also played a part in transforming the club's financial affairs. Having a winning team meant serious prize money was netted. The 2006 AGM recorded a profit for the year of just over £310,000, with a substantial part of that figure made up of earnings from the UEFA Cup run and also from the Setanta Cup triumph. Indeed, the all-Ireland win had swollen club funds by €130,000 (over £100,000). For the second year in a row, instead of racking up debt Linfield was actually making money. After a prolonged period of uncertainty the club was finally getting back on an even keel, and success on the pitch had played a major part in achieving this.[1]

Club finances were also boosted by another source of income. There was a huge rise in Northern Ireland international rent payment; this jumped during 2005/06 as the IFA contract (that for so long had hampered Linfield due to the associated overhead costs of maintaining Windsor Park) had now become beneficial. The lure of facing England in the 2006 World Cup qualifiers made Northern Ireland tickets the hottest in town, whilst television money skyrocketed. Suddenly the Blues' 15 per cent ground rent was worth a lot of cash. That year, the IFA paid Linfield just shy of £440,000. This was over five times the amount paid in 2003, when there was little interest in the national side and the terms of the Windsor agreement were hitting the Blues hard.[2]

Financially, everything seemed to have come good for Linfield by the mid-2000s. Success in the Setanta, a UEFA Cup run and the IFA contract paying dividends had all come together at once. The club was able to start bringing down its crippling debt and look to the future with confidence. Given this healthy outlook, Linfield would be able to function on a different level to the rest of the League. Indeed, such was the changed financial landscape, the Management Committee moved to back David Jeffrey on a vision he had long held for the Blues.

In the summer of 2006, Linfield began experimentation with full-time football. Jeffrey knew there was only so far the club could go as a part-time outfit. Whilst players had to juggle football and work commitments, the Blues would remain underdogs when competing against professional opposition. So prior to the start of the 2006/07 season, there was a tentative attempt to take the club down the full-time route. Going into that campaign, Linfield bestowed professional contracts on four players. Young striker Peter Thompson had signed full-time terms near the end of 2005/06. Then over the summer, midfielders Paul McAreavey and Michael Gault as well as goalkeeper Alan Mannus followed suit.[3]

With these players on board, David Jeffrey outlined how he hoped the addition of professionals would benefit the Blues. Speaking to the press, he explained: "I would like to have between six and eight full-time players in the next three years… But being full-time is not just a case of being fitter, it is about concentration levels as well… When you don't have to think about what you have to do in work on Monday morning then it helps players to cut out mistakes and improve [on] them." The Blues boss was looking to the future and anticipating that full-time players would take Linfield to the next level. Further European progression was always the aim. However, whilst the 2006/07 campaign started with preparations for what was hopefully to come, there was also a nod to the club's past. At the beginning of pre-season, the first team marked the 2005/06 Clean Sweep by recreating a 1962 open-top bus procession from the Shankill Road to Windsor Park. Unfortunately, 44 years on from the original parade, there was a much smaller crowd that gathered to salute Linfield's 2006 achievement.[4]

The reduced interest in Linfield's success was yet another indicator that in the intervening years, the appeal of local football had dropped significantly. One thing that had not diminished though, was the expectation that the Blues would challenge for the major honours. As the club began its 2006/07 campaign, there were the usual trophy-laden predictions. Linfield were odds-on favourite for retaining the Gibson Cup. However, the defence of the title got off to the worst possible start. Cliftonville arrived at Windsor on the opening day of the League

Championship and won 3-0. In doing so, the Reds played the Blues off the pitch. As Alex Mills of the *News Letter* put it: "The champions weren't only beaten... they were taken apart." After Linfield had swept aside all challengers during the previous season, the abrupt start to 2006/07 was unexpected.[5]

Jeffrey's men would rally in the coming months, but the form of 2005/06 was never replicated. In November the Blues crashed out of the League Cup at the semi-final stage. A loss on penalties to Glentoran ensured there would be no repeat of the Clean Sweep. A month later, Lisburn Distillery ended Linfield's County Antrim Shield interest – again in the semi-finals. By the turn of the year, the club's season was looking as if it could go either way. Already out of contention for two cups, Linfield sat in third place in the League. Still, there were plenty of games remaining for Jeffrey's side to turn things around, and there was also the Irish Cup to look forward to.[6]

The club's Irish Cup defence was supposed to get underway at Windsor with a game against junior side Oxford United Stars on 13 January 2007. This was postponed however, after the roof of the North Stand was damaged during a storm over Christmas. Linfield's New Year's Day League fixture with Limavady United had also been shelved after structural engineers declared the North Stand to be a Health & Safety risk. For half the month of January, the ground was out of action. This was embarrassing for the Blues, and not just because it meant the club could not fulfil two of its fixtures. The future of Windsor Park as the home of Northern Ireland had been fiercely debated since the late 1990s, and during this time, prominent names in the local game and media had called for the international team to leave Windsor. Thus when the stadium appeared unfit for purpose, it only lent credence to calls for Northern Ireland to find a new home.[7]

In 2005, Linfield had marked their 100th year of playing at Windsor Park. By then, it was fair to say that the ground was looking decrepit. Repair work would have the Blues back playing at Windsor within three weeks of the storm, but the damage to the North Stand's roof (two years after the centenary) only gave a superficial indication of the problems afflicting the stadium. There were other, fundamental flaws threatening the future of international football at the ground. The Railway Stand was deemed inadequate to hold spectators, with both Health & Safety and the Fire Authority condemning the stand's wooden structure. As things stood in early 2007, Windsor had only three operational stands and a capacity of just over 13,000.[8]

Worryingly, the Archibald Leitch designed South Stand (constructed almost 80 years beforehand) also appeared to be on its last legs. Like the Railway Stand, this was a wooden construction, and there was a fear that it would soon fail to meet the regulatory requirements. During the mid-1980s the stand had closed for a time so it could be upgraded in line with post-Bradford fire directives. Twenty years later, the structure was barely adequate. By 2007, extra stairways had to be erected in front of the stand to allow international games to pass Health & Safety testing. For the then Northern Ireland manager Lawrie Sanchez, the stadium had become an embarrassment. Sanchez told the *Sunday Life*: "Look at Windsor Park. I can't remember the last time I saw a wooden stand before I became… manager." He added: "We need a purpose-built stadium to take us to the next tier."[9]

Sanchez was not the first Northern Ireland manager to call for a new ground. In April 1998, Lawrie McMenemy was quoted backing "calls for a new international stadium". According to McMenemy, Windsor projected "an image of your country being second rate and a little bit tatty". A year later, he again bemoaned the stadium's facilities. At a fringe Labour Party Conference meeting, the Northern Ireland boss maintained that Windsor was "a good ground for a club team, but for an international stadium it's a disgrace". McMenemy's second outburst had followed a *Belfast Telegraph* story from early 1999, which claimed that the Province was in line for a purpose-built sporting arena. The newspaper's sports editor, John Laverty, maintained that Northern Ireland would "have a new national stadium inside the next five years".[10]

For two years there was little movement on this, but in August 2000 the Northern Ireland Office (NIO) announced that a "pre-feasibility study [had] been concluded by the Sports Council and the view is that the building of a new national stadium could succeed under certain circumstances". The NIO was opening up the debate to bring about the conditions that would see the construction of one stadium for football, the GAA (Gaelic Athletic Association) and rugby. This was a game changer. The prospect of a new national stadium seemed more likely – and Northern Ireland's future at Windsor began to look uncertain.[11]

In the years that followed the NIO statement, the location of Northern Ireland internationals became one of the hottest debates in local football. Essentially there were two options. Either spend money bringing Windsor up to standard, or support the creation of a new facility. On the mainland, significant capital had been (and was being) spent improving national stadiums, and there was a feeling that the Province should similarly benefit. Wales had just opened the 75,000-seater Millennium Stadium in Cardiff, whilst in October 2000, Wembley closed for major refurbishment. The big question for Northern Ireland was whether the IFA should follow the Welsh example and build a new stadium, or refurbish Windsor as the English had with Wembley.[12]

One of the foremost advocates for constructing a new national stadium was the *Belfast Telegraph*. During the early 2000s, the newspaper was sympathetic to calls for the building of such a facility. Then on 26 February 2003, a front-page headline read: "TELEGRAPH CAMPAIGN STARTS TODAY: THE CASE FOR A NATIONAL STADIUM." The paper maintained that football, GAA and rugby would be best served by one state of the art arena. According to an editorial, this was preferable to the status quo of hosting Northern Ireland games at Windsor, major Gaelic matches at Casement Park, and Ulster Rugby at Ravenhill. Like Windsor, the other two stadiums had seen much better days and were in need of refurbishment. However, the paper dismissed the thought of giving cash to the individual grounds. John Laverty exclaimed: "No amount of money will turn [these] pigs' ears into silk purses."[13]

For Laverty and the *Belfast Telegraph* there was another problem with Windsor. Aside from the stadium's decrepit structure, it was portrayed as "unwelcoming to many". Laverty conceded that the "'no-go area for Catholics' label [was], by and large, old hat". Yet he argued that this didn't "take away from the fact that Windsor [was] set in a predominantly loyalist area, with all but one of the access routes through that area". The paper's editorial line pulled no punches in its objection to international football remaining at Windsor, and this was a major concern for Linfield. At the time, the *Belfast Telegraph* had the largest circulation of any Northern Ireland newspaper. Therefore the agendas that it pushed had considerable weight behind them. If the newspaper's stance was worrying, the IFA's position was alarming. During the first half of the 2000s, the Association had sat on the fence over the future home of Northern Ireland internationals. Then in January 2006, the body gave its support in principle to the construction of a new national sports arena. After a five-hour meeting of the IFA's top brass, the chief executive, Howard Wells, informed reporters: "We have agreed to work with the government to further develop the stadium project."[14]

The "stadium project" that Wells referred to was set for the site of the former Maze Prison. HMP Maze had closed in July 2000, after the majority of inmates were released following the endorsement of the Belfast Agreement. It was thus a large location with ample land to develop on. There was, however, significant opposition to the project. Northern Ireland fans were overwhelmingly against the plans. A poll commissioned (prior to the IFA decision) by the Amalgamation of Official Northern Ireland Supporters Clubs, indicated that 90 per cent of members were against the move. Yet regardless of the expressed views of fans, the IFA was happy to back the government-proposed project. The Association's president, Jim Boyce, acknowledged that some supporters were "unhappy with the Maze site", though he maintained: "This is not a betrayal of them. We would never do that."[15]

According to Boyce, there was "no plan B" – the former prison would be transformed into a sporting arena. If he was right, Windsor's days as an international stadium looked numbered. Yet for that to happen, the IFA would have to work around the 104-year contract tying internationals to the ground. This was a major obstacle to overcome, and the Blues Board knew it. When stories about a national stadium had emerged in the late-1990s, the Management Committee sought legal advice and moved to shore up the club's position. Over the years that followed, the Board closely monitored developments and was quick to remind the powers that be of the contract's terms. For much of that time, the club had suffered financially because of those terms, but this had changed with Northern Ireland drawing England in the 2006 World Cup Qualifiers. The Blues Board was not simply going to walk away from the arrangement.[16]

If the IFA forced the issue and broke the agreement, Linfield would be in line for substantial compensation. There was, after all, over 80 years still remaining on the deal. On the other hand, there was a worry that the Association could claim that the club had neglected its obligations. Under the terms of the contract, Linfield was required to ensure that Windsor's "stands, offices and accommodation and the fixtures and fittings thereon and therein [were] in good order repair and condition". Given the stadium's dilapidated state, the club was barely fulfilling this side of the arrangement. Damage to the North Stand roof could be patched up, but it was obvious that much more work was required to preserve the ground's international status. If Windsor fell below the required standard, the IFA could claim that Linfield had in fact broken the contract.[17]

As things stood in early 2007, Windsor's future was mired in uncertainty. The IFA favoured leaving the ground, and the terms of the stadium contract appeared to offer it a potential way out. Yet in the year since local football's governing body had endorsed the proposed Maze project, very little movement was made on it. Indeed, the future home of Northern Ireland remained a live debate. Thus for the time being it was business as usual at a patched-up Windsor Park. Northern Ireland would continue to entertain international sides at the stadium, and the Blues would push on with domestic duties there. Linfield's first game back after the roof damage and forced interlude, was the postponed Oxford United Stars Irish Cup tie. On 16 January, Jeffrey's men began their defence of the cup with a comfortable 3-0 victory. A couple of weeks later, the Blues would triumph again in the other fixture deferred because of the storm damage. A last-gasp 3-2 League victory over Limavady took Linfield top of the table on 31 January for the first time that season.[18]

Given the exploits of the previous season, Linfield were expected to maintain that position at the summit of the Irish League. Winning had become a habit under David Jeffrey, and there was a presumption that this group of players would again bring home the Gibson Cup. Success had come to characterise Jeffrey's tenure as manager, although it seemed that competing in groundbreaking fixtures was just as common. The Blues boss had led Linfield back to the Brandywell and Solitude after 36- and 28-year absences respectively; he had also helped welcome Derry back to Windsor for the first time since the north-west club had left the Irish League. Then towards the end of February 2007, the latest in that long line of momentous games took place with the Blues entertaining Donegal Celtic. The West Belfast side had, of course, taken on Linfield at Windsor in the infamous 1990 Irish Cup game. However, back then Celtic had been a junior side; in 2006, the two clubs were facing off in the top flight.

The February game was the second match played between DC and the Blues that season. Before Christmas, Celtic had hosted Linfield and all had passed off without incident. Glenn Ferguson had settled that tie, scoring a free-kick to give the Blues a 1-0 win. Importantly though, it had been an occasion remembered for what happened on the pitch rather than off it. As Hoops chairman Raymond Bonnar put it: "Football reigned supreme." Three months later when the two clubs met at Windsor, Linfield would again emerge victorious, this time by a much more comfortable margin. On 24 February, the Blues dispatched the West Belfast side 3-0. A Steven Douglas penalty, then two strikes from Paul McAreavey, secured the points and kept alive the club's Gibson Cup challenge.[19]

In terms of the non-footballing aspects of the clash, things were very different from the Irish Cup match 17 years before. There was no rioting in the stands and no public disorder afterwards. The changed context of post-Troubles Northern Ireland had clearly helped take the sting out of the tie. That said, media reports condemned "a minority of [Linfield] fans" for sectarian chanting. The airing of such choruses indicated that whilst the everyday violence of the Troubles was gone, the Province was still a divided society. Attitudes that had pervaded Northern Irish life for years did not simply vanish with the coming of peace; in some regards, they had hardened. After the ceasefires, Belfast had witnessed a sharp rise in the number of 'peace walls' built to keep communities apart. Greater stability may have come to the Province, but age-old divisions had not yet left the stage. The unsavoury chants audible on Celtic's return to Windsor were evidence of that.[20]

When Linfield returned to Solitude in 1998, the local media had been ambivalent on the subject of "party songs". Steven Beacom of the *Belfast Telegraph* had maintained, "that sort of banter will never cease". However, nine years down the line a dim view was taken of such behaviour. This time, Beacom's paper declared that the inappropriate singing had "overshadowed" the win. Then in the game's aftermath, an embarrassed Blues Management Committee issued a statement conveying its disappointment at the chants. The Board also wrote to Celtic officials expressing regret at the "deplorable [and] disrespectful attitude of a small number of our supporters".[21]

Being able to hold contentious games without resulting disorder was an indication of how far Northern Ireland had come in a short period of time. The terrace chants at the Celtic match had though, shown there was still a distance to travel. As a club Linfield had undertaken a role in challenging such prejudice and bigotry. Through involvement in cross-community projects like Dunfield, the Blues demonstrated a commitment to confront issues that had for years plagued the Province. In August 2006, the club also launched the 'True Blues' initiative. This was an anti-sectarian strategy that aimed to "create a more vibrant, dynamic and inclusive culture" on match days. Societal ills would not disappear overnight, but Linfield was determined to address them.[22]

After the shaky start to the 2006/07 season, Jeffrey and his players had addressed the problems afflicting performances. The win over Donegal Celtic was the sixth on the bounce, and the 11th game without defeat. In fact, Linfield would not suffer another domestic loss that season. This helped the club to a second Double in two years. The League was secured on 14 April with a 2-1 victory over Glentoran at the Oval. A penalty converted by Oran Kearney and a clinical finish by Mark Dickson captured the points and the title. Dickson had signed from Larne during the previous summer, and it was his 15th strike of the campaign that sealed the Gibson Cup. At full time, a jubilant David Jeffrey roared: "We have exorcised the ghost of [Morgan Day]. That's well behind us now."[23]

Three weeks later, the Double was completed with a penalty shoot-out victory over Dungannon Swifts in the final of the Irish Cup. As 120 minutes of football could not separate the Belfast and Dungannon Blues, the game headed to spot kicks. For Linfield, the shoot-out got off to the worst possible start – Dungannon keeper Dwayne Nelson saved Linfield's first two efforts. After the second, David Jeffrey turned to his backroom staff and uttered, "That's it." Dungannon's first two kicks had been converted, so Linfield's hopes of claiming the cup looked dead and buried. That was before Alan Mannus surpassed Nelson's heroics. He saved Dungannon's next three penalties, whilst Glenn Ferguson, Mark Dickson and Pat McShane all converted for the Blues.[24]

In the game's aftermath, a delighted David Jeffrey told the *Sunday Life* that his players could "let their hair down" in the days that followed. However, there was a caveat. On the coming Thursday, all would have to report once more for duty – the season was not quite over yet. Just like in 2005, the Blues had reached the Setanta Cup final and had the opportunity to become all-Ireland champions. This was staged exactly one week after the Irish Cup decider. On the road there

Linfield had topped a four-team group that included Drogheda United, Derry City and Glentoran; then in the semis had dispatched Cork City 1-0. In the decider, Linfield would meet group opponents, Drogheda. The Blues had managed a 1-0 away win over Drogs in the opening group game, and had drawn 0-0 in the return Windsor fixture. But in the third meeting between the two sides, Linfield ran out of steam.[25]

Drogheda controlled proceedings for the majority of the showpiece (staged at Windsor), and had considerably more chances than their opponents. Yet just like seven days previously, the two finalists played out a draw. For the second week in a row, Blues fans would have to endure the nail-biting tension of penalties. This time, Linfield came up second best. In the fifth round of kicks, Aidan O'Kane missed for the Blues and Stuart Byrne converted for Drogs, handing the title to the Southern side. A reflective David Jeffrey admitted afterwards that, "Last week if we hadn't won the Irish Cup it would have been an injustice, today it would have been an injustice on Drogheda... They were excellent." Striker Mark Dickson was in full agreement. Pointing out that Drogheda were a full-time outfit, Dickson maintained, "They deserved the win." There was no shame in losing on penalties to the likes of Drogs. The Southern side's entire playing squad was professional, whereas Linfield were still tentatively experimenting with full-time football and only had seven pros on the books.[26]

Coming up just short against Drogheda was no small feat. If anything, it was a measure of the heady days that Linfield were enjoying in the mid-2000s. Two all-Ireland finals in three years, European progression, a Clean Sweep and two successive Doubles were all magnificent achievements. However, that team's appetite for success was not yet sated. In 2007/08 the Blues would pick up a League Cup followed by an incredible third straight Double!

The League Cup triumph came at the start of February 2008, and exemplified the never-say-die attitude that Jeffrey had instilled in his players. In the final played against Crusaders, the Blues would come from 2-1 behind during the closing minutes. Going into the game, few gave the Crues a chance. The North Belfast club had not beaten the Blues in almost five years. But when Seamus Browne put Crusaders ahead with 13 minutes left, it looked as if that sequence was about to be broken. That was before Glenn Ferguson turned the match on its head. Ferguson, a second-half substitute, was not long on the pitch when he grabbed the equaliser. Then with only four minutes remaining he doubled his tally, and clinched the cup for the Blues with a 3-2 victory.[27]

Ferguson's goals were his 500th and 501st of an incredible Irish League career. A decade earlier, David Jeffrey had bought the striker hoping he could provide three good years of service. Ferguson had surpassed all expectations, going on to enjoy 10 outstanding years at Linfield. As things stood he sat third in the all-time Irish League goal-scoring charts. By the end of his career, Ferguson had amassed 563 goals and was second in the record books. Only Jimmy Jones of Belfast Celtic and Glenavon fame would sit ahead of him. Back in 1998 Ferguson had cost an Irish League record fee. Considering all that he had achieved in the meantime, the outlay was a bargain. Spike was a Linfield legend and one of the greatest players the local game had ever witnessed. It was a travesty that he only earned five international caps.[28]

David Jeffrey could not speak highly enough of Ferguson. In his programme notes a week after the cup win, the Blues boss marvelled: "We will never see the likes of him again... His goal-scoring achievements have been phenomenal, but his overall play in support of his colleagues has also been tremendous." Club captain Noel Bailie was in full agreement. Bailie described Ferguson as "probably the best player I have ever played with", maintaining that the striker was "the focal point for us [creating] as many goals as he scores". As Jeffrey and Bailie pointed out, Ferguson was so much more than a "goal-getter". He was a linchpin whose all-round game was integral to the success the Blues had enjoyed during his time at the club.[29]

Back in the late 1990s and early 2000s, Ferguson had enjoyed partnering David Larmour and Chris Morgan. Linking up with Peter Thompson from 2004/05 onwards had proven even more fruitful. The veteran forward and Thompson seemed to have an intuitive knowledge of each other's game. This allowed the pair to rip Irish League defences apart, with both regularly featuring on the scoresheet. It was therefore little surprise when Thompson replicated Ferguson's achievement of attaining international recognition. Thompson would go on to win a total of eight Northern Ireland caps. The seventh of these came shortly before the player enjoyed a third straight Double with the Blues. On the night of 26 March 2008, Thompson came on as a substitute for David Healy in a 4-1 win over Georgia. Late in the game it was the Linfield striker who made it four when he grabbed his only international goal.[30]

The goal itself was rather scrappy – Thompson bundled a Keith Gillespie corner into the net. Yet regardless of its aesthetics, the effort was significant. This was the first time in almost a quarter of a century that an Irish League player had scored for Northern Ireland. Twenty-four years previously, Lee Doherty had struck on his debut for the international side, against Israel. Back then, Doherty of the Blues was joined on the pitch by two other Linfield teammates. Goalkeeper George Dunlop and striker Martin McGaughey were also part of the Northern Ireland side that dispatched the Israelis 3-0.[31]

When Thompson got his goal all those years later, again two other Bluemen would accompany him. Goalkeeper Alan Mannus and midfielder Michael Gault made second-half substitute appearances in the 4-1 win over Georgia. This made 26 March 2008 a particularly proud day for Linfield. Having three players representing Northern Ireland was an indication of just how dominant this Blues team was. It also bore witness to the advantages that full-time football was bringing. Mannus, Gault and Thompson were all on professional contracts, and it was a great boost for them to earn international recognition.

Just 24 hours prior to the trio playing their part in the Northern Ireland victory, they were helping the Blues to a 4-1 League win over Coleraine. Not surprisingly, Thompson was amongst the scorers on that occasion. The forward scored twice in a comfortable win that maintained the club's League challenge. All told, Thompson would weigh in with 44 goals that campaign. This invaluable contribution was crucial in helping secure the third straight Gibson Cup. When the title was clinched on the final day of the League season, with a 3-0 win away to Crusaders, it was one of the few occasions when Thompson's name was not on the scoresheet. Fittingly, his strike partner Glenn Ferguson scored twice that day, and when substitute Mark Dickson put away a third, the celebrations were already well underway amongst the travelling support.[32]

As had been the case during the three previous seasons, there was only so much post-title celebrating Linfield's players could take part in. The Irish Cup final would come seven days later, and as Glenn Ferguson maintained: "I think we'll have earned our place in history if we can beat Coleraine next week." Ferguson was referring to the potential of achieving a third straight Double. He pointed out in the *Sunday Life* that the last team to scale such heights was the Linfield side from 1891-93. Beating Coleraine and delivering a 'Treble Double' would thus well and truly mark that mid-2000s crop as special.[33]

When the showcase decider came about one week later on 3 May, nerves appeared to have got the better of Jeffrey's men in the first half.

 After the initial 45 minutes, Coleraine were 1-0 up and looked good for the lead. As the second half got underway, fans in the stands wondered whether Coleraine were about to bring the remarkable run of Doubles to an end. However, within six minutes the mood of supporters was much more upbeat, and this was down to one man. Just after the break, Peter Thompson grabbed his 43rd and 44th goals of the season to give Linfield a 2-1 win – clinching the cup and a third straight Double![34]

The Blues side of the mid-2000s had just achieved what no other Irish League team had been able to in over a century, and David Jeffrey was in the mood to celebrate. After the game he told the media: "This will take some beating... no one can take it away from this team... they deserve every single plaudit that they are given." Midfielder Michael Gault struck a similar note, maintaining, "It's a fantastic achievement which hasn't been done for over 100 years so credit to all the boys... What we have achieved is remarkable!" Yet perhaps the midfielder and his teammates' finest hour was to come a few months later – when the Blues earned a draw away to Croatian champions Dinamo Zagreb.[35]

In the first qualifying round of the 2008/09 Champions League, Linfield were paired with Zagreb, by far and away the toughest potential opponent. The Croats ran a professional outfit, had experience of the competition's group stages, and had just sold star midfielder Luka Modrić to Tottenham Hotspur for £16.5 million. Dinamo Zagreb operated on a completely different level to the Blues and had a squad packed with international talent. The Croatian side's first team included the likes of Igor Bišćan who had won the Champions League with

Liverpool, Boško Balaban who had played for Aston Villa, and Mario Mandžukić who would later win a Champions League medal with Bayern Munich. Everything pointed to an easy ride for the Croatians. Even inside the Blues camp there was little expectation of success. Reacting to the draw, Michael Gault told the press: "We have to be realistic and admit we're highly unlikely to get through but we won't lie down… They'll know they've been in a game."[36]

All went as expected in the first leg, held at Windsor, with Dinamo winning comfortably by a 2-0 scoreline. But in the away game, Jeffrey's men would produce one of the club's greatest European performances. Amidst a torrential downpour, Linfield fought back from conceding early to earn a 1-1 draw. Not long into the second half, Michael Gault brought the Blues level by heading home from a Conor Downey cross. As neither side scored again, Linfield held on for a famous draw against a side packed with quality. Not only had the Blues players over-achieved – they had done so in an extremely hostile environment.

David Jeffrey claimed the intimidation suffered by his team that evening was the worst he had ever experienced in Europe. Throughout the match, flares and firecrackers had littered the pitch, with the Blues boss admitting afterwards that he was "very concerned for the players' safety… Our goalkeeper Alan Mannus had to stand 25 yards outside his goal it was that bad." Michael Gault later joked, "Nothing scares big

Alan Mannus, but he was about 40 yards out of his box hiding behind me!" Given the crowd's hostility and the strengths possessed by

Dinamo, the draw in Zagreb was a fine achievement. The Blues had shown that with full-time football there was a possibility of making progress in Europe. Yet, instead of capitalising on such momentum, this turned out to be the beginning of the end for that mid-2000s team.[37]

Prior to the Zagreb encounter, Jeffrey had let go of veteran left-back Pat McShane. Then in between the home and away European legs, the Blues lost one of the stand-out performers of recent seasons. Stockport County of League One (England's third tier) had come in for Peter Thompson with a £100,000 bid, and this was too good to turn down. It also gave the striker a much-deserved opportunity. Thompson had torn Irish League defences to shreds, and it was only right he got the chance to test himself at a higher level. That said, getting a transfer to England's third tier was emblematic of the local game's decline; despite the respect Thompson commanded in the Irish League, it was only a team in one of the lower English leagues that was prepared to take a chance on him. Unfortunately for Linfield, the departure created a major void up front, and during 2008/09 this told. Without Thompson, Linfield struggled to attain the standards of recent campaigns.[38]

In 2008/09 the club failed to land a single piece of silverware. The Blues came close in the Irish Cup, suffering a last-minute defeat to Cliftonville in the semi-finals, whilst in the League, Glentoran pipped Jeffrey's men to the title by a single point. Regardless of how close the Blues came to victory, the bottom line was that at the end of the campaign, Windsor's trophy cabinet was bare. For a side that had won three straight Doubles and operated with eight full-timers, this was hard to take. It was therefore little surprise when over the summer months the playing staff at the club changed significantly. At the start of May, Oran Kearney, who had suffered with injuries over the previous two seasons, announced his retirement. A couple of days later, Paul

McAreavey indicated that he was "ready for a new challenge". He would express his sadness at leaving the club but maintained "the time is right to move on".[39]

Later that summer, goalkeeper Alan Mannus would follow McAreavey's lead. Yet the most sensational of the end-of-season departures was the release of veteran striker Glenn Ferguson. Spike's scoring record was already the stuff of legend, and he had just registered 24 goals in the past season. Although Ferguson was about to hit his 40th birthday, he was still one of the League's top performers. As Stuart McKinley put it in the *Belfast Telegraph*, "'Spike' is still THE mastercraftsman in the local game when it comes to knocking the ball into the net." The decision to release him was therefore one that stunned both Irish League football and the player himself. In the aftermath of receiving the news, Spike told the press that his "reaction was one of shock and disappointment".[40]

David Jeffrey had wanted to keep Ferguson at the club. The Blues boss was only too aware that Spike had turned his good Linfield sides into great ones. However, budgetary demands dictated that the Blues could not offer the player the wage packet he had been earning. In light of this, Jeffrey felt that because of who Glenn Ferguson was and what he had meant to Linfield, it would be "disrespectful" to ask him to sign on reduced terms. Having to tell Ferguson there was no contract for him was "horrible". The manager considered this one of his lowest times in the hot seat. Obviously it was also extremely tough for Ferguson to endure. The player was in the midst of a well-earned testimonial season, and not surprisingly was adored by fans. Ferguson had sparkled as the club's talisman for over a decade, but suddenly his time at the Blues was over. In the circumstances, any player would have struggled to accept such a call made by his manager.[41]

In the years following what was an acrimonious departure, Jeffrey and Ferguson have talked about what happened and cleared the air. The raw emotion of that time has been laid to rest and a reflective Ferguson can look back and shrug, "That's football, you just get on with it." However back in the summer of 2009, the turmoil surrounding his departure was reflective of the mood of apprehension at Windsor. The incredible run of success of the mid-2000s appeared to be over, and the team's future was uncertain. There was though, one silver lining. During the 2008/09 campaign the Northern Ireland government shelved the

Maze project (which the IFA had in principle supported). This did not necessarily mean that international football would remain at Windsor and that the worries over the club's home ground were gone. Nevertheless, the position had changed, and there was hope that the matter could still be resolved in the Blues' favour. Linfield's financial wellbeing was of course tied in with the stadium question. Hearing the news two years after the Association had committed to the project was therefore a major relief.[42]

Ever since the IFA backed siting a stadium at the former prison, the project had benefitted from significant political support. When Northern Ireland's Stormont Assembly reconvened in May 2007 after almost five years of suspension, a firm supporter of the Maze proposal was given the portfolio tasked with settling the stadium issue. This was DUP MLA (Member of the Northern Ireland Assembly) Edwin Poots, who was appointed Department of Culture Arts and Leisure (DCAL) Minister. At the time, the *Belfast Telegraph* maintained that moving Poots to this position had brought the "prospect of the Maze becoming Northern Ireland's national stadium... a step closer", and Poots certainly appeared to use his influence to push for the development of the former prison site. The *News Letter* reported in June 2007 that "the Government... stood accused of running scared of the stadium debate" after Poots (in his second month as minister) had out of the blue set a deadline of less than two weeks for tabling alternative plans to the Maze project. However, it was ultimately a deadline which carried no weight.[43]

On top of Poots' apparent attempt to railroad the decision, elements within the media continued their crusade to force the issue. In early 2007, Jim Gracey of the *Sunday Life* implored that the time was right to leave Windsor Park. Then in April 2008, he called on the Stormont Executive to ensure that a national stadium was built at the Maze. All the while, John Laverty at the *Belfast Telegraph* was maintaining: "there's no escape from the Maze". The journalist had even promised that if a Maze stadium did not get the go-ahead, he would "eat [his] laptop". Once again though, Laverty's confident predictions were proved incorrect – and as far as this author is aware, he never ate that laptop.[44]

The Maze project had benefitted from IFA backing as well as considerable political and media support. This had not been enough to make it a reality. There was, however, still a great distance to travel in settling the national stadium debate. Other possible Belfast sites were now very much in the frame. The Blues Board knew that the club still had a fight on its hands if the future of Northern Ireland internationals was to remain at Windsor. Linfield would have to make the case that refurbishing its ground was preferable to developing an entirely new arena. Given the amount of anti-Windsor feeling in the debate, this was far from an easy task.

Whilst there had been an escape from the Maze, there was still some way to go in safeguarding Windsor's future.

Chapter 12

# *Looking for the Next League*

One would have imagined that the phenomenal success of winning three straight Doubles would have been a once-in-a-lifetime experience. Achieving the feat in the years between 2006 and 2008 was, after all, replicating something that had only been attained once before, and that was over 100 years previously. Yet incredibly, Linfield fans would experience another three years of absolute dominance. From 2010 to 2012 the League title and the Irish Cup were resident in the Windsor trophy cabinet. This would make it six Doubles in seven years! Furthermore, as the team was enjoying an unprecedented run of success, the club's Board was edging closer to securing the long-term future of Linfield's famous old ground.

After the Stormont Executive indicated the Maze site would not be developed as a sports stadium, Linfield's Management Committee adapted its position on the IFA contract. Prior to then, they had maintained a public stance that was fiercely protective of the deal. The Northern Ireland team was bound to play home games at Windsor, and the Management Committee had advocated that this remain the case. However, with the Maze project out of the picture, they were afforded an opportunity to showcase how Windsor could be modernised. In June 2009 the Management Committee sent a blueprint of plans to DCAL. These outlined how the stadium could be upgraded to a 20,000-seater. The document claimed that this could be achieved with a budget of about £20 million. Importantly, the Board also served notice that it would consider renegotiating the IFA contract.[1]

Declaring that the club was prepared to move away from the contract was a bold initiative. For years, the Management Committee had not countenanced such a thought. It was therefore little surprise that when the media got hold of the plans, they were hailed as significant. On 12 June, the *Belfast Telegraph* described the declaration "as an attempt to move the debate for the stadium development forward". Judging by the IFA's reaction to the proposals, they certainly had that effect. The following day, IFA president Raymond Kennedy explained: "It gives us... something to go off... the ball is now in our court." Later that month at the Association's AGM, Kennedy informed assembled delegates that Windsor being upgraded was a possibility. There were though, two major caveats. Before any work could take place, Linfield had to demonstrate that revamping the old ground was the best option on the table. Secondly, the Blues had to follow through on renegotiating the current Windsor contract.[2]

The IFA deal was a sore point for much of the Irish League. Since the mid-2000s, the Blues had raked in substantial sums from the contract, and this had caused rancour with other sides. Unsurprisingly, back at the start of the decade when it brought in little money and the terms actually hurt the Blues, others had not shown the same level of interest. However, once the contract began to pay dividends this changed, and others were quick to point to the financial windfall the Blues received. Bobby Jameson of Portadown told the local press that Linfield's deal with the IFA left other "clubs out in the cold financially". He added, "there is a lot of disenchantment with the levels of money Linfield have pocketed".[3]

In early June 2009 the *Sunday Life* revealed exactly how much Linfield was making from the deal. The paper informed readers that the "Cash-Rich [Blues earned] a massive £558,323 for the use of Windsor in 2008". This was a major source of revenue for an Irish League side, and the worry for other clubs was that similar sums were likely to come in year after year. In 2007 the IFA had struck a lucrative television rights deal with Sky Sports, and Linfield was in line for its share – TV money was of course part of the Blues' 15 per cent international games rental fee. This meant the club would continue to reap hefty rewards for the foreseeable future. So when the Board indicated that the club was prepared to walk away from the contract, it was significant. The best part of 80 years remained on that deal, and Windsor had so far been maintained to the necessary international standards.[4]

Being able to say the stadium was at the required level put the Blues in a strong position, especially as worries over the ground's maintenance had, for a time, threatened the security of the deal. During the summer of 2007 the IFA had claimed that the club was neglecting its stadium duties, and on this premise the Association had sought a termination of the contract. Hard bargaining followed, with the Blues Trustees issuing a writ against the IFA. Delivered by Carson McDowell solicitors, it had the desired effect – the Association was soon backtracking on its position. By October 2008, Raymond Kennedy was vowing that the IFA would ensure Windsor was "up to scratch for international games in the short-term". This was a significant swing of momentum in the long-running national stadium debate.[5]

From a position of threatening Linfield over the contract, local football's governing body had – in the short term at least – about-turned. It seemed that relations between the Blues and the IFA were thawing. Linfield's Board thus seized upon an opportune moment to share its plans for the ground's redevelopment. The IFA wanted a modern stadium and the Blues Management Committee was adamant it could deliver on this. Yet other bids were vying for the Association's backing. After the Maze had fallen by the wayside, Belfast sites dominated the competition. Locations in the South of the city like Ormeau Park and the site of the former Maysfield leisure centre were mentioned, and so was East Belfast's Danny Blanchflower stadium at Tillysburn. It was the last of these options, the Blanchflower stadium, which presented the biggest threat to Windsor.

At the same IFA AGM that Raymond Kennedy mooted the potential redevelopment of Windsor, the president also informed delegates that the Blanchflower proposal was very much under consideration. By June of 2009, the IFA's decision on a national stadium was effectively a straight shoot-out between Windsor and the East Belfast option. A couple of months later, the Association made its call. On 7 September, the IFA released a statement supporting "the redevelopment of Windsor Park as the National Stadium for Northern Ireland". Given all that had gone on between Linfield and the IFA, this was quite a turnaround. The Association had backed the Maze, and attempted to terminate its contract with Linfield. Now here it was saying that the future of Northern Ireland home internationals remained at the current site.[6]

Receiving IFA support for the renovation of Windsor was something that the Blues hailed. *Look at Linfield* described the Association's decision as "a very welcome move", though it also acknowledged that there was much detail "still to be confirmed" and negotiations were needed to establish "how this redevelopment [could] be achieved". This cautious note was understandable. The Association's about-turn over the Maze project indicated that Windsor's revamp was far from being a certainty. In light of this, the Management Committee pushed ahead behind the scenes to do everything it could to ensure the redevelopment would take place. At a Board meeting on 12 October, club president Peter Lunn counselled that although the IFA had given a green light to Windsor, the Blues Management Committee had to move matters forward.[7]

Lunn's advice was apt given the fallout that resulted from the Association's decision to back the Windsor plans. Shortly after the resolution, the press was awash with reports that Glentoran had petitioned UEFA president Michel Platini, bemoaning Linfield's "fairy godmother" relationship with the IFA. Supposedly the Glens had written to Platini asking him to investigate the financial dealings between the Blues and the IFA. Platini proved reluctant to get involved in the dispute. Yet just by invoking UEFA's top man, the East Belfast side had given an indication of how high the stakes were. Furthermore, this correspondence with UEFA's president was not the only communication making the news at the time. Seemingly, letter-writing in protest against Linfield's relationship with the IFA was in vogue – as another letter along similar lines was circulated amongst the chairmen of Irish League clubs.[8]

This second petition, sent to Linfield's 11 top-flight rivals, pointed to the issue of stadium upkeep, and maintained that "without further work the capacity of [Windsor] will be reduced under the latest proposed health & safety legislation". It then added that this was "a clear indication that [the] substantial rent received by Linfield [had] not been used to keep the ground in 'good order repair and condition' as required in the contract". There was clearly considerable opposition to the IFA's decision to back the Windsor revamp, which meant that an already tough task of closing out the deal to see Windsor refurbished was made even more difficult.[9]

The Management Committee had its work cut out in the long term. Though in the short term, supporters had a bit of fun at the apparent spate of letter-writing. When Linfield hosted the Glens in the League on 17 October, fans brought flags and banners to the game with messages aimed at the Glentoran Board. One directed at the East Belfast side's chairman, Aubry Ralph, read: "Taxi for Ralph, Platini thinks you're a clown." As well as the written jibes, Radio Linfield (who provided the match-day entertainment) joined in with a pointed playlist. Included was Roxy Music's 'Jealous Guy', 'Stop Crying Your Heart Out' from Oasis, 'Money' by Pink Floyd and Elvis Presley's 'Return to Sender'.[10]

On a day when Linfield supporters had poked fun at their cross-city rivals through song and slogan, they also enjoyed the last laugh on the pitch. The Blues earned a 2-1 victory over the previous season's champions, but the win had come amidst a stuttering start to the campaign. During September the Blues had succumbed to a 4-0 drubbing away to Cliftonville, and to add insult to injury that game was beamed live across the UK on Sky Sports. The lucrative Sky contract (worth £10 million to the IFA), signed back in 2007, included provision for showing five Irish League games a season. This raised the League's profile and was obviously welcomed by all clubs, as they were afforded greater exposure. That said, a televised 4-0 hammering was never good for any team's morale![11]

Two months after the embarrassing defeat at Solitude, Linfield again went down in the League to the Reds. On 12 December, Cliftonville came to Windsor and turned the Blues over 2-1. That loss was followed by two more defeats. One came in a League Cup semi-final to Glentoran, and the other to Ballymena in the League. At Linfield, a run of this nature has always been enough to constitute a crisis. Consequently, as Christmas 2009 approached, David Jeffrey's position as manager came under scrutiny. On 21 December, the club's Team Committee (a sub-committee of the Management Committee) held "a full and frank discussion about... performances and the Manager's position". Jeffrey had obviously enjoyed terrific success as manager. However, in the past season his team had not won a trophy, and midway through the 2009/10 campaign his side was up against it.[12]

On the same day the Board discussed his position, the manager told the *Belfast Telegraph*: "You must keep believing, you must continue to know it will turn... And the only way it does turn is by working desperately hard... and then you want that wee bit of fortune." Jeffrey understood that he had to portray an upbeat image for the media. Though he also knew that if he "didn't win the League [he] was gone". There was no doubt that the manager, his backroom staff and his players would put in the effort to turn the campaign around. Whether or not that "wee bit of fortune" would come was another matter entirely.[13]

Up next on the Blues' agenda was a Boxing Day showdown away to Glentoran. If the club lost in this annual festive fixture, the rut would have stretched to four games. Jeffrey and his players were thus facing the possibility of a bleak midwinter. Yet on 26 December, Linfield's game at the Oval was postponed due to snow covering the pitch. A bleak midwinter had indeed arrived, though thankfully this was not an analogy for poor form on the pitch. The Province had just entered a prolonged cold snap which would decimate fixture lists. The extreme weather (by Northern Irish standards) ensured that after the loss to Ballymena on 19 December, the Blues would not play again until 16 January 2010. In a way, the club was afforded that "wee bit of fortune" Jeffrey was looking for. The enforced break allowed the players to regroup and come back refreshed and renewed in the New Year.[14]

When Jeffrey's men finally got back on the pitch, the pressure was still well and truly on. January 16th was Irish Cup fifth-round day and the Blues faced an away match with Donegal Celtic. The players simply had to hit the ground running in this game. As far as the club's ever-demanding fans were concerned, a win was a must – especially given that Celtic were at the time languishing in the second tier of the Irish League. Going into the game, supporters were obviously eager to see their team for the first time in the best part of a month. They were also very excited about a significant addition to the starting XI.

Lining up in the number nine shirt was striker Peter Thompson. After a year and a half in England, with Stockport County, the marksman was back in Belfast with the Blues. Earlier in January, Thompson had returned on loan until the end of the season, and in his first game back he scored to pick up where he had left off with the club. As the following day's *Sunday Life* maintained: "It was almost as if [the forward] had never left the place." His goal was Linfield's second in a comfortable 4-0 win. Scoring on his second debut for the club was no doubt a relief for Thompson. Returning to Windsor placed huge pressure on the striker – something right-back Jim Ervin had articulated to the press after Thompson's signing was confirmed. Ervin explained: "Everyone will expect him to be like he was in the past when he was scoring goals regularly", adding that there would even be "expectations that he's a better player" given his year and a half at Stockport.[15]

For Ervin and his teammates, the opportunity to work with Thompson once again was something to be relished. As the right-back pointed out, it was "a great signing... for Linfield", though he added, "I'm disappointed [for him] because I wanted Peter to do well in England." Thompson's return to Linfield after 18 months was not supposed to be in the script. However, it would be unfair to label that year and a half away a failure. The striker could boast the distinction of holding down a starting place at a professional club, and scoring six goals in the process. Unfortunately a serious injury had hampered his time in professional football. In January 2009, Thompson suffered a collapsed lung that kept him out of the Stockport side until almost the end of his first season. Then at the end of that campaign, the club entered administration. After that, the sale of assets was high on the club's list of priorities. Therefore when Thompson returned to the Blues, initially on loan, his employers were making a saving. County would benefit from a wage off the books, whilst Linfield were only too happy to have a proven goalscorer back at the Park.[16]

Thompson's return would help in lifting spirits at the Blues, but after the victory over Donegal Celtic, the pre-Christmas jitters appeared to have resurfaced. On 19 January, Linfield endured a 3-2 defeat to Crusaders in the final of the County Antrim Shield. This was followed by a 2-2 draw away to Glentoran in the rearranged Boxing Day fixture. The season's first two pieces of silverware (the League Cup and the Shield) had thus passed the club by, and the side had now gone five games without a win in the League. Against this backdrop the press speculated over the manager's position. Stuart McKinley in the *Belfast Telegraph* maintained that "Jeffrey [was] on the ropes." Midfielder Jamie Mulgrew was, though, quick to rubbish such reports. Mulgrew told the *News Letter* that the speculation was "well wide of the mark... We are glad he is manager and we [the players] want him to stay at the club." Over the weeks and months that followed, Mulgrew and his teammates demonstrated just how much they had wanted Jeffrey to stay.[17]

After the draw with Glentoran, 10 out of the next 13 League fixtures ended in victory. Included in this run were three 5-0 triumphs, over Newry City, Lisburn Distillery and Portadown respectively. Jeffrey's men had found a way to win, and were doing so with relative ease. The tenth in this series of victories was a 1-0 conquest of Dungannon Swifts on 10 April. This result ensured that three points from the final three games would secure the title. Given the despair around the club prior to Christmas, the turnaround was remarkable. However, two weeks would have to pass before the Blues had the opportunity to wrap up the Gibson Cup. In between the Dungannon fixture and the next League game, away to Crusaders, was another vital tie. On 17 April, Linfield secured passage to the Irish Cup final with a 4-2 semi-final win over Coleraine. Suddenly a fourth Double in five years had become a possibility.

When the League game with Crusaders came around a week after the semi-final triumph, supporters were hopeful that the first leg of what had been an unlikely Double could be attained with two games to spare. Unfortunately for the Blues fans who travelled to Seaview, this was not to be the case. Jeffrey's men would only earn one point as a 0-0 draw was played out. Second-placed Cliftonville secured a win in their match with Dungannon, meaning the title race went into the next round of games. Uncharacteristically, David Jeffrey was not overly concerned about missing out on the chance to secure the Gibson Cup. This was because the game with Crusaders was, incredibly, Noel Bailie's 1,000th for Linfield! As Jeffrey explained to the *News Letter*, "It may sound strange, but if we had secured the title, Noel's milestone might have been lost in the fanfare."[18]

By amassing 1,000 career appearances, Bailie had attained a truly amazing feat. Only a select few have ever reached the milestone. Bailie's achievement was, however, in a class of its own. Most players who reach the mark do so by turning out for different clubs, or by adding club and international appearances together. Linfield's captain had reached 1,000 appearances all in the royal blue of Linfield. For over two decades the defender had been a mainstay of the first team, and ever since making his debut in March 1989 he had represented the club with distinction. As an 18-year-old, Bailie told *Look at Linfield* that one of his dislikes was "losing". Over the two decades that followed, he certainly demonstrated that this was the case. More often than not, the Blues' number 11 was on the winning side with his club. Prior to the 2009/10 campaign, Linfield's captain had been part of eight League title and six Irish Cup winning teams.[19]

Reflecting on his achievement, Bailie "counted [himself] lucky in terms of injuries". He also quite rightly maintained: "You've got to have a bit of ability, the manager has to believe in you and you have to have belief in yourself. I believed that I could play for Linfield and I deserved to be at Linfield." Along the way, he had to make sacrifices. Bailie had endured over two decades of gruelling pre-seasons, and balancing work commitments with the club's training schedule required dedication. Representing Linfield for as long as he had was not easy, but Noel Bailie had been more than up to the challenge. His former teammate Glenn Ferguson (who had since moved to Lisburn Distillery, and would also achieve the 1,000-game feat) was full of admiration for the achievement. In the following day's press, Ferguson described Bailie as a "phenomenal player", pointing out that his record equated to "playing 50 games a season for 20 seasons. How good is that?"[20]

The 2009/10 season was Bailie's 22nd with the Blues. During that campaign, the club captain did not scale the heights of 50 games. Instead he only made 30 appearances (a number of which came off the bench). Bailie was 39 years old, and David Jeffrey had to be sparing in using him. The days of the club captain playing two games a week were over. It was therefore up to the younger members of the squad to shoulder some of the burden that Bailie had carried for so long.

Fittingly, a couple of days after the draw with Crusaders, it was one of this new generation of players that secured Linfield's title. On 27 April, the Blues defeated second-placed Cliftonville 1-0 at Windsor to mathematically make sure of the Gibson Cup. Just after the hour mark, Robbie Garrett struck what the *Belfast Telegraph* described as a "classy" volley to seal the tie and the title. Jeffrey's men had thus engineered quite the transformation. Young forward Michael Carvill put the change in fortune down to hard work and the team spirit at the club. As he explained, "Christmas time was hell [but] we all stuck together and stayed united."[21]

Carvill also stressed the importance of a mid-season meeting which the whole squad had attended. The attacker recalled how David Jeffrey had spoken candidly about the fragility of his position as manager. Then the floor was opened up for the players to pinpoint exactly what was going wrong. According to Carvill, in the main this consisted of "analysing how [badly] we were playing". The meeting stretched long into a cold January night, and David Jeffrey recalled how "harsh words [were] spoken", though he also maintained it was "a good, frank exchange". He reflected, "The young players must have realised that

being at Linfield is not a walk in the park – you've got to deliver." By capturing the League, the players had certainly responded to Jeffrey's challenge – though they were not finished there. A couple of weeks after securing the title, the Blues won the Irish Cup  to earn a fourth Double in five years. Jeffrey's men dispatched Portadown 2-1 in the final, with goals from Peter Thompson and midfielder Philip Lowry.[22]

Both of the cup final goalscorers had weighed in with their 10th strike of the season, and both tallies were impressive. Thompson had only been at the club since January, and Lowry was in his first campaign with the Blues. Symbolically, having these names on the scoresheet boded well for the coming seasons at Linfield. The opener from Thompson (who would soon be moving back permanently) came from a player that had done it all before with the Blues, and there were still plenty of others in that boat at the club. Included in this were the likes of defenders Noel Bailie, William Murphy, Jim Ervin and Steven Douglas, as well as midfielders Michael Gault, Damien Curran and Jamie Mulgrew. Clearly the know-how to win was in abundance in the Linfield squad.[23]

The second goal, which came via Philip Lowry's head, typified the hunger of recent additions to the squad. Right across the pitch, David Jeffrey had complemented his squad with players who were eager to be winners. At the back this was certainly the case for goalkeeper Alan Blayney and defenders Kris Lindsay, Chris Casement, JP Gallagher and youngster Billy Joe Burns. In midfield Jamie Tomelty, Robbie Garrett and Lowry himself possessed the skill and determination to succeed. Up front Mark McAllister, Paul Munster, Michael Carvill and Curtis Allen all weighed in with vital goals.

Once again, David Jeffrey had fashioned a potent blend of experience and desire in his Linfield side. In turn this would yield yet another League and Cup Double the following season. During the club's 125th anniversary in 2011, the title was secured with a game to spare, and the Irish Cup was captured thanks to a 2-1 final victory over Crusaders. At the end of the decider, the task of lifting the cup fell to acting captain, goalkeeper Alan Blayney. This was because Noel Bailie, the club captain, was an unused substitute on the day. In early April, Bailie had signalled his intention to retire at the end of that season. Thus his 1,013[th] appearance, which came against Portadown the previous Saturday, was his last in a distinguished career. Although Linfield's skipper did not make it onto the field in his final day as a player, it was fitting that he bowed out as part of a Double-winning squad.[24]

Replacing a player of Noel Bailie's ability and stature was impossible. The club therefore took a decision to retire his number 11 shirt. From the 2011/12 season onwards, no Linfield player would run out wearing the number that Bailie had made his own. David Jeffrey would have to make a call about which member of his squad inherited the captain's armband. Deciding who would get the nod was not easy. Bailie had been club captain for 15 years, and whoever took over had big shoes to fill. This was especially the case because Bailie was "not the typical captain". As David Jeffrey explained: "He was never one to bark orders at everybody on the pitch or to raise the roof before games. Noel was very much about example. In saying that, his communication skills were outstanding, he did everything very quietly, and he had the respect of everyone at the club." Following in these footsteps was a tough ask, something that Jeffrey and his backroom staff were well aware of. Consequently, considerable deliberation was given to who would receive the armband.[25]

Goalkeeper Alan Blayney had deputised for Bailie during the veteran skipper's last campaign. However, David Jeffrey was never really in favour of a keeper getting the captaincy full-time, "simply because of the positional side of things". Instead, the manager opted for an all-action midfielder – Michael Gault (who like Bailie, had come through the ranks at the Blues) was awarded the captain's armband. Jeffrey deemed Gault the best candidate for the job because of his "talent, experience and the desire to be captain of Linfield Football Club". Since breaking into the first team in the early 2000s, Gault had won six League titles, and was well respected in the dressing room. For Jeffrey, "Michael was the right man at the right time." Gault himself revelled in getting the captaincy. He described taking on the role as "the greatest thing that has happened to me" in football.[26]

Having a new club captain after Bailie's 15 years of service was a big deal. Yet no one at Linfield was expecting the story to make quite the splash that it did. On 10 August 2011, the *Irish News* made reference to Gault being "Linfield's first Catholic captain". Indeed, the publication deemed the appointment worthy of front-page billing. Reporter Simon Cunningham claimed it was all "a far cry from the days when it was unofficial club policy not to sign Catholic players". The "policy" that Cunningham alluded to had never existed, whilst Gault's place of worship was of no concern to David Jeffrey when he was choosing his captain. As the manager explained: "It makes absolutely no difference what religion you are. Whether you're Protestant, Roman Catholic, Hindu, Muslim or none, I've no interest... at Linfield, we are about one thing and that's winning trophies." For Gault, the story was an irrelevance. As far as he was concerned, he was "playing football with my mates [at] somewhere I loved being". He added: "Religion doesn't come into it for me." What was important was winning on the pitch, and Gault knew that the Linfield team he led had a lot to live up to.[27]

Aside from the accession to the captaincy, another major change at the club came during the summer of 2011. Linfield's six-year flirtation with full-time football ended. It should be pointed out that owing to financial constraints, the full-time venture had never really been anything other than an experiment. At no time were there ever more than nine members of Jeffrey's squad on professional terms. The club's budget dictated this, and ultimately forced the return to a semi-professional set-up. From 2011/12 onwards, all members of the playing staff would again be on part-time contracts. When looking back on the domestic success that came with it, the move to full-time football appeared to be a success. The first professional contract was awarded to Peter Thompson at the tail end of the Clean Sweep season. Then over the five seasons that followed, the Blues won a staggering four Doubles. The club had clearly reaped the benefits of having better-trained players; but there was a glass ceiling to this success. Domestic dominance was not accompanied by European progression or Setanta Cup triumphs.[28]

In each of the European campaigns, undertaken with a smattering of full-time players, the Blues had fallen at the first hurdle. The opponents the club came up against in Europe were all full-time outfits, therefore these performances were nothing to be ashamed of. The Setanta Cup on the other hand had provided slightly more favourable results for Linfield; though after reaching the final in 2007, the best subsequent performance was a 2010 semi-final appearance. Just like the opposition in European competition, the League of Ireland teams in the Setanta Cup functioned on a different level. Illustrative of just how far ahead League of Ireland sides were, was the 2011 achievement of Shamrock Rovers. That year, the Dublin outfit made it past all the qualifying rounds to reach the group stages of the Europa League. This – without question one of the most impressive Irish performances in Europe for decades – was attained with a full-time squad. The Blues simply did not have the means to compete with such a set-up. There was always less than half a squad training full-time at the club. Linfield's dabble with professional football was thus always doomed to failure.[29]

Not only were there insufficient players to make the venture a success; there was also no full-time coach to work outside of the club's three training nights. As David Jeffrey explained, the attempt at full-time football was like "a patchwork quilt... We had different people around at different times... My situation didn't lend itself, [assistant manager] Brian McLaughlin's didn't lend itself", whilst coaches Alfie Wylie and Dennis Shields could not always commit to the extra sessions. At times the players were even left to their own devices.

Looking back on the venture, Jeffrey's overriding feeling was one of "frustration, because we didn't really fully exploit the opportunity. We were never fulltime in the true sense of the word."[30]

However, it would be unfair to cast the dabble with professionalism in a wholly unfavourable light. As well as the considerable domestic success enjoyed during the period, the players who received a full-time deal relished the opportunities it presented. Peter Thompson credited going professional with preparing him for his move across the water. Similarly, Michael Gault appreciated the chance to do more technical work and generally improve as a player. It was armed with this experience that Gault assumed the club captaincy ahead of the 2011/12 campaign. Taking over the reins from Noel Bailie was never going to be easy, but judging by the early results that season, it appeared there had been a smooth transition. Domestically, the club got off to a solid start, with three straight League wins. This was followed by a 1-0 loss to  Glentoran at Windsor, but that failed to knock the Blues off their stride. After the defeat, four wins on the bounce saw the club give notice that it was not ready to relinquish the Gibson Cup.[31]

This early form would set the tone for the season to come. Linfield remained the dominant force in the local game, but there were notable chinks in the armour. On two occasions Cliftonville heavily defeated the Blues. A late-October 6-2 loss in the County Antrim Shield was soon followed in early November by a 4-2 beating in the League. These results caused obvious embarrassment. Yet even more worryingly, Linfield went down in every encounter with Glentoran that season. The last of these came in the final League match of the campaign; by then though, the title – Linfield's 51st – had long been sewn up.

The Blues' dominance ensured that the Gibson Cup returned to Windsor with four games to spare. Though Jeffrey's men were not finished there. The Irish Cup would also be lifted. In the by then almost customary cup final appearance, Linfield dismantled Crusaders 4-1 to take their 42nd Irish Cup. The win came courtesy of two goals from Mark McAllister, one from Jamie Mulgrew and a curling right-footed free-kick that Michael Carvill placed in the top left corner of the net. The convincing victory ensured Jeffrey's men had made it a third Double in a row – their sixth in seven years![32]

Winning three consecutive Doubles, and replicating the dominance of the mid-to-late-2000s side, was an incredible feat. Furthermore, it was not something that David Jeffrey had ever expected to happen. After the club failed to win anything in the 2008/09 campaign, he "was only looking for the next League". Jeffrey considered the 2009/10 Double "a bonus", then what followed in the subsequent two years the stuff of "dreams". He was the first to admit that this group of players were "not as ridiculously talented as the previous team" who won the first set of three Doubles, but he stressed: "they were [still] a good side, a very, very good side". According to the manager, what drove these players on was a fear of not living up to the club's previous success. Jeffrey explained, "They didn't want to be labelled failures."[33]

The winning formula that had brought the first of this set of Doubles in 2009/10 – blending hunger with know-how – was exploited in the two seasons that followed. The desire of Philip Lowry, who averaged 12 goals from midfield in the three seasons, typified the drive brought by those who had joined or come through the ranks. Across the park, other new recruits had pushed that Linfield squad forward. Goalkeeper Alan Blayney, defenders Billy Joe Burns, Chris Casement, David Armstrong and Albert Watson, midfielders Aaron Burns and Robbie Garrett along with forwards Mark McAllister, Michael Carvill and Daryl Fordyce, were all desperate to emulate what had gone before.

Marshalling the exuberance brought to the squad by the aforementioned additions were those who had 'done it all before'. Of these players, David Jeffrey maintained that centre-back "[William] Murphy was massive." The Blues boss further contended that Murphy's defensive partners, Steven Douglas and (before he retired) Noel Bailie, were both "Godfather" figures. In the midfield, the "consistency of [Michael] Gault and the real emergence of Jamie Mulgrew" were vitally important, whilst up front Peter Thompson had continued to plunder goals. Over those three Double-winning seasons, Thompson averaged just shy of 21 goals per campaign. Given that he arrived halfway through the first of these, and a kidney problem blighted his 2011/12 season, his scoring rate was impressive in the extreme.[34]

As with all success enjoyed under Jeffrey's stewardship, hard work had been integral. The Blues boss explained that this squad of players strove to "continually push the bar higher". On the pitch, this had reaped domination for the best part of a decade. However, it appeared that the club's supremacy was about to stretch even further. Near the end of the 2011/12 campaign there was a definite move toward the redevelopment of Windsor Park. Two and a half years after the IFA had resolved to back the revamp of the dilapidated stadium, the first tranche of funding for the project was released. The *News Letter* informed readers in early April that £1 million had "been released to allow the IFA to start its tendering process for the project", adding: "It is expected that work will proceed in August next year, with all construction work expected to be completed by summer 2015."[35]

Getting to that stage of the project had not been easy. Lengthy (and at times strained) negotiations had followed the Association's indication of support for redeveloping the stadium. Going into these discussions, the Board's stated intention was to "ensure that International football [remained] at Windsor Park and that the desirable and necessary improvements to the stadium [were] progressed to the benefit of all". Three-quarters of a year after publicly stating this position, the club and the IFA came to a draft agreement. At a meeting between the two parties on 16 June 2010, the parameters of a deal were reached. The controversial contract, which still had 78 years to run, would go, with a new arrangement taking its place. Linfield would lose its 15 per cent of international revenue, though government funding would pay for the revamp of Windsor, taking it to an all-seater capacity of around 20,000. Furthermore, the Blues would enter into a stadium management partnership with the IFA, and receive an annual indexed rent in the region of £200,000.[36]

Linfield would continue to own the land, though the IFA would assume ownership of the stadium buildings. This meant that in future the Blues would be constrained when making decisions about the ground. Windsor badly needed upgrading and the draft agreement meant that this could now proceed without cost to the club. Indeed, any subsequent required maintenance work would be carried out without expense for the Blues. Effectively the agreement safeguarded Linfield's material future, and at an Extraordinary General Meeting on 2 July 2010, club members backed the proposed deal. With this support secured, the next issue was ensuring that the government was happy to release the necessary funds. Stormont controlled the purse strings, and there was concern about handing over money to an IFA-backed project. This had come in the wake of the body's controversial sacking in October 2008 of Howard Wells, the Association's then chief executive. Wells had taken the matter to an industrial tribunal, only for the case to be settled by the IFA prior to its hearing. Doing so had been costly for the IFA. The *Belfast Telegraph* pointed out that "half a million pounds [was] squandered in [the] settlement".[37]

Such was the government's concern about putting up money for a project the IFA was a partner in, confirmation of funding only arrived six months after Blues members had backed the redevelopment. In the intervening time, government officials lobbied for change at the Association. Edgar Jardine, Deputy Secretary to the then Sports Minster Nelson McCausland, maintained in October 2010 that the IFA needed "to get its house in order". Top figures within the IFA had initially been reluctant to comply with this, but when they eventually caved in, Stormont was prepared to put up the funds.

On 16 December 2010, Finance Minister Sammy Wilson indicated in his draft budget that £28 million would be set aside for Windsor's revamp. Four months later, in March 2011, Nelson McCausland confirmed the money was secure when he announced that the IFA would receive £61.4 million for improving Windsor and other facilities. This funding was part of a larger £140 million package allocated to local sports. From this, the GAA also received £61.4 million for upgrading facilities, whilst Ulster Rugby was awarded £14.7 million.[38]

When the financial backing for Windsor had been secured there was still some time to go before all was officially agreed for pushing ahead. In fact there was almost a year between McCausland's confirmation, and the binding deal on the redevelopment being reached. This only came at the end of February 2012, after the other Premiership clubs gave their support to the new arrangement. With that in place, a new 51-year contract between Linfield and the IFA could be signed. The revamp of Windsor had thus finally been the green light. What had been delivered was, as a *Look at Linfield* editorial of 3 March 2012 stated, "in essence all that was set out and agreed by Linfield members" back in July 2010.[39]

Everything had seemingly fallen into place – and it appeared that in the not too distant future, Windsor would become a state of the art facility.

Chapter 13

# *When the Castle Came Tumbling Down*

The unprecedented success of six Doubles in seven years, which Linfield had enjoyed under David Jeffrey, was brought to a shuddering halt during the 2012/13 campaign. Supporters accustomed to a dominant Blues team were suddenly confronted by a changed reality – other teams had stolen the march on Linfield. This was something that was hard to come to terms with at Windsor, and furthermore was analogous of an uncertain period off the pitch – the planned redevelopment of Windsor was thrown up in the air. Mercifully, Windsor would ultimately undergo its much-needed revamp. However, David Jeffrey, the man who had guided Linfield through all its recent triumphs, would not be the manager to take the Blues into this new era.

Linfield's players had sported a white and red away strip when they lifted the 2012 Irish Cup. Yet as with any success attained by the club, the trophy was adorned with blue ribbons. Given events in Munich a couple of weeks later, it seemed the hue was in vogue that spring of 2012. In mid-May, blue was once again the colour as Chelsea triumphed over Bayern Munich in the Champions League final. Understandably, the victory in itself was cherished by all connected with the West London side. Importantly though, it also ensured that the Stamford Bridge outfit would again sit at Europe's top table the following season. Chelsea had finished their 2011/12 domestic campaign in sixth, outside the top four Champions League qualifying places. However, by winning the UEFA competition, the club secured passage to the 2012/13 edition of the tournament. In doing so, it pushed fourth-placed Tottenham Hotspur into the Europa League places. Considering the disparity in prestige between the two competitions (not to mention the long-standing rivalry between the two sides), this was something that Chelsea fans revelled in and Tottenham fans despaired of.

The ramifications of Chelsea's victory would, however, go much further than one-upmanship in the English Premier League. Those near the bottom of the UEFA coefficient rankings (the statistics used to assess the standings of individual teams and member associations) also felt a knock-on effect. Unfortunately for the Belfast Blues, the impact was far from ideal. The calculations worked out after Chelsea's triumph placed Linfield in the very lowest Champions League qualification tier. Since 2009/10, an extra preliminary round had operated in the competition, and it was minnows from countries such as San Marino and Andorra who entered here. Prior to 2012, Linfield's coefficient had been high enough to ensure entry at what had become the second round. Yet this was about to change as the Blues dropped further still in European competition.[1]

Of course, the calculation made in light of Chelsea's triumph was not the only factor at play. Consistently poor Irish League performances in European competition had taken their toll; and on top of this, ahead of the 2012/13 season, that first qualification round had expanded, from four to six sides. It was thus a combination of different elements that coalesced to bring about the depressing reality. Linfield found itself amongst the six lowest-ranked Champions League teams, and entered the competition at the very start of July. When the draw was made in late June, the Blues were paired with Faroese side, B36 Torshavn. Although there was little glamour attached to the tie, there was a feeling that the match-up could at least allow for European progression.

The optimism around Linfield's chances was somewhat tempered by the Faroe Islands' side already being in the midst of their domestic campaign. As new Linfield forward, Matthew Tipton, explained: "Torshavn are into their season so they will be up to speed. We have only had two friendlies, and you need competitive games to get you going." Participating in a summer league gave the Faroese opposition an advantage, but Linfield had the upper hand in respect of their squad. Whilst Tipton was right to point to Torshavn's inevitable superior fitness levels, there was a confidence inside the Linfield camp. So when the first leg, at Windsor, ended 0-0 on 3 July, David Jeffrey was quick to air his frustration. He told the *News Letter*, "I'm so disappointed. We created numerous chances... but just couldn't put the ball in the net."[2]

One week later in the Faroe Islands, Jeffrey went through exactly the same emotions. Several chances were created, but his players could not score. That said, neither could Torshavn, which meant the tie went to extra time, then penalties. In the lottery of a shoot-out, Linfield's teenage goalkeeper Ross Glendinning was the hero. The young keeper saved twice, as the Blues emerged victorious by a 4-3 scoreline. If the manner of progression was far from impressive, the significance of the result was in no doubt. This was the first time that Linfield had won a round in the competition since the tournament had become the Champions League. In 1993, the Blues had progressed at the expense of Dinamo Tbilisi, but that was after the Georgians were expelled for an attempt to bribe the referee. Almost 20 years on, Linfield had finally tasted victory in Europe's premier club competition.

An exuberant David Jeffrey could not contain his delight after the game. Reflecting on the Blues' progression, the manager pointed out: "It's not only a great result for Linfield Football Club, but for the Irish League in general." By winning the tie, the Blues had achieved what was expected, but Jeffrey was right to stress the importance of having done so. Such results could only improve the club's coefficient and also the ranking of the Irish League as a whole. Significantly, on the same night that Linfield were progressing, Portadown would do the same in the Europa League. A 2-1 aggregate victory saw the Ports knock Macedonian opposition out of the competition. Upon learning of this, David Jeffrey was as thrilled for the mid-Ulster side as he was for his own team. He described Portadown's success as "fantastic news for our much maligned and criticised" local game.[3]

Regrettably, both Linfield and the Ports would fall at the next stage of their respective competitions. Nevertheless, these first-round victories contributed to raising the Irish League's coefficient over the coming seasons. It was also a positive experience for the likes of Linfield to once again progress in a UEFA competition. If dropping down a further preliminary stage was on one hand unappealing, it had brought with it certain advantages. After the high of making it past Torshavn, there was a sense of inevitability to the elimination that followed in the second round. Cypriot side AEL Limassol comfortably dispatched the Blues 3-0 on aggregate. As had become the norm, European football was over before July was out, and thoughts soon turned to the domestic season.

In six out of the seven previous seasons the Blues had dominated, and the pundits fully expected that this run would continue. *News Letter* columnist Liam Beckett affirmed that "Linfield [would] start the season as hot favourites." Furthermore, he quipped, "I'm sick sore and tired [of] people from various clubs asking me the same bloody question virtually every day: Who's gonna be second this season?" Not only did Beckett's column highlight Linfield's utter dominance of Northern Irish football; it also conveyed exasperation at the reality. Unsurprisingly, those outside Windsor were not enamoured by Linfield's recent feats. One letter sent to the Blues Board ahead of the 2012/13 domestic campaign summed up this feeling. In the correspondence, a Mr G. Wilson complained that the success of the current Linfield side was killing any competition in the League.[4]

Despite the widespread expectation of yet another season in which Linfield cruised to the title, David Jeffrey was not as confident. The Blues boss felt that in winning the previous season's Double, he had "squeezed" as much as possible out of that side. He reflected: "I didn't think there was any more to get out of them." Jeffrey though, was not about to break up that team. His management had been grounded on the mantra, "If you win games, you win trophies: if you win trophies, you win contracts." It was a philosophy that had served him well and he was not for changing it. Jeffrey was not ready to "look around eight or nine boys in the eye and say, 'Well you won another Double, but all the best.'" If he had done so, he would have compromised the principle he had built his success on. Caught in a catch-22, Jeffrey resolved to stick with his current squad and see how they fared. In an effort to keep things fresh, he added midfielder Ryan Henderson from Donegal Celtic as well as striker Matthew Tipton from Portadown to the group.[5]

Ominously, the first League game of the campaign ended in a 2-0 defeat away to Ballymena. This was followed by a 0-0 draw with Coleraine which meant that, including European involvement, Linfield had not scored in the first six matches of the season. It was only in the seventh, and in the 606th minute of football played, that the club's scoring duck was broken. Forward Gary Browne opened Linfield's campaign account in a comprehensive 4-0 win over Donegal Celtic in late August. Sadly though, the result was not the beginning of Jeffrey's men getting their season back on track. Inconsistency would be to the fore throughout, and there were some real lows along the way. A 3-1 home defeat to newly promoted Ballinamallard at the start of October was particularly galling for fans accustomed to League and Irish Cup success. After the Mallards loss, David Jeffrey had lamented to the *Belfast Telegraph*: "we cannot keep going like this". But despite his protestations, the players just couldn't respond and put a run of results together.[6]

Given the team's inability to hit any sort of form, the chances of winning a title were diminishing with every faltering result. On 10 November, Jeffrey's men travelled to a Cliftonville side that had started the season with purpose. What unfolded at Solitude was tough viewing for Linfield supporters. The Reds took the Blues apart, winning 3-0. This was the point at which it was becoming apparent that the Gibson Cup would be leaving Windsor come the spring. Reacting to the defeat, a dejected David Jeffrey sighed, "We now find ourselves 12 points behind [leaders Cliftonville] and it is not a nice position to be in." A couple of weeks later, *Look at Linfield* admitted that, although "we are still in November... our chances of retaining the title are now almost gone". With defeat a regular occurrence, the mood around Windsor was pretty low. As David Jeffrey put it: "When the castle came tumbling down, that was wick!" Before the month was out, things would get worse still.[7]

The Blues had made it to the County Antrim Shield final, and even though a sense of gloom hung over the club, there was an expectation that on 27 November, Linfield would lift the trophy. In the decider the Blues were up against Ballymena United, a club that had failed to win any silverware in 23 years. That statistic was about to change, with the Sky Blues taking the Shield on a penalty shoot-out. As one accustomed to winning, David Jeffrey found it "difficult to stand... and watch our opponents go up and lift the trophy". Blues captain Michael Gault similarly struggled, as he bemoaned: "We just haven't been winning games like we have done in the past... We need to step up and fight back." Two days after the loss, Jeffrey held a meeting with his players at training and attempted to gee them up. Though try as he did, he seemingly could not force anything more out of that group of players.[8]

At the very start of December, Linfield travelled to bottom-of-the-table Lisburn Distillery, and were lucky to emerge with a point. Only a late equaliser saved the Blues from the ignominy of defeat against a team stuck at the foot of the Irish League. In the immediate aftermath of what was an embarrassing performance and result, an impromptu meeting took place with members of the Board's Team Committee, the playing squad and Jeffrey. The upshot of the private summit was that the Blues boss offered his resignation. A frustrated David Jeffrey had felt that no matter what he was trying, nothing seemed to work. His players though, were not prepared to see their manager leave like that. Captain Michael Gault and veteran defender William Murphy spoke to him on behalf of the team, and implored him to stay. The message from the players was simple: they accepted responsibility for the team's failings, and resolved to put them right. In light of the intervention, Jeffrey was given 24 hours to reconsider his offer.[9]

Humbled by the response of the players, David Jeffrey withdrew his resignation and continued as Linfield manager. The draw with Distillery may have been one of the real lows of his tenure at the club, but in the short term at least, it galvanised the team. Over the Christmas and New Year period, the Blues' form improved. That said, there was never a consistent run throughout the campaign; and when in mid-January Crusaders knocked the Blues out of the Irish Cup, the last opportunity for domestic silverware had gone. After the loss to Crusaders, the only thing left to play for (pride aside) was the all-Ireland Setanta Cup. Considering the struggles of the 2012/13 campaign, Linfield were not expected to have much of an impact in the 2013 version of the tournament. It was therefore no surprise that the Blues would exit the cross-border cup at the first hurdle.[10]

Having won the 2012 Irish League, Linfield began the 2013 Setanta Cup as a seeded side – giving them direct entry into the quarter-final stage. Here the club had been drawn to face Dublin outfit, Shamrock Rovers. Although Linfield's early-March defeat was almost expected, the manner of the loss was another thing altogether. Rovers won the first leg of the tie 4-1 in Dublin, then the return game 3-1 at Windsor. This gave the Southern side a 7-2 victory on aggregate. Obviously the scoreline did not reflect well for local football, but unfortunately was in keeping with the two other Irish League sides involved in the quarters. Crusaders were dismantled 4-1 by Cork City, whilst Glentoran were thumped 8-0 by Sligo Rovers! Underwhelmed by the performance of Northern Irish sides, journalist Steven Beacom was scathing in the *Belfast Telegraph*. An exasperated Beacom exclaimed: "They are full-time in the Republic compared to the part-timers up here, so the argument will go what do you expect?" He then snapped: "Well a bit more... to be honest."[11]

Beacom's frustration was borne out of more than the disappointing results of Irish League teams during that particular season. Aside from Linfield in 2005, only Crusaders, seven years later, had brought the Setanta Cup north. Southern sides had dominated the tournament, with Northern Irish representatives at times appearing to do little other than make up the numbers. The predictability of the competition did nothing for its prestige; and as interest declined, so did the prize-money on offer. When Linfield had lifted the trophy in 2005, the club pocketed over £100,000. Almost a decade on, Setanta were only offering a fraction of that figure. This drop in cash incentives made the competition much less appealing, and contributed to the Blues eventually pulling out. Ahead of the 2014 cup, the prize money for winning the tournament stood at a mere £25,000. Linfield would qualify for that 2014 edition by virtue of a third-place finish in the Irish League, yet the club rebuffed Setanta's overtures.[12]

A statement on the withdrawal indicated that the Board had "decided, reluctantly, not to accept the… invitation to participate in the proposed 2014 Setanta Sports Cup", citing "a much-reduced prize fund available to clubs competing". Furthermore, the statement made reference to the "scheduling of… games in the spring". At that time of the season, Northern Irish sides were prioritising the conclusion of the League and Irish Cup. Therefore it was a tough ask to expect part-time players to be at their best when competing against full-time opposition from the Republic who were only starting off their season. The Board's comments were not limited to the timing of the tournament and the available prize money. The statement added that "the considerable difficulties faced by our supporters travelling to attend [Setanta] games" had also played its part in the decision.[13]

Just holding a cross-border competition was witness to the normality ushered in by the political changes in Northern Ireland during the 1990s. Yet this did not mean that all games would pass off without incident, and both legs of the Linfield-Shamrock Rovers 2013 quarter-final were testament to that. After the first leg in Dublin, the *Irish News* highlighted obscene chanting from both sets of supporters as well as clashes between Linfield fans and the Gardaí. Then in the return game at Windsor, Shamrock Rovers fans broke through a temporary fence in the North Stand to hurl missiles at the home support. The situation was only brought under control when riot police stepped in. The negative media generated by both matches did little for the reputation of the tournament. Also it would do nothing to ease what the Board identified as "the considerable difficulties" faced by fans when travelling across the border.[14]

If the early-March visit to Dublin was mired in controversy, the opposite was the case for a friendly away-day the following month. Near the end of the season Linfield played their first ever match at Ibrox Stadium, the home of Scotland's most successful club – Glasgow Rangers. The game was organised by Rangers as a thank you for the help that Linfield had provided in the Glasgow club's hour of need.

Back in 2012, a creditors report declared debts of over £130 million at Rangers. The staggering level of money owed by the Gers had forced the club into administration, and ultimately liquidation. In the midst of the crisis, Linfield hosted Rangers at Windsor in a fundraising friendly, with all proceeds going to the Glasgow club. This had come at the end of the 2011/12 campaign, and approximately £100,000 was raised by the game (which ended 2-0 to the Gers). Considering the level of outstanding debt, the match with Linfield did little to alleviate Rangers' financial difficulties. Nevertheless, the generosity of the gesture was greatly appreciated by the Glasgow side; and such was the gratitude felt by Rangers, that club official and revered former player Sandy Jardine had offered a return game.[15]

True to Jardine's word, Rangers hosted Linfield on 10 April 2013. Less than 12 months had elapsed since the clubs had last met, but the Gers side that lined up in the Ibrox game was virtually unrecognisable from the team that had travelled to Windsor. Only four of the Rangers XI from the game in Belfast would start in Glasgow that April evening. This was on account of the mass exodus from Ibrox that followed the end of the 2011/12 campaign. As punishment for the club's financial turmoil, Rangers had been expelled from the Scottish Premier League, then demoted to the Third Division (Scotland's fourth tier). Faced with the prospect of languishing in lower-league football, the majority of the club's first-team squad had left. It was, though, one of the players who had started both games for Rangers that got the opening goal in the Ibrox fixture. Ulsterman Chris Hegarty would head the ball home just before the break to put the Scottish side 1-0 up. Then at the game's death, teenage substitute Andy Murdoch made it 2-0 with an effort from 20 yards out.[16]

Linfield could have felt aggrieved by a couple of decisions that went against them on the night. A penalty shout was denied, whilst a Peter Thompson header that found the net was flagged for offside. Yet as Gers manager Ally McCoist stated afterwards: "The result was immaterial... the important thing was the two clubs getting together." More than anything, the game was all about the occasion, especially for the 700-plus Linfield fans that travelled from Northern Ireland. Blues vice-chairman and long-time Rangers fan Billy Kennedy described the evening as "just unbelievable". There was though, one thing missing from this gala friendly, and that was the presence of Malcolm Brodie. As a stalwart of Irish League journalism and a lifelong Gers supporter, the veteran reporter would have revelled in the Ibrox fixture. Sadly Brodie had passed away just a couple of months beforehand, at the end of January.[17]

Malcolm Brodie's contribution to the coverage of Northern Irish football was without compare. Brodie had set up the sports department at the *Belfast Telegraph* and was a driving force at *Ireland's Saturday Night*. He had also worked as a freelance journalist for a host of other newspapers, including the *Daily Telegraph* and the *News of the World*. Brodie was famed for his reporting on World Cups, having attended every tournament from 1954 in Switzerland, to Germany 2006. On account of his service to the game, FIFA presented Brodie with a replica of the Jules Rimet (the first World Cup) trophy in 2004. Given his profile, Brodie's unstinting support for the Irish League had been invaluable during his career. It should also be noted that throughout the protracted debate over the future of Northern Ireland home internationals, he was always a firm advocate of redeveloping Windsor Park. Amidst what Brodie called "the constant propagating and the spin for the 'only show in town' scenario of a new multi-purpose stadium", he had maintained that "the upgrading of Windsor [was] the obvious avenue to go down".[18]

Ultimately, the powers that be had agreed with Brodie's summation, and plumped for Windsor's redevelopment. Yet getting to the stage where work could actually begin had proved extremely difficult. Striking a new agreement between Linfield and the IFA had not been easy, whilst securing the finances was just as tough. Seemingly though, the green light for the project had come at last when all Irish League Premiership clubs gave their backing to the proposals, back in February  2012. Over the 12 months that had followed, the groundwork for the revamp got underway in earnest. This was a thorough endeavour. According to Jim Gracey of the *Belfast Telegraph*, "no stone [was] being left unturned before the first brick [was] laid". At the end of 2012 the planning application for Windsor was submitted. As Raymond Holbeach from design consultants RPS explained, after "an intensive period of community and statutory body consultation as well as completion of environmental and transport assessments", all was in order to proceed.[19]

The required permission was granted less than 11 weeks after the relevant paperwork was submitted. Stormont's Environment Minister, Alex Attwood, confirmed the news on 20 February 2013. This was the quickest ever turnaround of a Major Planning Application (what is known as 'an Article 31 case') in the Province. After receiving the go-ahead it appeared the project was all set, with work scheduled to begin on 9 September. However, there was yet another twist in the stadium saga – one which threatened to scupper the entire redevelopment. North Belfast side Crusaders was in the process of legally challenging the project's government funding (which amounted to £25 million). The Shore Road club was seeking a judicial review, and had instructed solicitors on the matter. With this came the real possibility that the upgrade of Windsor could be stopped right in its tracks.[20]

News of Crusaders' legal move hit the papers at the tail end of the 2012/13 campaign. With Linfield and Crusaders scheduled to meet on the League's final day at Windsor, a game that was until then effectively a dead rubber, suddenly had an edge. Going into the fixture, the Crues sat in second and the Blues were well adrift in third. Whatever the result, these positions would not change. In any other context, the match would have had a lacklustre end-of-season feel to it. The legal action had changed that significantly. Ahead of the game, Linfield's Board informed Crusaders officials that they were not welcome in the Directors' Box. A club spokesman explained: "We are very disappointed… We reckon the spirit of the game was breached by [the] decision to seek a judicial review… We stand by our decision not to hold out the hand of courtesy."[21]

In this frosty atmosphere, Linfield were beaten 2-1. It was a result that piled further misery on what had been a disastrous playing campaign for the Blues. After starting out as champions, Linfield finished the season on 62 points, a massive 29 points behind winners Cliftonville. If cracks had appeared during the previous campaign's Double, gaping crevasses were apparent in 2012/13. Jeffrey and his backroom staff would have a huge job of rebuilding over the summer months. Meanwhile, the Board was facing up to the reality that all the hard work put into Windsor's redevelopment plan could be lost. It would be fair to say that the 2012/13 season had been one to forget, both on and off the field of play.

In late May, High Court Judge Seamus Treacy granted Crusaders leave to seek their judicial review. The Crues had therefore won the right to legally challenge the government's funding for the Windsor project. The action had been brought on three grounds. Crusaders argued that the deal struck on the redevelopment lacked transparency; that the money which the IFA would pay to Linfield as part of the deal represented state aid; and that the funding arrangements breached competition law. While Mr Justice Treacy rejected the contention on competition regulation, he upheld the two other claims. Windsor's redevelopment plans were now well and truly in disarray. There were particular worries at Linfield Board level that because the argument on state aid was upheld, the Stormont Executive was duty-bound to make contact with the European Commission on the matter. This had the potential to delay matters for 18 months.[22]

Whether or not 18 months would elapse before the future of the revamp was decided, it was clear that bulldozers and builders would not be starting on Windsor come 9 September 2013. The judicial review's hearing was set for 16-18 December; there was thus an anxious seven months ahead for all connected with the club. Yet concerns over halting the redevelopment reached much further than the corridors of Windsor Park. Right across the local game there was anxiety about the implications of Crusaders' move. This disquiet was something that Jim Gracey of the *Belfast Telegraph* captured in his response to the news that the judicial review would go ahead. Gracey was adamant that "the courts of law with the attendant legal costs" was not "the place" to consider "the destination of funding in football... From the outside it looks like money going out of football to stop money coming into football." In the same paper, Graham Luney decried the Shore Road side for "flying this flag alone". He maintained that "if the major construction work which Windsor badly needs fails to proceed, the knives will be out for the Hatchet men".[23]

The powers that be were also aligned against the action taken by Crusaders. Stormont's DCAL Minister, Sinn Féin's Carál Ní Chuilín, had promised to "fight for Windsor Park". However, it would not come to a square-off between the different sides in the dispute. By mid-summer, the mood music emanating from the Shore Road was much changed. On 15 July, Crusaders members met to hear how the judicial review was proceeding, but also to consider the offer of a revised financial settlement for Irish League clubs. After listening to what was on the table, Crues members moved to support the deal, and backed down on the judicial review. Speaking to the press after the meeting, chairman of the Shore Road club, Stephen Bell, insisted: "Crusaders FC can take pride in the action we have taken. The proposals before us have the potential to benefit the entirety of the football family. Understanding the imperatives for all parties, and the urgency associated with the decision, we will nonetheless take time with our legal team to shape the right deal for the football family."[24]

Bell was making the case that Crusaders had saved "the entirety of the [local] football family". It was an argument which was ridiculed in the *Belfast Telegraph*. Jim Gracey ranted that there was an attitude "coming out of Seaview... that we should be grateful to Crusaders for their climbdown from the legal action that threatened the new Windsor Park project, scores of jobs, community benefits and a new beginning for football here... Glad, yes. Grateful, no... One minute they are prepared to sacrifice the biggest ever investment in the game here... the next they are the self-appointed saviours of the game... What's not to be grateful for?" Given that the Shore Road club had held the local game hostage over the spring/summer of 2013, Gracey's anger was understandable. Crusaders could have raised their objections in February 2012, when Irish League clubs had backed the redevelopment. Instead the Crues chose to oppose the plans only after everything seemed in place for the project to commence.[25]

Due to Crusaders' intervention, work on Windsor's revamp would not get underway until May 2014. This was almost nine months later than scheduled. It was thus unsurprising that the bad blood between the Crues and Blues at the end of the 2012/13 campaign would spill into the following season. When Crusaders hosted Linfield in the sides' first meeting of 2013/14, the vast majority of Blues fans boycotted the fixture. A paltry sum of around 130 Linfield supporters turned up at Seaview for the game played on 24 August. As the Shore Road club were used to Linfield bringing in excess of 1,000 fans, the snub gave an indication of the feelings aroused by Crusaders bringing the judicial review. On the pitch, the home team emerged with a 2-0 win. The defeat was the Blues' second on the bounce, and after a draw with Glentoran in the next League fixture, Linfield dropped to bottom of the table. With four matches gone at the start of the 2013/14 domestic campaign, Linfield had the unenviable position of gazing at all the other sides ahead of them.[26]

The disastrous start to the Irish League was a far cry from the club's Europa League exploits a month earlier. At the beginning of July,

Linfield had progressed past the first qualifying round with a 5-0 aggregate victory over ÍF Fuglafjørður of the Faroe Islands. Not only was the scoreline extremely comfortable; the 2-0 away-leg triumph was a significant milestone. This was the club's first European competition win on foreign soil since defeating Norwegian side Vålerenga in 1966. Winning out in the Faroes was no small feat, yet the achievement seemed small fry set against the exploits of the next round. Two weeks after the victory in the Faroes, Jeffrey's men would record one of the club's greatest European wins. In the first leg of the second preliminary round, Linfield travelled to Greece and defeated Skoda Xanthi 1-0. To put into context just how impressive the result was, that season's UEFA coefficient standings had the Irish League ranked in 47th place, and the Greek league in 12th. Furthermore, the win brought about a Northern Irish first: this was the first time an Irish League side had recorded three European wins in a row.[27]

The Blues team that had won out in Greece looked very different to the side that had competed in 2012/13. During that season to forget, the trio of Albert Watson, Daryl Fordyce and Robbie Garrett had left to play in Canada; Watson and Fordyce on a permanent basis, Garrett on loan. Then at the campaign's end, a number of other players left. Included in the exodus were striker Gary Browne, midfielders Damien Curran and Ryan Henderson, as well as defenders Nathan  Hanley, David Armstrong and Johnny Black.

There were also two figures that David Jeffrey had described as "colossal" who left in the aftermath of 2012/13. These were long-serving defenders Steven Douglas and William Murphy. Douglas joined back in 2003, and Murphy in 1997. Both had played significant roles in the considerable success enjoyed by Linfield during their stays at the club. Douglas had been so keen to pull on the Blue jersey that he offered to pay part of his transfer fee when he joined; whilst Murphy would always be remembered as a rock at the back during some of the club's most successful years, and furthermore as part of the 2005/06 Clean Sweep first XI.[28]

After the extensive clear-out, Jeffrey brought in a number of replacements. At the back, goalkeeper Jonathan Tuffey arrived from Scottish side St Johnstone. Then ahead of him, in came defenders Sean Ward from Glentoran, Matthew Clarke from Glasgow Rangers and Kyle McVey from Coleraine. The midfield was strengthened with the return of Aaron Burns from Portadown and the signing of James Knowles from Cliftonville. Up front Andy Waterworth (like Sean Ward) joined from Glentoran.[29]

Judging by the success out in Xanthi, the recruitment policy appeared to bear early fruit. Aaron Burns put the Blues in front on 25 minutes, and afterwards the new-look side managed to keep the Greeks at bay. Securing the win was a truly outstanding achievement, one which David Jeffrey raved about.

He told the *News Letter* that "courage, bravery and commitment of hard work [as well as] on some occasions very good football" had

earned the victory. Going into the return leg, Jeffrey reiterated just how impressive the win in Greece had been. Ahead of the game at Windsor, he described the result out in Xanthi as "ridiculous, especially when you consider the gulf that exists between our respective leagues – in terms of standard, finance, expectations, facilities and all that is involved in the running of the clubs". Jeffrey then

maintained that if the Blues were to progress, "We [would] need another performance of that magnitude." Getting past the Greeks would be tough, but it was not impossible. There was a belief amongst the players that it could be done. New recruit Sean Ward explained: "We didn't want to wake up on Friday [the day after] with the usual patronising stories of 'Blues go down with a fight'… We wanted to read about the club making history."[30]

Ward's aspirations were sadly unrealised, as Linfield were knocked out after extra time on the away-goals rule. Xanthi had taken a 26th-minute lead, but then just before the break the Greek side was reduced to 10 men after Konstantinos Fliskas fouled Michael Carvill. Losing a man forced Xanthi to sit back, and nullified their attack. In a cagey second half, neither team scored and the game went to extra time. Almost 10 minutes into the extra half hour, Linfield fans had been on their feet as Michael Gault volleyed home from 15 yards.

Prior to the European campaign, Gault had joked with the press that he "was still talking about [his 2008] Zagreb goal", adding that he needed "some other goals to talk about". The Xanthi strike provided just that, but also gave the Blues a lead with just over 20 minutes of the tie remaining. Windsor had erupted with Gault's strike, but minutes later, just before the first half of extra time was out, Xanthi struck. This put the Greek side ahead 2-1 on the night, and drew the clubs level 2-2 on aggregate. Given that Xanthi had scored twice at Windsor, they were leading on away goals. With neither team finding the net in the second half of extra time, the Greeks would progress to the next round.[31]

To go toe-to-toe with the likes of Skoda Xanthi and fall just short was extremely impressive. As David Jeffrey remarked afterwards: "We didn't fall gallantly on our sword after a brave effort, we were very unlucky to go out." Xanthi knew they had been in a fight, and were relieved to make it to the third qualifying round. Sean Ward explained that "their reaction at the end told the real story... [Their] celebrations in the dressing room went on for a full 30 minutes. They were singing and dancing, literally going crazy." This European campaign of 2013 was one that boded well for the domestic season ahead. Thus it was no surprise that Jeffrey's players were soon able to turn around their poor start. After falling to last spot with only four games gone, a revival in fortunes saw the Blues march up the League table. By October Linfield sat top, and were in the midst of a run of form which had been unattainable in the previous campaign.[32]

Come the end of 2013, Linfield had maintained their lead and had opened up a six-point gap on second-placed Cliftonville; this would extend to eight points early in the New Year. It was all quite a turnaround from the previous season, and was evidence that Jeffrey's rebuild was progressing well. Indeed, two more players – Northern Ireland international winger Ivan Sproule, and defender Jimmy Callacher – would come in during January to further strengthen the team Jeffrey was assembling. That said, there were still question marks hanging over his side. Worryingly, Linfield could not seem to get it together when they faced reigning champions Cliftonville in the League. Even though the Blues had a comfortable enough lead going into the New Year, the Reds had come out on top in the two League meetings thus far that season. Although Linfield had improved in a short period of time there wasn't the invincibility of previous sides. In the uncertainty of it all, the press was again speculating on Jeffrey's future. On 14 January 2014, Graham Luney pondered in the *Belfast Telegraph* whether the Blues boss would "be sacked" should Linfield fail to win the Gibson Cup.[33]

The pressure was on, and it was starting to tell. On two occasions in January, Linfield dropped points when they had been in control of games. A 1-1 draw with Crusaders came on the same day that Luney had speculated over Jeffrey's future. Then a week and a half later, relegation-threatened Ards travelled to Windsor and earned their first away-point of the season. Linfield had been 3-1 up in that game but could not see it through – as the Strangford side equalised with seconds left on the clock. At the beginning of February, the ropey form dipped further. A 1-0 loss to Cliftonville at Solitude consigned Linfield to a third straight League defeat against the Reds that season. Going into the game, Reds defender Marc Smyth had maintained that, given the recent record between the two clubs, the Solitude side was confident of prevailing. It was Smyth who scored the winner on the day, and afterwards he boasted: "I thought Linfield were beaten before they came out."[34]

Smyth's comments played into a narrative that this Linfield team, whilst much-improved, didn't have what it took to be winners. In the aftermath of the Cliftonville defeat, the *Belfast Telegraph*'s Steven Beacom queried the team's mental resolve. Acknowledging that although David Jeffrey and experienced players like Gault and Mulgrew had done it all before, Beacom wondered whether "the rest of the Blues [had] the bottle?" A week after the loss to Cliftonville, the Blues went down again; this time at home to Ballymena in a sixth-round Irish Cup tie. With the cup defeat, the pressure at Windsor reached fever pitch, and speculation over Jeffrey's future as manager was splashed all over the papers. Indeed, Mark McIntosh of *The Sun* went so far as to describe Jeffrey as a "Dead Man Walking".[35]

Behind the scenes, Jeffrey's position was discussed at Board level. Of course, this had happened on previous occasions. Back in April 1999, the Management Committee considered Jeffrey's future after he had failed to land the League title in his second full season in charge. Ten years later in December 2009 they had done so again, just prior to the club's second run of three straight Doubles. This time, however, there was a different dynamic to the discussions. Jeffrey had always maintained he wanted to be at Linfield "as long as people at the club [thought he could make] a significant contribution". In February 2014, he did not feel that he had the backing of the Board. Given that reality, he resolved to leave. On the Wednesday after the Ballymena defeat, the Blues boss confided in his family that regardless of what happened, he would be stepping down. The following night, before training, he spoke with members of the Board and indicated his decision to leave at the end of the campaign.[36]

On the Friday evening of 14 February, Jeffrey drafted a statement for public consumption, and choreographed how the news of his forthcoming resignation would be released. The entire Board would be informed the next morning, at a meeting scheduled to consider stadium development. Then, as it was a match day and the players were at Windsor for a League game with Ballinamallard, Jeffrey would speak with his squad before the main business of the afternoon. Once they were made aware of his decision, the prepared statement was to be released on the club website. Jeffrey knew only too well that his resolution to leave would attract a media storm. By February 2014, he had occupied the Linfield hot seat for over 17 years. This made him the longest-serving manager in the club's history. Therefore, because of his reign, because of all he had achieved, and because the goings-on at Linfield have always attracted interest, news of his intended departure would dominate the local press. The inevitable media reaction was something that after all those years in charge, he could take his stride. Informing his players was another matter. For David Jeffrey, relaying his decision to his squad was always going to be the toughest part of that Saturday.[37]

Jeffrey had always had a strong rapport with his sides, and they had loved playing for him. So it was hardly a surprise that when the manager spoke to the group he broke down, and members of his squad did likewise. According to midfielder Jamie Mulgrew, the dressing room went "numb". Club captain Michael Gault was both "shocked and gutted" by what he heard. David Jeffrey was the only manager Gault had known in senior football, and he considered his boss to be a father-like figure. The reaction from Gault was indicative of the affection that Jeffrey was held in, but also of the respect that long-serving squad members had for their manager. Even those who had recently joined were similarly affected. Sean Ward, who had arrived from the Glens during the previous summer, considered Jeffrey's decision as "a massive loss for all of us". Right across the playing staff – from veterans of numerous campaigns to players just in the door – Jeffrey's message was hard to take.[38]

The emotions and disappointment expressed by the players were testament to David Jeffrey's man-management skills. Striker Andy Waterworth (who was only in his first year at the club) intimated that such was the belief Jeffrey instilled in his players, "you actually would fight and die for him". Jeffrey made his players feel valued, respected and even that they were world-beaters. Sean Ward joked that the boss had "you believing you were the third best player in the world… Only third, because you realised yourself, I'm not better than Ronaldo or Messi." Ward maintained that much of this stemmed from Jeffrey's way with words and his ability to rouse a dressing room. Yet this was only a fraction of David Jeffrey's role whilst Linfield boss. As Michael Gault explained, Jeffrey was more than just a "great manager, he was a friend as well". Jamie Mulgrew insisted that each player knew the manager "always cared about you".[39]

David Jeffrey loved the company of his players and he took an active interest in their personal lives. Jeffrey wanted to know that off the field, all was well with his squad members. This was something that both Gault and Ward put down to his nine-to-five job as a senior social worker. Ward stated that Jeffrey could read someone very quickly. This allowed the manager to forge a bond with each individual as well as the squad as whole. On top of being a motivator and a friend to his players, David Jeffrey had the trust of his squads, and they respected his fairness. Jamie Mulgrew stressed that Jeffrey was "always fair… and if you stepped out of line, he never bore a grudge". Sean Ward explained that "Davy always said every player had his trust." Knowing that was something his squad had always appreciated.[40]

For a whole host of reasons, David Jeffrey's players loved being a part of his sides. The devastation in the dressing room that Saturday afternoon was thus to be expected. Yet, ever focused on achieving success, once the tears had dried Jeffrey said to his men: "Right: enough of this." There was a game to be won, and his Blues side did just that, beating Ballinamallard 6-0 to maintain their title challenge. After the win, Linfield sat in second place, one point behind leaders Cliftonville, but importantly with a game in hand. Jeffrey's players were desperate to get the Blues back into first place and maintain that lead. They wanted to see their manager go out on a high. With this resolve as extra motivation, the Blues went on an unbeaten run.[41]

Linfield would not taste defeat in the seven games that followed Jeffrey's indication he was stepping down. Included in this run was a penalty shoot-out victory over Crusaders in the final of the County Antrim Shield. The win gave Jeffrey his 31st piece of silverware as Linfield manager, drawing him level with Roy Coyle in the number of honours lifted. Sadly though, Jeffrey was not going to make it to trophy number 32. His Linfield side of 2013/14 would come up short.

The unbeaten stretch of seven matches had returned the club to first place, and had opened up a two-point gap on Cliftonville. However, the Reds would break that run, seize the advantage in the title race, and take the Gibson Cup. On 29 March, Cliftonville beat Linfield 3-1 at Windsor in what was ultimately the decisive fixture of the season. On the day, the Reds' goals came from Liam Boyce and Joe Gormley. Over the year and a half that followed, both of these players moved into full-time football on the mainland: Boyce to Scotland's Premier League, signing with Ross County, whilst Gormley moved to Peterborough United in England's League One. The Boyce-Gormley partnership was one of the great Irish League forward lines, and in 2013/14 it was the difference between the Reds and the Blues.[42]

After the late-March game at Windsor, Cliftonville made sure of the title with four straight wins in their remaining matches. Unfortunately the Blues could not match this; indeed, their campaign fizzled out. As the Reds powered to Gibson Cup glory, Linfield fell to second place. Along the way the Blues won twice, drew once and lost once. The defeat, which came in the penultimate game of the season, was particularly galling. Mathematically this secured the title for the Reds, and also came against Glentoran in Jeffrey's last ever home match.

Not only was it Jeffrey's final match at Windsor, it was also the club's last at the stadium before the major redevelopment work began. Such were the hitches and delays to this point that the last Linfield match at the old stadium came after the first rugby game (an Ulster vs Saracens Heineken Cup tie) was staged at the new Ravenhill (or as it became known, the Kingspan). This despite rugby and football getting monies for their redevelopments at the same time! On 22 April 2014, Blues fans said goodbye to their famous old ground and to Jeffrey's reign there. What they witnessed was described in the press as a "truly shocking" performance. Glentoran eased to a 2-0 win, and David Jeffrey left the Windsor pitch for the final time in defeat.[43]

As a dejected Jeffrey walked back to the dressing room, there were two things he took solace in. Firstly, the memories of all the good times he had enjoyed at Windsor; secondly, the reaction of supporters. Jeffrey remembered eight years previously when his side clinched the Clean Sweep against the same opposition. He thought: "Well, I mightn't have given what you wanted today, but in 2006 against our oldest enemy, we beat them – not just in the Irish Cup final, to do the Double – we beat them to do the Clean Sweep! Now tell me, how much better does that get?" Such memories were not lost on supporters, and they cheered and clapped their manager as he left the pitch. Jeffrey was humbled as the crowd "stood and they applauded, and applauded, and applauded". What he came away thinking was, "My goodness gracious me. Look at the number of people standing there. We've been beaten by our Big Two rivals, the League is totally gone, and yet they are taking the time to show their appreciation." The fans' reaction transformed the manager's emotions. Shame in what had gone on in that day's game was replaced by pride, and total respect for those who had stayed behind.[44]

Chapter 14

# *Linfield Will Rise Again*

Fortunately, David Jeffrey's last involvement as Blues boss was not the woeful showing against Glentoran. Half a week after losing to the East Belfast side, Jeffrey brought his Blues team to Lurgan for his final engagement on club duty. On this occasion, Linfield would beat Glenavon by a convincing 5-2 scoreline to ensure that Jeffrey bowed out with a win. After the game, the end of an era was signalled, as for one last time Jeffrey took the applause of the Blues support. Minutes later, a new era began. At 5:00pm on Saturday 26 April 2014, Linfield announced that their new manager would be former Northern Ireland striker, Warren Feeney. Less than a quarter of an hour after the Glenavon game had finished, the Blues Board was confirming what had been one of the worst-kept secrets in local football. Warren Feeney would be coming home to manage the team he had supported as a boy.[1]

After Jeffrey had indicated he would be standing down, the Linfield Board advertised his position, then whittled their way through the applications. Incredibly, this was the first time in 24 years that the club had undertaken such a process – both Trevor Anderson and David Jeffrey had been promoted from within. Feeney's route to the Blues hot seat was thus significantly different to that of his two predecessors. What he did share with Anderson and Jeffrey was limited managerial experience at the time of taking up the job. Feeney's apprenticeship had been short, serving less than a year as assistant manager of English non-league side, Salisbury City. Furthermore, he was still in the process of completing his UEFA Pro Licence (a necessary requirement for managing in the top division of any member UEFA state). That said, his playing CV was impressive. Feeney had spent his entire career in the professional game on the mainland, plying his trade with Bournemouth, Stockport County, Luton Town, Cardiff City and Plymouth Argyle amongst others. He had also represented his country on almost 50 occasions.[2]

Warren Feeney was also steeped in the history and traditions of Linfield. His father, Warren Feeney Senior, had represented the Blues, and so had his grandfather, Jim Feeney. As a boy, Warren was a regular at Windsor Park, where he cheered on his Linfield idols. One of his most cherished memories as a fan was the climax of the 1993/94 season, when Linfield clinched the title ahead of Glenavon and  Portadown on the final day. A young Warren Feeney was so caught up in the euphoria that he had (along with hundreds of other fans) made his way onto the pitch to celebrate with the players. Linfield was in Feeney's blood. So when the position of manager was advertised, the former international striker put his name forward. He thought, "When a club like this comes along, you might only get one chance at it… this is my club, this is what I want to go for." Feeney interviewed well, impressed the Board, and on the back of this was offered the position.[3]

The new manager would inherit the job at a time of great upheaval. The redevelopment of Windsor began in early May, and work – which included re-laying the pitch as well as tearing down the South and Railway Stands – would render the stadium off-limits until mid-September. This meant that all of the club's early-season League games had to be played away from Windsor, and also that 'home' European commitments would have to take place at an alternative venue.

Linfield had to get used to life on the road – including the club's Europa League campaign, the Blues would play away from Windsor in the first 11 games of 2014/15. They would do so with a much-changed playing outfit. Over the spring-summer of 2014, Warren Feeney remodelled the squad that he had inherited from David Jeffrey. Nine first-team players left during that period. Amongst them were Kyle McVey, James Knowles and Matthew Tipton, who had been at the club for a relatively short time. There were also those who had served for a number of years, having been part of very successful sides. Philip Lowry left for Derry City, Billy Joe Burns joined Crusaders, Alan Blayney moved to Ballymena, whilst Robert Garrett and Mark McAllister headed to Portadown.[4]

Controversially, Blues captain Michael Gault would also join Garrett and McAllister at the mid-Ulster side. This was because a contract offer for the seven-time League winner was withdrawn at the end of the 2013/14 campaign. Feeney's reign had thus started with significant squad trimming and the loss of the club's skipper. Keen to stamp his own identity on the team ahead of a European campaign, the manager brought in new faces to replace those who had left. At the back, Rangers defender Chris Hegarty (who had scored against the Blues in the 2013 friendly between the two clubs) joined, whilst Jamie Richards signed on loan from Plymouth. In the midfield, Stephen Lowry (brother of the departing Philip) came in from Coleraine and later that summer he would be joined by free agent and winger Kirk Millar. Then up top, another free agent Sammy Morrow signed a one-year deal. Judging by Linfield's showing in the Europa League, there were grounds for optimism at the outset of Feeney's stewardship. The Blues made it past Faroese side B36 Torshavn in the opening qualifying round. Then in round two, they produced a stunning first-leg performance against Swedish side AIK Solna.[5]

On 17 July, Linfield played their 100th match in European competition – going into the game, the significance of this statistic was not lost on the players. Indeed, as striker Andy Waterworth has pointed out, the club's heritage in European football is something that Linfield players are always well aware of: "As players we feel we don't always live up to the club's size" in such competition. Yet that evening at Mourneview Park (where the Blues were playing their home European fixtures), Waterworth and his teammates would in fact exceed all expectations. AIK went into the game as clear favourites. They were after all a full-time side with seven internationals, and even had a player, Celso Borges, who had just made it to the quarter-finals of the World Cup with Costa Rica. But it was Feeney's men that looked the stronger, as they won 1-0. Linfield contained AIK throughout the game, and as the *Belfast Telegraph* stated, Blues "keeper Johnny Tuffey would have anticipated a busier evening". The only goal on the night came in the 87th minute, when substitute Waterworth beat the Swedish defence and then their keeper with a powerful run and finish.[6]

For the second season running, Linfield had pulled off a quite remarkable result in Europe. The win in Xanthi followed by this victory over AIK were incredible achievements for a part-time outfit. However, just like against Xanthi, taking the tie on aggregate proved beyond the reach of Linfield. Out in Sweden, AIK won 2-0, meaning it was the full-timers who progressed to the next round. The step up in class from the Irish League to AIK Solna and Skoda Xanthi was huge. For Linfield's part-timers to have beaten both sides within the space of a year was a credit to the club and to Northern Irish football more generally. By the same token, there was no shame in going out to sides that could boast a wealth of international talent, and had players without work commitments, who trained daily.

As a part-time club in the modern era, the Blues will almost certainly never again scale the heights of previous Linfield teams. Reaching the quarter-final of a European competition is out of the question. Indeed, making it through the qualifying rounds seems unlikely. Circumstances would have to change beyond all recognition for the latter to happen. A side like Linfield, with a turnover of less than £1 million, cannot bankroll a squad of full-time players to compete at the required level. Irish League clubs are thus resigned to early-summer European exits – that is just the reality. However, allowing for lowered expectations in European competition (and the glamour that goes with it), the local media's coverage of Northern Irish teams in UEFA competitions has been disappointing. When Waterworth scored past AIK, the goal was not screened on either BBC Northern Ireland or UTV. Local television had no highlights package of the game whatsoever. Defeating Solna was a significant achievement, but as former Blues boss turned *Sunday Life* columnist David Jeffrey put it, "judging by the [media] coverage... you'd be forgiven for wondering if the Blues... had even been in action at all".[7]

At a time when football was enjoying almost saturation levels of television coverage, the fact that Waterworth's winner did not grace the small screen was telling. It seemed that local broadcasters were not fussed on sending cameras to what was a significant fixture. This could not have contrasted more starkly with the profile of the game on the mainland. During that 2014/15 season, the English Premier League would announce a domestic TV deal worth £85 million per club per year! This staggering level of investment, which Sky Sports and BT Sport were stumping up between them, indicated just how valuable an asset football could be. In 2014, Northern Irish sides – and indeed the local game in general – could only dream of such prestige and glamour. It was thus a disappointment that around the time England's top-flight clubs were signing their eye-watering television rights deal, Sky Sports pulled its coverage of the local game. Not only was this a financial setback for the League (teams had been earning £5,000 a game on Sky), it was a blow in terms of exposure.[8]

Losing the Sky Sports coverage was far from ideal, yet as one media partnership was ending, another was beginning. At the outset of the 2014/15 campaign, the Irish League struck a long-term agreement with Trackchamp to stream games live on the internet. Over the course of a season, cameras situated at each ground would screen more than 250 matches to a worldwide audience on the web. The move was innovative, and was soon hailed as a success. Not long after the deal was signed, some games were pulling in online viewing figures of 35,000. This provided a real boost to local football. However, the good news was not confined to the League's international presence. The 2014/15 campaign witnessed a considerable jump in attendances at games across the Irish League. By the halfway point of the season, gates were up just shy of 13 per cent on the same time the previous year. Given the dramatic rise in crowds, League bosses had much to be happy about.[9]

The rise in attendances had coincided with – and also seemed to vindicate – a restructuring of the local game's governance. Back in 2013, a newly formed body, the Northern Ireland Football League (NIFL), had assumed responsibility for the Irish League, and there was cautious optimism that it could, in the words of *News Letter* columnist Liam Beckett, "arrest the gradual decline in our sport". For years, perceptions of decline, and of course actual decline, had blighted the local game.[10]

Way back in 1985, former Blues midfielder Peter Dornan was bemoaning that, "Football is stagnant here." Yet over the decades that followed, things had only appeared to worsen. The depressing developments in European competition were symptomatic of this. Complaints about standards were commonplace, but prescriptions to remedy the ailments were hard to come by. Along the way, government bodies charged with finding solutions had fallen by the wayside. At the turn of the Millennium the Stormont Executive, directed by the then Sports Minister Michael McGimpsey, appointed a Task Force to advise local football on its future. Ultimately, this had proved nothing more than a talking shop. Indeed, the Task Force commissioned report would do little other than gather dust. So in 2013 it was hoped that NIFL could succeed where those who had gone before had failed.[11]

Essentially, NIFL was undertaking a job of rebranding and reinvigorating the Irish League. Given the associated difficulties of such a venture, those at the top of the organisation brought on board experience to help see their vast assignment through. Peter Dornan, who had berated the local game's stagnation in the mid-1980s, was appointed an independent director of the body. Away from football, he had carved out a successful legal career. Someone like Dornan could thus bring both an impressive playing CV and considerable professional expertise to the table. NIFL also engaged the services of those outside Northern Irish football. UEFA advisory manager Tom Gorrisen, who had helped reshape the Europa League and European Championships as well as football in Belgium and the Netherlands, was brought in as a consultant. NIFL managing director Andrew Johnston explained that having this input from Europe's governing body was vital. In early December 2013 he stated: "UEFA share our ambitions and they're happy to help us in every way possible."[12]

Johnston was speaking at what was dubbed the launch of NIFL's new vision. Less than half a year after assuming responsibility for the day-to-day business of the League, the body was outlining its plan of action and also instigating a consultation process. On the night of 4 December 2013, Johnston indicated that "the time [was] right for a review... the status quo [was] no longer feasible". The review that he was referring to would be far-reaching, and would involve stakeholders right across the game. During early 2014, clubs, supporters, the media and sponsors were all invited to air their views on the future of local football. After the consultation period ended, the data collated was analysed, then shaped into proposals that were brought before NIFL's June 2014 AGM. These included provision for capping the size of squads, the introduction of a four-team playoff for a Europa League spot, as well as mandatory Thursday and Friday night League games.[13]

These were radical proposals, and considering that local football had not always embraced change, it was a shock that they were approved by almost 90 per cent of clubs. Acknowledging this, NIFL chairman Adrian Teer maintained that the "overwhelming [vote] was maybe a surprise", though he also stated that "the endorsement [was] a very welcome one". NIFL's Andrew Johnston would echo these sentiments, and described the vote as "a huge step in the right direction". It was therefore on the back of a momentous decision that the 2014/15 domestic season began, and given the dramatic bounce in attendance, it seemed fans were receptive to the changes. Of course, there were other factors that brought more supporters through the turnstiles, and when the gate figures were released in March 2015, Andrew Johnston was quick to acknowledge them. Johnston pointed to clubs improving their engagement with their local communities, as well as upping their game on social media. He also attributed the rise to "the competitiveness of the season and the fact [that by then] six teams [had] led the League".[14]

Linfield were one of those six teams; however, by March they sat in second place, behind leaders Crusaders. It would be fair to say that up to this point, Feeney's first campaign had been a mixed bag. A late-August exit to second-tier Ballyclare Comrades in the League Cup was the low point of a rocky beginning to the campaign. Yet after this unsure start, Feeney's men hit form, and by the end of the year the Blues sat top of the Irish League. Unfortunately it was a position they could not maintain. New Year's Day 2015 saw Linfield go down 2-1 away to Crusaders, and this signalled the start of another sticky patch. Defeat brought the North Belfast side within a point of the Blues, and as Linfield would struggle to hold their form, Crusaders soon went top. Not even the signing of former Northern Ireland international (and life-long Linfield fan) Grant McCann could halt the Blues' indifferent run of results. In joining Linfield, McCann was fulfilling a childhood dream – though his time at the club was short-lived. During a one-month spell he would pull on the blue shirt on six occasions, before returning to coach at his former club, Peterborough United.[15]

In Grant McCann's brief stay, the club won three games, drew two and suffered one loss. This form was clearly far from that of a title-winning side. Furthermore, the two draws and the loss had one worrying theme – in each of the matches, the Blues had taken the lead but had failed to see off their opponents. The draws had come against Ballinamallard and Cliftonville, whilst Portadown had fought back to win 2-1 at Windsor after conceding early on. Not only were the Blues struggling to see out a lead; it seemed at times that Feeney's men were only performing in one half of a game.

This trend continued in the first match that followed McCann's departure for Peterborough. At the end of February, Linfield travelled to Portadown for an Irish Cup seventh-round fixture. On this occasion, it was not a case of Linfield throwing away a lead; instead the match was effectively over when Portadown went 3-0 up in the 43rd minute. As Warren Feeney fumed after the game: "We gave ourselves a mountain to climb with that first-half performance." A much-improved second-half display reduced the deficit to 3-2 by the end of the game, but this was not enough to keep the Blues in the cup.[16]

On too many occasions throughout 2014/15, the Blues could not maintain the intensity needed over 90 minutes to win matches; and just as this had cost them in the Irish Cup, it would ultimately derail their title bid. After going down 1-0 to Glenavon on 28 March, Warren Feeney admitted that Linfield's League challenge was over. Crusaders had taken full advantage of Linfield's post-Christmas form, and with five games left sat nine points ahead of the Blues. Mathematically Linfield could still catch the Crues, but given how the North Belfast side was playing, Feeney knew the game was up. If that final weekend in March had brought about a sobering realisation for Linfield fans, the opposite was the case for Windsor Park's other residents – the Northern Irish national team. The day after Linfield went down 1-0 to Glenavon, Northern Ireland would defeat Finland 2-1 to stay second in their Euro 2016 qualifying group. The win extended their lead over third-place Hungary to four points. Given that the qualification process was now halfway, and that two teams from each group would automatically be going to the finals the following summer, Northern Ireland were sitting in a very strong position.[17]

Caught in the excitement of it all, supporters in Windsor's North and Kop Stands (the only two parts of the ground open with the on-going redevelopment) cheered each goal with gusto and partied at the final whistle. As was always the case, the celebrations were loudest and most boisterous in the Kop. Indeed, such was the excitement generated that some fans claimed they had felt the structure shake. Whether or not that actually happened, evidence of damage to the Kop was visible less than 48 hours after the game. Cracks appeared at the side of the stand, and worryingly, over the days that followed, they got bigger. As thoughts turned to the potential disaster that had been avoided, the IFA was quick to point out that prior to the game the stadium had passed all relevant safety assessments. That said, it was clear that the Kop (like the South and Railway Stands before it) would have to come down. The cracks pointed to structural subsidence, therefore this was not a case of patching things up. A new stand would have to be built.[18]

On the plus side, Windsor would be getting three brand new stands instead of two. Yet this also meant that the completion date for the refurbished stadium would be set back significantly. Before the damage to the Kop had occurred, it was expected that the new Windsor would be finished by the autumn of 2015. Now almost a whole year would be added on. This was obviously a huge cause of frustration. Playing at a stadium undergoing renovation had already brought many practical challenges. The first 11 games of 2014/15 had been played away from Windsor, and with the Kop coming down, so were the last seven. As Linfield's title challenge fizzled out, it did so on the road. Keen to stress that he was "not one to make excuses", Warren Feeney refused to blame his side's second-place finish on the stadium disruption.[19]

Crusaders had been the most consistent team throughout the season, and Feeney acknowledged that they were worthy champions. He explained that the Shore Road men had "a strong squad" and were "very good at what they did". Yet whilst the Blues boss was right to stress that the Crues were deserved Gibson Cup winners, the upheaval of Linfield's stadium redevelopment should not be downplayed. Aside from having to play away from Windsor at the start and end of the 2014/15 season, when the Blues did play at home they were doing so in unfamiliar surroundings. With the South and Railway Stands bulldozed, Windsor was an open stadium exposed to the elements. As Warren Feeney put it, Linfield were effectively "playing on a building site". That was never easy to get used to, and nor were the temporary changing rooms that were used during the redevelopment. Feeney explained: "Psychologically, players are used to their own routines at a home ground." With all the upset of the on-going building work, these could never be established.[20]

The dislocation that resulted from playing at Windsor was, however, nothing compared to the difficulties that were encountered when trying to prepare for games. During 2014/15 the Blues trained at eight different venues. Midgley Park – the club's training ground, located behind the Kop Stand – could not be used owing to the stadium construction work. According to Feeney, his players "felt like cuckoos at times", given the nomadic nature of club training. Yet it was more than a case of having to get used to new surroundings on a regular basis. On occasion, players did not even know where an evening's training venue was until four o'clock that afternoon. Andy Waterworth explained that at one point, a venue was switched from a grass pitch to an artificial surface at the last minute, meaning players turned up with the wrong footwear to train in. As Waterworth sighed, "It just wasn't Linfield." Similarly, Jamie Mulgrew contended: "I think the new manager already had enough of a job in trying to make his own stamp on the team, without having to deal with all [these training difficulties] as well."[21]

It would be fair to say that Windsor's redevelopment had caused havoc for the Blues in Feeney's first season. However, the IFA had also suffered in all this. Without the South Stand in operation, the stadium's capacity for Northern Ireland internationals stood at just over 10,000; this was 4,000 less than it had held before the refurbishment began. Then when the Kop had to come down, the capacity fell to the 6,000 mark. Given that Northern Ireland were due to play their next European Championships qualifier at Windsor in June, against Romania, local football's governing body had a dilemma on their hands. Four thousand tickets had been sold for the Kop Stand, and the IFA would somehow have to accommodate these fans. There was talk in the press of moving the game to rugby's Kingspan stadium, or even outside the Province. Yet incredibly, in the 10 weeks that followed the cracks appearing in the Kop, the IFA had Windsor ready to host the Romanians.[22]

IFA chief executive Patrick Nelson explained that in the three weeks after the damage had been spotted, a "project team [had] worked tirelessly [on] a plan" to sort out the mess. This entailed accelerating work on the Railway Stand as well as on the corner between the Railway and South Stands. This would allow fans with Kop tickets to move to the other end of the ground. The plan was executed with precision, and on 13 June Northern Ireland welcomed the Romanians to Windsor. At the end of 90 minutes the teams had played out a 0-0 draw, ensuring that Northern Ireland's strong qualification campaign rolled on. For those at the game and those who watched on television, it was apparent that Windsor's redevelopment – Kop catastrophe aside – was progressing well. The partially completed Railway Stand looked impressive, and this boded well for the remaining work. After the despair of having to tear down a stand, there was now a buzz and an air of excitement about the progress being made on the stadium.[23]

However, this buzz around the refurbishment was accompanied by unease at Linfield over what appeared to be an attempt by some within the IFA to diminish the club's identity at Windsor Park. As *Sunday Life* columnist and former Blues boss David Jeffrey railed: "The [IFA] are slowly making sure Linfield FC, once proud owners of the venue, are losing all identity from the famous stadium. Sure, we have a Chief Executive who refuses to call it by its proper name and instead constantly refers to it as the National Stadium". For whatever reason, there seemed to be a concerted effort to drop the name 'Windsor Park' when referring to the ground. This contravened the terms of the stadium agreement, and was demeaning to the Blues. Linfield had played at Windsor since 1905, and the ground was an integral part of the club's history. So when it appeared there were elements at the IFA attempting to change the stadium's title, a backlash was only natural.[24]

For Linfield manager Warren Feeney, such posturing was an unwelcome distraction. With the Blues and the IFA sharing the stadium, he could not get his head around why some were snubbing the ground's name. A frustrated Feeney explained: "It's Windsor Park, it always will be Windsor Park... Linfield play at Windsor, Northern Ireland play at Windsor; that's not going to change." Yet for all the protestations coming from Linfield quarters, the apparent efforts to dilute the ground's identity continued. Indeed by March of 2016, the press was reporting that the relationship between the club's Board and the IFA had broken down over the issue. The *Belfast Telegraph* told its readership that the "name of the stadium [was causing] particular problems". Elaborating on this, the paper revealed that such was the concern at Board level, the Blues had lodged "an official complaint to the IFA".[25]

Regrettably, the disagreement over Windsor's title was far from the only matter that the club and local football's governing body were at loggerheads over. Issues around the colour of seats in the stadium, as well as when Linfield were allowed to train at the ground, had provoked acrimonious disputes between the two parties. In the course of sharing a stadium, hitches along the way were only to be expected. Yet as Linfield chairman Jim Kerr told the press: "While we may agree to differ on certain things, I would hope that going forward we can have a positive relationship." Effectively, Kerr was implying that the IFA needed to start treating their partners at Linfield with respect.[26]

The straining of relations was not healthy for Windsor's future; nor was it befitting of the stadium under construction. As the June 2015 Northern Ireland vs Romania game had shown, an impressive ground was taking shape – and Windsor was becoming a stadium that both Linfield and Northern Ireland could be proud of. Warren Feeney indicated at the start of the 2015/16 campaign that his team was once again enjoying their football at the Park. Considering that his side won their first seven domestic games on the bounce, his players' contentment was appreciable, though there was surely more to this strong start than the improvements made to Windsor. This was Feeney's second season in charge, and his players were getting to know their manager better. Also, the Blues boss had added to his squad to further mould his team. After releasing forward Peter Thompson (who went out with a record of 230 goals in 431 matches), Feeney brought in defender Mark Stafford, midfielder David Kee and striker Guy Bates. And with thumping wins over the likes of Coleraine (3-1), Portadown (3-0) and Ballymena (4-0), it seemed all was well at Windsor. However, in mid-September Feeney's side would endure a major wobble.[27]

Linfield travelled to Seaview on 12 September and were dismantled 3-0 by reigning League holders, Crusaders. According to the *News Letter*, the scoreline reflected "the utter dominance of the champions", whilst Crues boss Stephen Baxter crowed: "We won every key battle and we were strong all over the pitch." The frailties of the previous campaign appeared to be alive and well; and though Feeney's side responded with a 5-1 victory over Warrenpoint, Linfield would concede three in each of the two League games that followed. In the first of these, the Blues defeated Glenavon 4-3 at Windsor. Then in the second, on 3 October, they drew 3-3 (after being 2-0 up) away to Cliftonville. At the end of an absorbing encounter, Warren Feeney came over to the Linfield fans for what turned out to be the last time. Going into the game, speculation had been rife that Feeney would be leaving to become assistant manager at Newport County, a team that resided in League Two (England's fourth tier). Until then the Blues boss had been coy with the press on the subject, but at the start of the next week, he made the jump.[28]

At Newport Feeney would link up with John Sheridan, a manager he had played under at Plymouth Argyle. This was obviously appealing, but it was the lure of a return to the professional game and moving back to his family – who had stayed on the mainland all the time he was at Linfield – that was too much for Feeney to resist. After signalling that he was leaving, he told the press: "It was the right opportunity for me to move home with the kids and also to get back into full-time football." The Blues Board had offered an improved contract extension, yet this could not dissuade Feeney, and as a resigned editorial in the Linfield programme explained, the club had "reluctantly accepted [his] understandable request".[29]

Reflecting on the departure, *Belfast Telegraph* journalist Graham Luney chose to play devil's advocate. Luney posed the question: "How many of us would turn down an exciting job offer that makes sense from a financial and family perspective?" He then remarked that it was revealing when "a side struggling at the bottom of League Two [Newport were already relegation candidates] can entice away the manager of the biggest and most successful club on the Island of Ireland. And not just any manager – someone who has always supported Linfield." This reality check was depressing, especially given that Feeney was moving to an assistantship, not a full managerial role. After only a year and a half at the semi-professional Blues, he had jumped at the chance to get back into the full-time game.[30]

The experience of Feeney walking out on Linfield was chastening. However, it did not stop the club's Board from appointing another ambitious young manager who had recently finished a professional playing career on the mainland. On 14 October (eight days after Feeney left), the Blues announced that David Healy would become their new manager. For Linfield fans, and for that matter, general Irish League supporters, Healy needed no introduction. Famous for his winner against England in 2005 and his hat-trick against Spain in 2006, David Healy was footballing royalty in the Province. Indeed with 36 strikes to his name, the former forward was Northern Ireland's all-time leading goalscorer.

In his club career, Healy had turned out for Preston North End, Leeds United, Fulham and Sunderland amongst others. He had also played for two of his supported teams – Manchester United and Glasgow Rangers. As Healy explained: "Ask anyone from Northern Ireland, you support a Scottish club, an English club and a Northern Irish club... I was fortunate to play for my English club, Man United, albeit three times. I was fortunate again to join a boyhood supported club, Rangers... Then to be offered the chance to manage my Northern Irish club [Linfield] was something I could not turn down."[31]

In his teenage years, David Healy made it along to watch the Blues whenever he could. As a trainee at Manchester United and living away from home, this was something that was not always easy. Back when he was 18 years old and had 10 days off at Christmas, he had struggled to source a ticket for a Boxing Day clash at the Oval. In this instance, Healy turned to a friend he had known since playing with Northern Ireland schoolboy squads – one Warren Feeney. Fortunately, after they met on the Newtownards Road, a ticket was sorted.[32]

Almost 20 years later in the autumn of 2015, Healy and Feeney would again meet with Linfield of central importance to the rendezvous, but in rather different circumstances. The (by then) former internationals had remained close throughout their careers, and prior to leaving his position at the Blues, Feeney wanted to sound Healy out on taking the manager's job. Over a game of golf, Feeney explained that it looked like he would be leaving to link up with his former manager John Sheridan at Newport County. Feeney then asked his old friend if he fancied taking up the reins at the Blues. Healy's response was: "Absolutely no chance Warren! Are you mad?"[33]

Since retiring from playing football, Healy had coached at Fleetwood Town and with Northern Ireland development squads. These were roles which he considered "cosy", and his initial reluctance to contemplate the pressure-cooker atmosphere of Linfield was understandable. Yet the more he thought about what Feeney had suggested, the more appealing it became. A couple of days after Feeney had walked, Linfield Board member Jack Grundie asked Healy if he would like to get a coffee. Grundie had for years served in various IFA roles as well as on the Linfield Board, and was someone who David Healy knew well. That said, the former international striker thought to himself, "Jack, I've known you for 10 years, and you've never asked me for a coffee." Thus fully aware that Grundie had approached him on Linfield's behalf, Healy agreed to meet with three of the club's Board members the next day. Preliminary discussions about the vacant position were held, with both parties asking questions of the other, before another meeting, the following week was arranged. By the time this came about, Healy had made up his mind – he would become the club's new boss.[34]

When Healy informed his father that he was taking the job, he was met with the question, "Are you sure this one is for you?" Whilst extremely proud that David had been offered the role, Clifford Healy knew his son would at times endure harsh criticism. The Linfield faithful would expect success, and the glare of the local media would, as always, be focused on Windsor. That was simply part and parcel of the Linfield remit, and given Healy's prominence in Northern Irish football, press interest would be raised even further. Yet despite how well known he was, there were elements in the local media that had misjudged and misread the new Blues boss. There was a perception that as a 'nice guy', David Healy would struggle at Linfield. *Sunday Life* sports editor Paul Ferguson encapsulated this viewpoint when he wrote that if the new manager was to succeed, "he will need to develop a new thick skin and quickly".[35]

Because Healy had always come across as polite in front of the camera, and because as a player he was not one to waste words, the misconception held that he was soft. Yet this was far from the case, and very soon his new team would see there were no grounds for the fallacy. After a solid enough start to life under the new manager (the Blues won three of their first four games), a disastrous stretch followed, and the players soon felt Healy's wrath. During November his side played four games and lost the lot. In the first half of the month, the club went down at Windsor to Crusaders and Cliftonville, then went on to lose at Glenavon and Portadown. It was after the third of these defeats, away to Glenavon, that Healy's players learnt first-hand that their new boss was no soft touch. At full time, the young manager let fly with a 15-minute tirade in the Mourneview dressing room –  telling his players in "no uncertain terms" that "standards were not good enough".[36]

Now, as Linfield were beaten at Portadown a week later, the Blues boss could have been forgiven for wondering what he had to do to get a win – especially given that the press was stating this was the club's worst losing streak since 1997. Yet rather than wallowing in the despair of it all, Healy came out fighting. In the Sunday papers he maintained: "People enjoy kicking Linfield when they're down, but Linfield will always bounce back… Linfield will rise again." The manager was desperate for a resurgence in form, and a week later he got it. A 1-0 home win over Coleraine at the start of December would signal the beginning of a two and a half month unbeaten stretch in the League.[37]

When the next loss came, it did so (once again) away to Portadown, and was in fact one of only two League defeats between the start of December and the end of the Gibson Cup campaign. Healy had successfully galvanised the squad he inherited, and with the additions of midfielder Ross Gaynor who arrived from Cork, and youngster Paul Smyth who graduated through the Windsor youth set-up, his Blues team looked very strong. However, the second loss after Christmas, which came on 9 April, arrived in what was pretty much a title-defining match against Crusaders.

Going into the encounter, the Crues sat five points clear of the second-placed Blues, and it seemed for most of the game that this margin would be maintained. Then in the 89th minute, the Shore Road men went ahead through Gavin Whyte, before Jordan Forsythe made sure of the result deep into added time. Crusaders had won the game 2-0 and stretched their lead to eight points with only four matches remaining. It was thus clear that for the second year running, they would be lifting the Gibson Cup. Ultimately it was the wretched November that had cost the Blues. Such a run was always going to be hard to come back from, meaning that despite the strong showing in the second half of the season, the Blues had come up short.[38]

Unfortunately, going close without succeeding was something Linfield had become accustomed to. This was, after all, the club's third straight runners-up finish. Furthermore, the Blues had fallen short in that season's County Antrim Shield, and were about to do so in the Irish Cup as well. On 7 May 2016, Healy's side went down 2-0 to Glenavon in the showpiece final. After starting brightly Linfield soon lost their way, and were well off-pace in a game that the Lurgan side dominated. Healy's men had flattered to deceive on the big occasion, and they knew it. Captain Andy Waterworth was ashamed of how his team had fared. Likewise Sean Ward ruefully bemoaned that "too many of us didn't turn up", whilst for veteran Jamie Mulgrew the loss brought about the "lowest" feelings he had experienced during his career.[39]

Not one to mince words, David Healy blasted his side in the following day's papers. A furious Blues boss exclaimed: "Right now, I'm hurting… We didn't put up the sort of fight I expect from a Linfield side." He added: "We don't have the ability to get over the line." The "ability" which Healy spoke of had been lacking for four seasons (in that time the club had lifted a solitary County Antrim Shield). This was something that had to be rectified. Thus the smarting manager went on: "As a football club, Linfield have always fought back. And as a manager, I will fight back from this… Next year is going to be a massive season for this football club and it is a massive season for me, personally." Healy knew that success was a prerequisite at Linfield, and he would have to deliver it soon. Therefore as soon as the season had passed, he was scouring the transfer market, looking at how he could

strengthen his squad. Half a month after the disappointment of the cup final, he moved to make his first signing and brought in a player with experience of the highest level. In late May, former Manchester United, West Ham United and Olympiacos goalkeeper, Roy Carroll, agreed terms with the Blues.[40]

With Carroll joining, the club was getting the service of a player who (at Manchester United) had won both an English Premier League and an FA Cup. Not only that, he was signing a couple of weeks before heading to France for the European Championships, as part of the Northern Ireland national squad. Carroll had earned his place on the back of his performances with League Two side, Notts County, but at the tournament he would be registered as a Linfield player. In a way there was a certain symmetry with how Mark Caughey had gone to the World Cup in Mexico 30 years earlier. Caughey's performances with the Blues during the 1985/86 season had propelled him into Billy Bingham's squad, but by the start of the tournament he had moved to Scottish side Hibernian.[41]

Back in 1986, Mark Caughey was a young man who hoped that by leaving Linfield, he could carve out a career in the professional game.

At 38, Roy Carroll on the other hand was coming home to the Province in the twilight of his career. Not only were their individual circumstances vastly dissimilar, there was also a telling difference about the respective squads they were a part of. In 1986, Caughey was not alone as a player who had starred in the Irish League and made it onto the plane to Mexico. Veteran Coleraine keeper Jim Platt was also included in the squad. Thirty years later, Michael O'Neill found no space for any player that had just finished the Irish League season.

Unquestionably, in the years between Linfield's 1986 centenary and Roy Carroll joining in 2016, the local game had drifted further and further away from top-level football. By 2016, Northern Irish sides are well used to the depressing reality of entering (and exiting) European competition in the qualifying rounds. Although back in the mid-1980s local clubs had experienced little joy in European football, they nevertheless competed (by virtue of an open draw) with the 'big boys'. What is more, the changes brought about in European football have in these 30 years contributed to a widening financial gap between the haves and the have-nots. The Irish League is in many ways so much worse off than it was in the mid-1980s. The routine glamour friendlies that a club like Linfield could boast of back then are gone. 'Big' clubs are rare visitors these days, and they are unlikely to take a chance on players from the League. The days of someone like Tommy Wright leaving to sign for Newcastle United in England's top flight, or George O'Boyle moving to a club like Bordeaux, appear to be over.

Yet despite these realities, the Irish League in 2016 seems much more self-assured than it was 30 years previously. Peter Dornan's 1985 charge that "Football is stagnant here" could not be levelled today. Indeed, when during the 2015/16 campaign former Northern Ireland international Colin O'Neill rubbished the local game, his assertions were confidently rebuked by a wide cross-section of the League. In early November 2015, O'Neill told the press that the quality of local football was "awful" and had been "deteriorating for some time". Two days later, the *Belfast Telegraph* was carrying rebuttals from supporters, players, management and administrators. Perhaps the most confident counter came from former Linfield striker, and by then Crusaders manager, Stephen Baxter. The Crues boss maintained: "Our product has never been on a better footing and can go forward from strength to strength."[42]

Baxter's assertion was, of course, partly grounded in the rising number of punters coming through the gates at Irish League games. For years the local game had watched crowds dwindle; but over the past two seasons, the marked increase in attendances had been notable. In keeping with this trend, the 2016 Irish Cup final was the best attended in 10 years – 12,000 fans would pack into the nearly complete, new Windsor Park for the decider. And whilst defeat on the day was a bitter pill for Blues fans to swallow, as they surveyed the stadium taking shape there was much to be excited about.[43]

The new Windsor is something that Linfield can be proud of. With its completion in the autumn of 2016, the facilities for fans and players alike provide outstanding benefit for the club. From the offices, to the shop, to the stands which generations of supporters will occupy every other Saturday – the stadium offers a bright future for the Blues. Furthermore, the club will be able to stamp an identity on the ground, and new memories will soon be created to go alongside all those special days and nights at the old Windsor. Moving from the old to the new has been tough, and the team's struggles on the pitch are emblematic of this. However, as Blues manager David Healy stated in November 2015, "Linfield will rise again."[44]

# Notes

### Introduction
[1] *Look at Linfield* 19 Oct. 1985; Brodie, *Linfield: 100*, p. 2.

[2] *Ireland's Saturday Night*, 4 May 1985.

[3] *ISN* 4 May 1985; Brodie, *Linfield: 100*, p. 186

[4] *ISN* 4 May 1985; Spaaij, *Understanding Football*, pp. 76, 82; Jefferys, *Sport and Politics*, p. 183.

[5] Goldblatt, *The Game*, p. 13; *Daily Telegraph* 15 Feb. 2013; Ridley, *Golden Sky*, p. 5; Rodríguez, Késenne, and Koning (eds), *Competitive Sport*, *Birmingham Mail* 21 July 2011; *Observer* 3 Apr. 2005; p. 39; Hornby, *Fever Pitch*, pp. 158-59.

[6] *ISN* 17 Aug. 1985.

### Chapter 1
[1] *Belfast Telegraph* 26 July 26 1985.

[2] *LAL* 14 Sept. 1985; Martin McGaughey interview with author 11 Oct. 2016.

[3] *BT* 20 Nov. 1985; Martin McGaughey interview with author 11 Oct. 2016.

[4] *LAL* 16 Nov. 1985; *BT* 23 Dec. 1985; LFC minute book 1985-93, entry 24 Feb. 1986; Lee Doherty interview with author 8 Feb. 2014; Roy Coyle interview with author 22 Apr. 2014.

[5] *BT* 18 Apr. 1986; *Belfast News Letter* 18 Apr. 1986; David Jeffrey interview with author 26 June 2014.

[6] *LAL* 31 Aug. 1985; *BT* 20 June 1985; LFC minute book 1985-93, entry 20 Mar. 1986.

[7] Markovits, and Hellerman *Offside*, pp. 168-69; *ISN* 22 June 1985.

[8] *LAL* 6 May 1986.

[9] *BT* 17 May 1986,

[10] *ISN* 20 May 1986.

[11] Committee of Inquiry into Crowd Safety, p. 29; LFC minute book 1985-93, entry 8 July 1985.

[12] *BT* 19 Mar. 1986.

[13] *ISN* 16 Aug. 1986.

[14] *BT* 18 Aug. 1986; *BNL* 20 Aug. 1986; Roy Coyle interview with author 22 Apr. 2014; George Dunlop interview with author 22 Apr. 2014; Lee Doherty interview with author 8 Feb. 2014.

[15] *BT* 19 Aug. 1986; LFC minute book 1985-93, entry 8 Sept. 1986; *BT* 20 Aug. 1986.

[16] *BT* 27 Sept. 2006; *BT* 8 Sept. 1986.

[17] *BNL* 11 Sept. 1986; *BT* 11 Sept. 1986; LFC minute book 1985-93, entry 8 Sept. 1986.

[18] *BNL* 11 July 1986.

[19] *BT* 18 Sept. 1986.

[20] *BT* 2 Oct. 1986; Roy Coyle interview with author 22 Apr. 2014.

[21] George Dunlop interview with author 22 Apr. 2014; David Jeffrey interview with author 26 June 2014.

[22] *LAL* 17 Jan. 1987.

[23] George Dunlop interview with author 22 Apr. 2014; Lee Doherty interview with author 8 Feb. 2014; Martin McGaughey interview with author 11 Oct. 2016; David Jeffrey interview with author 26 June 2014.

[24] The IFA implemented the 3pm kick-off throughout the 1985/86 season. *LAL* 26 Dec. 1986; *ISN* 31 Jan. 1987.

[25] *ISN* 21 Mar. 1987; *BNL* 23 Mar. 1987; *BNL* 11 May 1987.

[26] *LAL* 12 Nov. 1988; *LAL* Nov. 25 1997.

[27] *BT* 29 May 1987; *BNL* 29 May 1987.

[28] On top of the North American tour, other opportunities were rebuffed. The Blues turned down two exhibition games in Malta during the Christmas period of 1986. Then in March 1987, an invitation to a 10-team tournament in Iraq was rejected. The tournament offered attractive financial remuneration and the opportunity to test the club against the Iraqi international team. However, the off-season timing of the games, 16-26 June, precluded Linfield's participation. *LAL* 26 Dec. 1986; *LAL* 7 Mar. 1987; *LAL* 14 Dec. 1985; *LAL* 26 Mar. 1988; *BNL* 11 July 1987; *BNL* 27 Feb. 1988; *BT* 23 July 1988.

## Chapter 2

[1] *BT* 26 Aug. 1987.

[2] *LAL* 29 Aug. 1987; *BNL* 28 Aug. 1987; *BT* 27 Aug. 1987.

[3] *BNL* 5 Sept. 1987.

[4] The UTV apology and assurance were recounted in quotes attributed to John Crossen. Magee, 'English Beer', p. 132; Scott, *End to End*, p. 411. *BNL* 5 Sept. 1987.

[5] *BNL* 16 Sept. 1987; *BT* 17 Sept. 1987; *BT* 1 Oct. 1987.

[6] *BT* 1 Oct. 1987; *BT* 16 Nov. 1987.

[7] Gillespie, *Years of Darkness*, p. 182; *BNL* 3 Dec. 1987.

[8] *BNL* 4 Dec. 1987.

[9] *BNL* 18 Jan. 1987.

[10] *BNL* 3 Feb. 1987; *BT* 3 Feb. 1987.

[11] *LAL* 26 Mar. 1987.

[12] *BT* 25 Apr. 1988; LFC minute book 1985-93, entry 26 May 1987.

[13] *BT* 9 June 1988; Roy Coyle interview with author 22 Apr. 2014; *BT* 4 July 1988.

[14] Derek Brooks, Linfield secretary, reiterated Coyle's claim that religion never entered into transfer negotiation in the *Sunday News* article. Brooks added it was "irresponsible" of the paper to raise the issue. *Sunday News* 10 July 1988; Roy Coyle interview with author 22 Apr. 2014.

[15] Honved were at the time a world-renowned name, made famous by the exploits of star striker Ferenc Puskás – an architect of Hungary's famous 6-3 demolition of England at Wembley in 1953. Puskás was celebrated worldwide as footballing royalty in the aftermath of the game. O'Hara, 'Other Foot', p. 11; Lendvai, *Hungarian Uprising*, pp. 3-4; Fink, Hadler and Schramm (eds), *1956*, p. 16; Brodie, *Linfield: 100*, p. 98.

[16] Esplin and Walker 'Introduction', p. 6; Murray, *Bhoys, Bears*, pp. 31, 44-45.

[17] *SN* 17 July 1988.

[18] *BT* 17 Aug. 1988; *ISN* 3 Sept. 1988; *BT* 5 Sept. 1988; LFC minute book 1985-93, entry 21 Nov. 1988; LFC minute book 1985-93, entry 24 Apr. 1989; *BT* 6 Oct. 1988.

[19] *LAL* 27 Aug. 1988; *BT* 11 Oct. 1988.

[20] David Jeffrey interview with author 26 June 2014; Lee Doherty interview with author 8 Feb. 2014.

[21] *BT* 2 Nov. 1988.

[22] *Irish News*, 30 Nov. 1988; *BNL* 30 Nov. 1988; *BNL* 1 Dec. 1988; *BNL* 2 Dec. 1988.

[23] *BT* 2 Dec. 1988.

[24] *BT* 2 Dec. 1988.

[25] Hill, *Out of His Skin*, pp. 183-184; Black, Crabbe, and Solomos, *Changing Face*, p. 55.

[26] The FA identify 1993 as the year that the body acted to rid the game of racism. Racism in Football, p. 5; *BNL* 11 Jan. 1989.

[27] *BNL* 10 Dec. 1988.

[28] *LAL* 2 Jan. 1989; David Jeffrey interview with author 26 June 2014; Lee Doherty interview with author 8 Feb. 2014.

[29] *LAL* 23 Dec. 1989.

[30] For more on the Hillsborough Disaster, see Scraton, *Hillsborough*. *ISN* 15 Apr. 1989; *ISN* 22 Apr. 1989

[31] *BT* 16 May 1989; Roy Coyle interview with author 22 Apr. 2014.

### Chapter 3

[1] *ISN* 22 Apr. 1989; *BT* 27 July 1989.

[2] *LAL* 19 Aug. 1989; *BT* 8 Sept. 1989; *BT* 12 July 1989.

[3] French side Bordeaux also offered free use of their ground for the fixture. The good relationship between the two clubs after the George O'Boyle transfer was very much in evidence, though Linfield chose to return to Wales for the second game of their European ban. LFC minute book 1985-93, entry 20 July 1989; *LAL* 13 Sept. 1989; *BNL* 12 Sept. 1989; *BT* 14 Sept. 1989; *BNL* 14 Sept. 1989. Smith, *Post-Soviet States*, pp. 28-30; Ponton, *Soviet Era*, pp. 72-73.

[4] *LAL* 7 Oct. 1989; David Jeffrey interview with author 26 June 2014; *BT* 25 Sept. 1989.

[5] *LAL* 7 Oct. 1989; *LAL* 18 Nov. 1989; O'Dochartaigh, *Germany Since,* p.67; George Dunlop interview with author 22 Apr. 2014.

[6] *LAL* 7 Oct. 1989; David Jeffrey interview with author 26 June 2014; Lee Doherty interview with author 8 Feb. 2014; *BT* 26 Sept. 1989.

[7] *BT* 26 Sept. 1989; LFC minute book 1985-93, entry 20 July 1989; *LAL* 7 Oct. 1989; *BNL* 28 Sept. 1989.

[8] *BT* 22 Sept. 1989; *BNL* 6 Nov. 1989.

[9] *BT* 2 Dec. 1989; *LAL* 16 Dec. 1989.

[10] *BNL* 13 Jan. 1990; Roy Coyle interview with author 22 Apr. 2014.

[11] Wangerin, *Soccer*, p. 225; *BT* 5 Feb. 1990.

[12] For more on the Linfield Belfast Celtic riot of 1948, see: Flynn, *Political Football*, pp. 123-48; Coyle, *Paradise Lost*, pp. 77-94; Brodie, *Linfield: 100*, pp. 75-80; Hennessey, *Northern Ireland*, pp. 92, 97-100; *LAL* 24 Feb. 1990.

[13] Celtic officials queried whether there was an option of playing the game behind closed doors. *IN* 16 Feb. 1990; *BT* 14 Feb. 1990.

[14] *BT* 16 Feb. 1990.

[15] *ISN* 17 Feb. 1990; *BNL* 19 Feb. 1990; *IN* 19 Feb. 1990.

[16] *BNL* 19 Feb. 1990; *ITN News Report*, 17 Feb. 1990; *Sunday Life*, 18 February 1990; *IN* 19 Feb. 1990; *SL* 25 Feb. 1990; *Andersonstown News*, 24 Feb. 1990.

[17] *IN* 19 Feb. 1990.

[18] *IN* 19 Feb. 1990; *BT* 21 Feb. 1990.

[19] *IN* 19 Feb. 1990; Cronin, 'Catholics and sport', p. 32.

[20] *LAL* 24 Feb. 1990.

[21] *BT* 23 Mar. 1990; George Dunlop interview with author 22 Apr. 2014

[22] *BT* 30 Mar. 1990.

[23] *BNL* 31 Mar. 1990; George Dunlop interview with author 22 Apr. 2014; *BNL* 4 Apr. 1990; *BT* 4 Apr. 1990; Lee Doherty interview with author 8 Feb. 2014.

[24] *ISN* 31 Mar. 1990; *ISN* 7 Apr. 1990; *BNL* 9 Apr. 1990.

[25] LFC minute book 1985-93, entry 9 Apr. 1990; *BNL* 9 Apr. 1990; *LAL* 17 Apr. 1990; *BNL* 18 Apr. 1990.

[26] *BT* 18 Apr. 1990; *BT* 19 Apr. 1990; *BT* 20 Apr. 1990; Roy Coyle interview with author 22 Apr. 2014.

[27] David Jeffrey interview with author 26 June 2014.

[28] *BNL* 26 Apr. 1990; *BT* 26 Apr. 1990.


**Chapter 4**

[1] *ISN* 5 May 1990.

[2] *LAL* 18 Aug. 1990; *BNL* 31 July 1990.

[3] Brodie, *Linfield: 100*, pp. 141-40; Eric Bowyer interview with author 22 Apr. 2014; *BT* 28 May 1990.

[4] *BT* 28 May 1990; *BNL* 29 May 1990.

[5] *LAL* 18 Aug. 1990.

[6] *LAL* 6 Oct. 1990; *ISN* 6 Oct. 1990; *BT* 7 Nov. 1990.

[7] *BT* 25 Feb. 1991; *BT* 8 Mar. 1991; *ISN* 9 Mar. 1991.

[8] The US faced little competition in bidding for the 1994 World Cup. Only Brazil and Morocco had mounted serious challenges. Brazil's bid lacked government backing, and Morocco's proposal was based on infrastructure that existed mainly on paper. The US offer appeared the safe option. This was important for FIFA. Only a few years earlier, Columbia had withdrawn as hosts of the 1986 finals; FIFA needed a bid it could trust. Wangerin, *Soccer*, p. 228; *LAL* 23 Mar. 1991; Eric Bowyer interview with author 22 Apr. 2014; *LAL* 30 Mar. 1991.

[9] Horton, *World Cup*, p. 50; Wangerin, *Soccer*, p. 229; *BT* 29 Apr. 1991.

[10] Wangerin, *Soccer*, p. 245.

[11] *BT* 29 Apr. 1991; *BNL* 29 Apr. 1991; Tennessee Athletics. 'Neyland Stadium', utsports.com, http://www.utsports.com/facilities/neyland/ accessed 8 Oct. 2016; *BT* 1 May 1991; Eric Bowyer interview with author 22 Apr. 2014.

[12] *ISN* 4 May 1991; *BNL* 4 May 1991.

[13] *ISN* 12 Oct. 1991; *BNL* 14 Oct. 1991.

[14] *BT* 3 Dec. 1991; *BT* 4 Dec. 1991.

[15] *BT* 5 Dec. 1991; *BNL* 5 Dec. 1991.

[16] *LAL* 21 Dec. 1991; *One Team in Ulster* 18, 1991.

[17] Jary, Horne, and Bucke, 'Football "Fanzines"', p. 581; Steve James cited in Jenkins and Holly (eds), *Survival*, p. viii; Gillespie, 'Fanzines', pp. 1, 15.

[18] *OTIU* 18, 1991.

[19] *OTIU* 18, 1991.

[20] Eric Bowyer interview with author 22 Apr. 2014; *OTIU* 18, 1991.

[21] In the fanzine, the Bowyer interview appeared in block capitals. *OTIU* 18, 1991.

[22] *SL* 5 Jan. 1992.

[23] *IN* 6 Jan. 1992.

[24] *SL* 26 Jan. 1992; *IN* 3 Mar. 1992.

25 *IN* 3 Mar. 1992.

26 *IN* 15 Feb. 1992.

27 LFC minute book 1985-93, entry 28 Nov. 1991; *BT* 14 Feb. 1992; *LAL* 18 Feb. 1992.

28 *IN* 3 Mar. 1992; *IN* 16 Mar. 1992.

29 *IN* 16 Mar. 1992; McManus, *MacBride Principles*, p. 90.

30 The *Irish News* published Linfield's "Right to reply" in full. This statement was approved unanimously" by Linfield's Management Committee. *IN* 19 Mar. 1992;
LFC minute book 1985-93, entry 16 Mar. 1992.

31 Bairner and Walker maintain that the club was "justifiably criticized over many years" for its sectarian image. However, the prominence of Gerry Morgan at Linfield over a 40-year period should not be "dismissed as unimportant or simply ignored… the relationship between sport, especially football, and society is frequently more complex than initial appearances might suggest". Bairner and Walker 'Football and Society', p. 96; *IN* 19 Mar. 1992.

32 *IN* 19 Mar. 1992

33 *IN* 19 Mar. 1992.

34 Gillespie, *Years of Darkness*, pp. 214, 217; *IN* 19 Mar. 1992; *BT* 6 Nov. 1991.

35 *IN* 23 Mar. 1992; Eric Bowyer interview with author 22 Apr. 2014; *OTIU* 18, 1991.

36 *BT* 15 Apr. 1992.

37 *LAL* 18 Feb. 1992; *BT* 1 May 1992.

38 *ISN* 2 May 1992; Eric Bowyer interview with author 22 Apr. 2014.

39 *ISN* 2 May 1992; *BT* 4 May 1992; *ISN* 9 Jan. 1993.

## Chapter 5

1 *BT* 23 Mar. 1992; *BT* 9 June 1992; *BT* 4 July 1992.

2 *IN* 4 July 1992; Gillespie, 'Fanzines', p. 13; *The Blues Brothers* Nov. 1994.

3 *IN* 30 July 1992; *IN* 13 Oct. 1992; *BT* 4 July 1992.

4 *BT* 19 Mar. 1992; *SL* 2 Aug. 1992.

5 *Ireland's Saturday Night* spelt "boos" with an "h". *ISN* 12 Sept. 1992; *OTIU* 18, 1991.

6 *BNL* 23 Sept. 1992; *BT* 24 Sept. 1992; *ISN* 26 Sept. 1992.

7 *ISN* 24 Oct. 1992.

8 LFC minute book 1985-93, entry 26 Oct. 1992; *BT* 24 Oct. 1992; *BNL* 27 Oct. 1992; *BT* 27 Oct. 1992; *ISN* 31 Oct. 1992.

9 *LAL* 18 Jan. 1992; *BT* 27 Oct. 1992.

10 Trevor Anderson interview with author 18 Nov.2014; *BT* 25 Nov. 1992; *BNL* 1 Dec. 1992.

11 *BT* 14 Dec. 1992; *BNL* 15 Dec. 1992; *BT* 18 Dec. 1992.

12 Trevor Anderson interview with author 18 Nov.2014; *BNL* 18 Dec. 1992; *BNL* 21 Dec. 1992.

13 *BT* 15 Jan. 1993.

14 Noel Bailie interview with author 22 Apr. 2014.

15 *BT* 7 Jan. 1993; *ISN* 9 Jan. 1993; McManus, *MacBride Principles*, p. 89.

16 Trevor Anderson interview with author 18 Nov.2014; *BNL* 29 Mar. 1993.

17 *ISN* 17 Apr. 1993, *BNL* 19 Apr. 1993.

18 *BNL* 19 Apr. 1993; *LAL* 17 Oct. 1998; *BT* 19 Apr. 1993.

19 Dessie Gorman interview with author 21 Feb. 2015.

[20] *ISN* 17 July 1993; *BT* 29 June 1993.

[21] *BNL* 15 July 1993; *ISN* 24 July 1993; *BT* 11 Aug. 1993.

[22] Zürcher, C., *Post-Soviet Wars*, pp. 2, 115-16; *Moscow Times* 11 Aug. 1993; *Independent*, 22 Aug. 1993.

[23] *LAL* 24 Aug. 1993; *BNL* 17 Aug. 1993; *BT* 17 Aug. 1993.

[24] *LAL* 24 Aug. 1993.

[25] *BT* 18 Aug. 1993; *Independent*, 22 Aug. 1993.

[26] *ISN* 26 June 1993; *LAL* 14 Aug. 1993; *ISN* 31 July 1993.

[27] *BNL* 19 Aug. 1993; *BT* 19 Aug. 1993; *LAL* 24 Aug. 1993.

[28] *BT* 2 Sept. 1993; *ISN* 28 Aug. 1993.

[29] *BNL* 2 Sept. 1993.

[30] *BNL* 4 Sept. 1993; *ISN* 2 Oct. 1993; *ISN* 4 Sept. 1993; *BNL* 7 Sept. 1993; *BNL* 10 Sept. 1993; Wilson, *Behind the Curtain*, p. 235.

[31] *BT* 17 Sept. 1993.

[32] *BT* 17 Sept. 1993.

[33] Trevor Anderson interview with author 18 Nov. 2014; The Chris Lightbown article was reproduced in *LAL* 16 Oct. 1993.

[34] Chris Lightbown in *LAL* 16 Oct. 1993.

[35] *BT* 27 Sept. 1993; *BT* 18 Sept. 1993; FCK Magasinet 29 Sept. 1993.

[36] *BT* 30 Sept. 1993; Lindsay McKeown interview with author 22 Apr. 2014; *BT* 11 Oct. 1993.

[37] *LAL* 16 Oct. 1993; *BNL* 1 Oct. 1993.

[38] Chris Lightbown in *LAL* 16 Oct. 1993.

[39] *BT* 11 June 1993; *BNL* 20 Nov. 1993; *BT* 28 Dec. 1993.

[40] *BNL* 10 Jan. 1994; *BNL* 14 Jan. 1994; *ISN* 15 Jan. 1994.

[41] *BT* 22 Apr. 1994; *ISN* 23 Apr. 1994; *BNL* 25 Apr. 1994.

[42] *BT* 27 Apr. 1994; *BT* 29 Apr. 1994.

[43] Trevor Anderson interview with author 18 Nov. 2014.

[44] *ISN* 30 Apr. 1994.

[45] *ISN* 30 Apr. 1994; *BNL* 2 May 1994.

[46] *ISN* 30 Apr. 1994.

[47] *BNL* 2 May 1994; *BNL* 5 May 1994.

[48] *ISN* 7 May 1994; BNL 9 May 1994.

[49] Lee Doherty interview with author 8 Feb. 2014; Alan Dornan interview with author 22 Apr. 2014; *BT* 9 May 1994.

**Chapter 6**

[1] At the 1993 Irish League AGM a promotion and relegation proposal was agreed by a 15-14 majority. It was then rubberstamped the following year. *ISN* 29 May 1993; *BT* 28 May 1994; The European Model, p. 4; Cain and Haddock, 'Similar Economic', p. 1125; Ferguson, *Here for a Season*, p. 25; For examples of *Look at Linfield* promotion and relegation calls see *LAL* 31 Oct. 1987; *LAL* 31 Jan. 1989 and *LAL* 24 Aug. 1991; *ISN* 31 May 1987; *BNL* 20 May 1988; *ISN* 12 Mar. 1988; *BT* 15 Aug. 1988.

[2] *LAL* 14 Aug. 1993; *BT* 28 May 1994.

[3] The 'Big Five' (Arsenal, Everton, Liverpool, Manchester United and Tottenham Hotspur) were the small band of elite clubs that drove the establishment of the Premier League. Bose, *Game Changer*, p. 64; Walvin, *People's Game*, p. 200.

4 Southampton would finish the 1994/95 campaign in a respectable 10th position, which in hindsight made the achievement of beating the Saints all the more impressive. *ISN* 30 July 1994.

5 *ISN* 13 Aug. 1994.

6 *ISN* 13 Aug. 1994.

7 *BNL* 16 June 1994; *BT* 3 Dec. 1994; *BT* 5 July 1994; *BT* 10 Aug. 1994.

8 *ISN* 10 Sept. 1994; *BT* 12 Sept. 1994; *BT* 14 Sept. 1994.

9 The ruling on player illegibility was one of many consequences of the 1995 Bosman ruling. *BNL* 27 Sept. 1994; *Independent* 20 Dec. 1995; Storey, 'Football, Place', p. 88.

10 *BT* 28 Sept. 1994; *BNL* 28 Sept. 1994; *BT* 14 Sept. 1994.

11 *BNL* 8 Aug. 1994; *BT* 9 May 1994; *LAL* 25 Mar. 1995.

12 Brodie, *Linfield: 100*, p. 185; *ISN* 6 May 1995; *BNL* 6 May 1995.

13 *ISN* 6 May 1995.

14 *ISN* 6 May 1995; *BNL* 8 May 1995; *BNL* 8 May 1995; *BT* 3 Jan. 1995; *BT* 15 June 1995.

15 *BT* 15 June 1995; *ISN* 18 Sept. 1993; *ISN* 17 June 1995.

16 *ISN* 17 June 1995.

17 The Bosman ruling (which would transform the status of end-of-contract players) was only making its way through the European courts in June 1995. Therefore it had no bearing on the matter. *BNL* 6 July 1995; *ISN* 24 June 1995; *BT* 7 Aug. 1995; Groeneveld, 'Matters of', pp. 32-33.

18 *BT* 4 July 1995; *BT* 30 June 1995; *BT* 30 Aug. 1995.

19 *BT* 7 Aug. 1995; *BNL* 11 Sept. 1999; *BT* 27 Oct. 1995; LFC minute book 1993-99, entry 4 Oct. 1995; LFC minute book 1993-99, entry 7 Nov. 1995; *BT* 16 Nov. 1995; *BT* 10 Oct. 1995.

20 LFC minute book 1993-99, entry 22 Nov. 1995; *BNL* 20 Nov. 1995.

21 *BT* 12 July 1995; *BT* 8 Aug. 1995.

22 Pat Fenlon interview with author 21 Dec. 2013.

23 *BT* 21 June 1995; *BT* 3 Aug. 1995; *BT* 21 Aug. 1995; *BT* 27 Oct. 1995.

24 *BT* 27 Dec. 1995.

25 *BT* 19 Mar. 1996; *ISN* 9 Mar. 1996.

26 *LAL* 27 Apr. 1996; *BNL* 16 Apr. 1996.

27 At the time, significant change also came off the field. Before the 1996 AGM, chairman David Campbell stood down on health grounds. A couple of weeks later, Billy McCoubrey was appointed to the position. *BT* 30 Apr. 1996; *ISN* 18 May 1996; *ISN* 4 May 1996; *BT* 23 July 1996; *BT* 6 June 1996; *BT* 31 July 1996; *BT* 22 Aug. 1996; *LAL* 26 Dec. 1996; *BT* 27 Sept. 1996; *LAL* 1 Sept. 1996.

28 *BT* 3 Aug. 1996.

29 LFC minute book 1993-99, entry 7 Nov. 1996; LFC minute book 1993-99, entry 2 Oct. 1995; *ISN* 21 Sept. 1996.

30 *ISN* 21 Sept. 1996; *BNL* 12 Nov. 1996; *BNL* 27 July 1989.

31 *ISN* 28 Dec. 1996; David Jeffrey interview with author 26 June 2014; *BT* 6 Jan. 1997.

32 Trevor Anderson interview with author 18 Nov.2014; *ISN* 4 Jan. 1997.

33 Dessie Gorman interview with author 21 Feb. 2015; Pat Fenlon interview with author 21 Dec. 2013; Noel Bailie interview with author 22 Apr. 2014.

34 *ISN* 24 Aug. 1996; Trevor Anderson interview with author 18 Nov.2014

35 *BNL* 6 Jan. 1997.

36 *LAL* 11 Jan. 1997; David Jeffrey interview with author 26 June 2014.

[37] David Jeffrey interview with author 26 June 2014; Dessie Gorman interview with author 21 Feb. 2015; *BT* 7 Feb. 1997.

[38] *LAL* 8 Feb. 1997; David Jeffrey interview with author 26 June 2014.

## Chapter 7

[1] A 10-year-old Michael Owen famously smashed an Ian Rush goalscoring record for Deeside Schools. Rush had scored 72 goals whilst Owen hit 92. After this, comparisons between the two were commonplace. *DT* 19 Mar. 2013; *BT* 25 July 1997; *The Guardian* 14 Jan. 1997.

[2] A few weeks after the Liverpool game the chairman of the Football Trust, Tom Wharton OBE, officially opened the new Kop Stand. The Trust had contributed £1.5 million – 75 per cent – of the funding for the structure. The first game played after the official opening was a Northern Ireland international, a 3-1 defeat for the home side in a 1998 World Cup qualifier against Germany. *BT* 23 July 1996; *BT* 11 Aug. 1997; *BT* 28 July 1997; *BT* 28 July 1997; Honigstein, *Englischer Fussball*, p. 81; Cornwall 'The Making', p. 97.

[3] *BT* 10 Sept. 1997; *BNL* 10 Sept. 1997; *LAL* 13 Sept. 1997.

[4] David Larmour initially arrived on a short-term deal, but this was improved to a three-year contract after an impressive first month. Lee Feeney's signature was secured after Linfield fought off Glentoran's challenge. *BT* 28 Oct. 1997; *BT* 26 Nov. 1997; *BT* 26 Aug. 1997; *ISN* 27 Sept. 1997.

[5] LFC minute book 1993-99, entry 24 Sept. 1992; *BNL* 4 Jan. 1997; LFC minute book 1993-99, entries 22 July 1993,10 Mar. 1997.

[6] David Jeffrey interview with author 26 June 2014; *BNL* 10 Dec. 1997; *BT* 8 Jan. 1998.

[7] Glenn Ferguson interview with author 8 Feb. 2014; *ISN* 17 Jan. 1998; *BT* 15 Jan. 1998.

[8] Supporters at Linfield have always been to the fore in raising monies for the club. At the turn of the Millennium, a Special Efforts Committee would help raise over £400,000 in two years for the club. *LAL* 13 Jan. 2001; *BNL* 16 Jan. 1998; *BT* 15 Jan. 1998; *LAL* 14 Feb. 1998.

[9] *BT* 18 Feb. 1998.

[10] *BT* 6 Mar. 1998; *BNL* 6 Mar. 1998.

[11] Glentoran fans in the North Stand caused £7,500 worth of damage. *ISN* 28 Mar. 1998; *ISN* 7 Mar. 1998; *BT* 9 Mar. 1998; *BNL* 9 Mar. 1998.

[12] *ISN* 14 Mar. 1998; *Walsh*, 'Introduction', pp. 13, 18.

[13] Behlmer 'Introduction', p. 2; Selznick, *Global Television,* p. 98; Cox, 'The Search', p. 78; *DT* 16 Apr. 2010; Ridley, *Golden Sky*, p. 9.

[14] Linfield took its own measures after the riot. £30,000 was spent on security, including placing a fence between the Kop and North Stand. *BT* 12 Mar. 1998.

[15] *ISN* 28 Mar. 1998.

[16] David Jeffrey interview with author 26 June 2014.

[17] *BT* 23 July 1998; *ISN* 25 July 1998.

[18] *BT* 30 July 1998.

[19] At the end of the 1997/98 campaign, David Jeffrey was informed that he had to cut his wages budget by £50,000. *BT* 5 May 1998; *BT* 29 Apr. 1998.

[20] Referenda on the Agreement took place on both sides of the border. In Northern Ireland 71 per cent voted 'Yes', whilst in the Republic of Ireland there was overwhelming endorsement. McKittrick and McVea, *Making Sense*, p. 259; *ISN* 20 June 1998.

21 One Cliftonville 'home' game against Linfield was switched to Bangor, but otherwise all took place at Windsor. *BT* 21 Nov. 1998; *BT* 25 Feb. 1987.

22 *ISN* 26 Mar. 1994.

23 *BT* 12 Apr. 1994; LFC minute book 1993-99, entry 14 Mar. 1994.

24 LFC minute book 1993-99, entry 25 July 1994; *BNL* 30 May 1994; LFC minute book 1993-99, entry 29 Aug. 1994.

25 *BT* 7 July 1995.

26 In early 2000, Lee Clegg was cleared of all charges relating to his 1993 conviction. *TG* 1 Feb. 2000; *BT* 7 July 1995; *ISN* 15 July 1994; *DT* 13 Sept. 2007; *Independent*, 25 Jan. 1995.

27 Bryan, *Orange Parades*, pp. 1-3.

28 *BT* 23 Jan. 1996.

29 *BT* 21 Apr. 1998; LFC minute book 1993-99, entry 12 May 1998.

30 McKittrick and McVea, *Making Sense*, pp. 349, 262.

31 In the aftermath of the 1970 Irish Cup final, the press was awash with condemnation of the events outside Solitude. The *Irish News* castigated the "vicious hooligan element [who] left a trail of destruction behind them", *IN* 6 Apr. 1970; *ISN* 24 Oct. 1998; *BT* 4 Nov. 1998.

32 *ISN* 21 Nov. 1998; *BT* 4 Nov. 1998; *LAL* 28 Nov. 1998; *An Phoblacht* 26 Nov. 1998; *BT* 20 Nov. 1998.

33 *BT* 20 Nov. 1998; *AP* 26 Nov. 1998; *ISN* 21 Nov. 1998.

34 *ISN* 21 Nov. 1998; *IN* 23 Nov. 1998; *BT* 23 Nov. 1998.

35 *BT* 19 Apr. 1999.

36 For speculation on Jeffrey's future see *BNL* 26 Apr. 1999; *BT* 26 Apr. 1999.

### Chapter 8

1 Noel Bailie interview with author 22 Apr. 2014; *LAL* 21 Aug. 1999; *LAL* 25 Sept. 1999.

2 Early on during season 1999/2000 the Finance Committee was expressing "grave concern" about the club's economic position. LFC minute book 1999-2003, entry 6 Sept. 1999; *BT* 18 Dec. 1998; *BNL* 18 Jan. 1999; *ISN* 24 July 1999; *BT* 5 Aug. 1999; *ISN* 7 Aug. 1999.

3 *ISN* 21 Aug. 1999.

4 *BT* 28 Sept. 1999; *BT* 8 Oct. 1999.

5 *ISN* 27 Nov. 1999; *BT* 1 Nov. 1999.

6 *ISN* 8 Jan. 2000.

7 Linfield's team of 1952-56 set the original post-war record of 39 unbeaten home League games. Derry City hold the all-time Irish League record of 47 games unbeaten at home. The Candystripes achieved the feat during 1934-38. *ISN* 19 Feb. 2000; *BNL* 28 Feb. 2000.

8 *ISN* 26 Feb. 2000; *ISN* 25 Mar. 2000.

9 *ISN* 15 Jan. 2000; *BT* 9 Feb. 2000.

10 *BT* 29 Mar. 2000.

11 *BT* 29 Mar. 2000.

12 *ISN* 1 Apr. 2000; *ISN* 8 Apr. 2000.

13 *ISN* 1 Apr. 2000; *BT* 3 Apr. 2000.

14 Glenn Ferguson interview with author 8 Feb. 2014.

15 David Jeffrey interview with author 26 June 2014.

16 *BT* 19 Apr. 2000; LFC minute book 1999-2003, entries 28 Oct. 1999, 4 May 2000.

[17] Jeffrey wanted to sign Darren Lockhart and Darren Fitzgerald in the summer of 2000. However, he failed due to lack of club finances – both players would join rivals Glentoran. *BNL* 22 June 2000; *BT* 5 May 2000; *ISN* 13 May 2000; *BT* 17 May 2000.

[18] *BNL* 18 May 2000; *BNL* 11 Aug. 2000.

[19] *ISN* 1 July 2000.

[20] *BNL* 13 July 2000; *BT* 13 July 2000.

[21] *BT* 20 July 2000.

[22] *BT* 20 July 2000.

[23] *ISN* 22 July 2000.

[24] *ISN* 22 July 2000.

[25] *BT* 3 Aug. 2000.

[26] *BNL* 18 May 2000; *BNL* 26 Nov. 2012; *When Saturday Comes* Sept. 1999.

[27] *ISN* 5 Aug. 2000; *BT* 7 Aug. 2000.

[28] *BT* 7 Aug. 2000.

[29] *WSC* Sept. 1999.

[30] Sondaal, 'Football's grobalization', p. 488; Rookwood and Chan '39th game', p. 899.

[31] In 1999 Linfield earned in the region of £50,000 from the Challenge, in 2000 the figure was £40,000. *WSC* Sept. 1999; LFC minute book 1999-2003, entry 29 June 2000; *ISN* 11 Nov. 2000; *BT* 27 Nov. 2000.

[32] *BNL* 27 Dec. 2000; *BT* Dec. 27 2000; Gavin Arthur interview with author 3 Aug. 2013.

[33] *BNL* 22 Feb. 2001.

[34] Woods, *Manufactured Plague*, pp. 137-45; *BT* 2 Mar. 2001.

[35] *ISN* 21 Apr. 2001.

[36] *BNL* 23 Apr. 2001, Noel Bailie interview with author 22 Apr. 2014.

### Chapter 9

[1] LFC minute book 1999-2003, entry 26 Mar. 2001.

[2] LFC minute book 1999-2003, entry 31 May 2001; *BNL* 23 June 2001.

[3] *BT* 19 July 2001; *BNL* 16 July 2001; *BT* 12 July 2001.

[4] *BT* 17 July 2001; *ISN* 21 July 2001; *BT* 19 July 2001.

[5] *BNL* 20 July 2001; *ISN* 21 July 2001.

[6] *BT* 23 July 2001; *ISN* 21 July 2001.

[7] *BT* 21 Feb. 2001; *BT* 30 May 2001; *BNL* 5 Oct. 2001.

[8] *ISN* 16 June 2001; *BT* 4 July 2001.

[9] Rowbottom, *Foul Play*, p. 66.

[10] *BT* 12 July 2001; *BNL* 15 Aug. 2001; *ISN* 24 Nov. 2001.

[11] *ISN* 24 Nov. 2001; *BT* 12 Oct. 2001.

[12] *BT* 10 May 2002.

[13] *BNL* 10 May 2002; *ISN* 11 May 2002.

[14] *BNL* 13 May 2002; *ISN* 11 May 2002; *BT* 13 May 2002.

[15] *BT* 15 May 2002.

[16] Michael Gault interview with author 6 Jan. 2014.

[17] *BT* 29 May 2002; *BNL* 31 May 2002; *BNL* 4 June 2002; *BNL* 18 June 2002; *BT* 11 Apr. 2003.

[18] *BT* 14 Mar. 2003.

[19] *LAL* 29 Apr. 2003; *ISN* 3 May 2003; *BT* 3 May 2002.

20 *ISN* 3 May 2003; *BT* 14 May 2003.

21 For more information on former Linfield chairman Harry Midgley MP, see: Graham Walker, *Harry Midgley*; Brodie, *Linfield: 100*, p. 16; The Bank indicated that if the club's overdraft facility exceeded £750,000 this would force the sale of Midgley. LFC minute book 1999-2003, entry 28 Apr. 2002; LFC minute book 1999-2003, entry 22 May 2002.

22 *BT* 14 May 2003.

23 LFC minute book 1993-99, entries 21 Apr. 1988, 22 Apr. 1993, 22 Nov. 1993; LFC minute book 1999-2003, entry 17 Mar. 2003.

24 LFC minute book 2003-06, entry 24 July 2003; Richard Johnson interview with author 16 June 2015.

25 Wagg, 'Nowt for', p. 146; Phillips, *Fit to Bust*, pp. 55-56; *Observer* 7 Mar. 2004; *London Evening Standard* 9 Jan. 2012.

26 *ISN* 19 July 2003.

27 *BNL* 24 Sept. 2003; *BT* 24 Sept. 2003.

28 *BNL* 27 Sept. 2003; *ISN* 27 Sept. 2003.

29 David Jeffrey interview with author 26 June 2014; *BT* 7 Oct. 2003.

30 *BNL* 22 Oct. 2003; *BT* 3 Nov. 2003.

31 Glenn Ferguson interview with author 8 Feb. 2014; David Jeffrey interview with author 26 June 2014.

32 Phil Charnock interview with author 15 Apr. 2014.

33 *BT* 27 Dec. 2003.

34 In early January the *Belfast Telegraph* reported that Linfield was "set to land a £2 million windfall" with the sale of Midgley. The paper claimed that an offer was on the table and would probably be "too good to turn down". The story indicated that Linfield needed the cash, but did not convey how serious the club's financial position was. *BT* 7 Jan. 2004; LFC minute book 2003-06, entries

27 Nov. 2003, 8 Dec. 2003, 18 Dec. 2003; Richard Johnson interview with author 16 June 2015.

35 The worries of the mid-1980s about falling attendances at local games only continued to worsen as the years went on. In the early 1990s Linfield's Management Committee had reflected on depressing slumps in the uptake of season tickets. A decade later they would establish a sub-committee "to investigate ways and means of attracting more spectators to home games". LFC minute book 1985-93, entry 26 Sept. 1991; LFC minute book 1999-2003, entry 5 Nov. 2001.

Richard Johnson interview with author 16 June 2015.

36 *ISN* 17 Apr. 2004.

37 *ISN* 24 Apr. 2004.

38 *ISN* 1 May 2004.

39 In mid-March 2004 the club's overdraft facility was still around the £700,000 mark. LFC minute book 2003-06, entry 18 Mar. 2004; *ISN* 24 Apr. 2004; *ISN* 12 June 2004.


**Chapter 10**

1 *ISN* 23 Apr. 2005.

2 *ISN* 23 Apr. 2005.

3 *BT* 11 June 2014; *ISN* 12 June 2004; *BNL* 10 Nov. 2004; *BNL* 28 Dec. 2004.

4 *ISN* 23 Apr. 2005; *BNL* 25 Apr. 2005.

[5] *BT* 19 Apr. 2005; *BT* 25 Apr. 2005.

[6] Noel Bailie interview with author 22 Apr. 2014; Glenn Ferguson interview with author 8 Feb. 2014; William Murphy interview with author 26 Apr. 2014.

[7] Although an all-Ireland competition appeared unlikely in the aftermath of 1980, the Blues remained hopeful of taking part in such tournaments. In March 1990, Shelbourne had invited Linfield to participate in a Belfast/Dublin City competition. The Management Committee backed the club's involvement, however, nothing came of this. LFC minute book 1985-93, entry 19 Mar. 1990; *Irish Times* 12 Mar. 2005.

[8] Gillespie, *Years of Darkness*, pp. 272-74.

[9] Gillespie, *Years of Darkness*, pp. 275-78.

[10] By September 2000, Cliftonville vs Linfield at Solitude could kick off at 3pm on a Saturday. As the *Belfast Telegraph* put it, "at last [the fixture] has become a game of football again". *BT* 15 Sept. 2000; Co-operation Ireland, *Committed to*, p. 3.

[11] Brodie, *Linfield: 100*, p. 115.

[12] *DT* 6 Oct. 2014; *Observer*, 1 Sept. 2002; Keane and Dunphy, *Keane*, p. 231; *Daily Mail* 16 Oct. 2002.

[13] Keane and Dunphy, *Keane*, p. 102

[14] Keane and Dunphy, *Keane*, p. 102.

[15] *Observer*, 8 Sept. 2002.

[16] The 1998 Windsor game between Linfield and Derry City finished in a 2-2 draw. It was held in support of John Easton's testimonial season. *BT* 3 Nov. 1998; *BNL* 4 Aug. 2004; *BNL* 22 Feb. 2005; Duke and Crolley, *Football, Nationality*, pp. 71-75.

[17] On one occasion the RUC escorted a Garda team as far as the Brandywell gates because of a loyalist paramilitary threat. When competing in Europe the club was able to circumvent UEFA rules requiring a police presence during fixtures, by stationing officers in the vicinity of the ground. McLlister, 'The Red Army', p. 11; McCann, 'Two Tribes', p. 25; *ISN* 16 Nov. 1991.

[18] Ashe, 'From Paramilitaries', p. 300; *BT* 23 Feb. 2005.

[19] *BT* 23 Feb. 2005; *BNL* 23 Feb. 2005.

[20] *BT* 23 Feb. 2005; *BNL* 23 Feb. 2005.

[21] For media reaction to the match, see *BT* 23 Feb. 2005; *Derry Journal* 25 Feb. 2005; *IN* 23 Feb. 2005; *Londonderry Sentinel*, 2 Mar. 2005.

[22] David Jeffrey interview with author 26 June 2014.

[23] The Republic's move to summer football was initially an experiment, though such was its success, the FAI announced in 2006 that summer football was there to stay. Changing the season's timing had a positive impact on football in the Republic. In three seasons, the League jumped five places in UEFA's coefficient table. By the mid-2000s, the Republic's Celtic Tiger was in its last throes, though few at the time realised it. Indeed, an *Economist* survey of Ireland 'The Luck of Irish' in October 2004 maintained that the Republic's economy had "a number of plus points that [would] help it grow [further]". *DM* 18 Dec. 2008; *Economist* 16 Oct. 2004; Donovan and Murphy, *Celtic Tiger*, p. 171.

[24] *WSC* Jan. 2005.

[25] *BT* 19 May 2005; Michael Gault interview with author 6 Jan. 2014.

[26] *BNL* 31 July 2004; *BNL* 23 Dec. 2004.

[27] *LAL* 10 May 2005.

[28] *BT* 23 May 2005.

[29] *BT* 23 May 2005; David Jeffrey interview with author 26 June 2014.

[30] *BT* 14 July 2005.

[31] *BNL* 9 July 2005; *BNL* 11 Aug. 2005.

[32] *BNL* 26 Aug. 2005.

[33] David Jeffrey interview with author 26 June 2014; *BNL* 27 Dec. 2005.

[34] *BNL* 27 Dec. 2005; *BT* 30 Dec. 2005; *ISN* 31 Dec. 2005.

[35] *BT* 8 Feb. 2006; *ISN* 18 Mar. 2006.

[36] *BNL* 20 Mar. 2006.

[37] *ISN* 6 May 2006.

[38] *BT* 8 May 2006; Noel Bailie interview with author 22 Apr. 2014.

[39] *ISN* 15 Oct. 2005; William Murphy interview with author 26 Apr. 2014; David Jeffrey interview with author 22 July 2014.

[40] Noel Bailie interview with author 22 Apr. 2014.


**Chapter 11**

[1] *ISN* 6 May 2006; *BT* 17 May 2005.

[2] Richard Johnson interview with author 4 Aug. 2015;  LFC minute book 2003-06, entry 14 Dec. 2006.

[3] *BT* 6 Mar. 2006; *SL* 21 May 2006; *BT* 7 Aug. 2006.

[4] *BT* 7 Aug. 2006; *BNL* 10 July 2006.

[5] *BT* 20 Sept. 2006; *BNL* 25 Sept. 2006.

[6] *SL* 7 Jan. 2007.

[7] *BNL* 1 Jan. 2007; *BT* 13 Jan. 2007.

[8] *BT* 13 Mar. 2007.

[9] According to Gavin Mortimer, Glaswegian architect Archibald Leitch "was responsible in some measure for the creation of twenty nine stadiums, from the Art Deco glamour of Arsenal's Highbury to the splendour of Manchester United's Old Trafford". Mortimer, *A History*, p. 60; Brodie, *Linfield: 100*, p. 13; *BT* 27 Mar. 27; *SL* 4 Feb. 2007.

[10] Sanchez was also not the last Northern Ireland manager to call for a new stadium. Nigel Worthington, who followed Sanchez, also made that call. *BT* 27 July 2007; *LAL* 9 Oct. 1999; *BNL* 15 Jan. 2001; *BT* 24 Apr. 1998; *BNL* 29 Sept. 1999; *BT* 21 Jan. 1999.

[11] Shortly after the NIO statement, the former Maze prison site was mentioned as a potential location for a new national stadium. *ISN* 26 Aug. 2000; *BNL* 31 Aug. 2000.

[12] The Millennium Stadium cost £121 million to construct. £46 million of this was public money that came from the Millennium Commission. £750 million was spent redeveloping Wembley. Of that figure, about £170 million was public money (this was made up of funding from the National Lottery as well as the Government and London Development Agency). *DT* 20 July 2012; *TG* 25 Sept. 2002; Johnes 'Every day', p. 58.

[13] *BT* 21 Sept. 2001; *BT* 26 Feb. 2003.

[14] During 2002 the total average net circulation per *Belfast Telegraph* issue was 109,629. ABC Ltd, *Standard Certificate*, p. 2; *BT* 23 Feb. 2003. For examples of IFA ambivalence on the future of Windsor Park as an international stadium, see: *BNL* 13 Jan. 2004; *BNL* 16 Jan. 2004; *BT* 20 Jan. 2006.

[15] In the months following the IFA decision, The Amalgamation of Official Northern Ireland Supporters Clubs continued to be a vocal critic of the Maze project. During this time there were strained relations between the Amalgamation and the Association. *BNL* 31 May 2006; *BNL* 16 Nov. 2006; *BT* 17 Jan. 2006; *BT* 30 May 2006; McKeown,

'Bulldozing History', p. 5.

[16] *LAL* 28 Sept. 2001; LFC minute book 2003-06, entry 13 Dec. 2004; *BT* 17 Jan. 2006; LFC minute book 1999-2003, entry 1 June 1999.

[17] The contract required Linfield's Trustees to maintain the stadium. The terms were reproduced in the *Sunday World*, see *Sunday World* 21 Sept. 2008.

[18] *BT* 26 Oct. 2006; *BNL* 1 Feb. 2007.

[19] The overriding media consensus on Linfield's trip to Donegal Celtic in November 2006 was positive: see *AN* 20 Nov. 2006; *IN* 20 Nov. 2006; *BNL* 20 Nov. 2006; *BT* 20 Nov. 2006.

[20] By 2011, twice the number of Belfast peace walls existed than had been the case at the height of the Troubles. Brewer, Higgins and Teeney, *Religion, Civil Society*, p. 5; *SL* 25 Feb. 2007.

[21] *BT* 23 Nov. 1998; *BT* 26 Feb. 2007; *BNL* 26 Feb. 2007; LFC minute book 2007-10, entry 27 Feb. 2007.

[22] *BNL* 5 Aug. 2006.

[23] *SL* 15 Apr. 2007.

[24] *SL* 6 May 2007.

[25] *SL* 6 May 2007.

[26] *SL* 13 May 2007.

[27] *SL* 3 Feb. 2008.

[28] *BNL* 4 Feb. 2008; McLaughlin (ed.), *Soccer Yearbook*, p. 98.

[29] *LAL* 9 Feb. 2008; *BT* 14 Dec. 2006.

[30] *BNL* 27 Mar. 2008; *BNL* 25 Apr. 2015.

[31] *BT* 27 Mar. 2008.

[32] *SL* 4 May 2008; *SL* 27 Apr. 2008.

[33] *SL* 27 Apr. 2008.

[34] *SL* 4 May 2008.

[35] *SL* 4 May 2008.

[36] It should be noted that when Zagreb had qualified for the Champions League group stages in 1998 and 1999, this was under the name Croatia Zagreb and not Dinamo Zagreb. *DT* 29 Apr. 2008; *BT* 2 July 2008.

[37] *Ulster Star* 24 July 2008; *BT* 24 July 2008; Michael Gault interview with author 6 Jan. 2014.

[38] *BT* 16 May 2008; *BNL* 15 July 2008.

[39] *BNL* 1 May 2009; *BNL* 7 May 2009.

[40] *BT* 22 May 2009; *BT* 23 May 2009; *BNL* 22 May 2009.

[41] After leaving Linfield, Ferguson played on for two more seasons at Lisburn Distillery. When he retired at the end of the 2010/11 season he had amassed over 1,000 career appearances. Ferguson's 1,000th career appearance came when he turned out for Lisburn Distillery in a match against Newry City on 28 August 2010. In February 2009 the Finance Committee heard "there would have to be a significant reduction of 10-15 per cent [wage costs] for next season". LFC minute book 2007-10, entry 19 Feb. 2009; David Jeffrey interview with author 22 July 2014.

[42] In late January 2009 the media got wind that the Maze project would not be followed through on. See *BNL* 29 Jan. 2009; Glenn Ferguson interview with author 8 Feb. 2014.

[43] *BT* 16 Apr. 2007.

[44] *SL* 28 Jan. 2007; *SL* 27 Apr. 2008; *BT* 26 June 2007; *BT* 26 Feb. 2008.

**Chapter 12**

[1] *BT* 12 June 2009.

[2] *BT* 12 June 2009; *BT* 13 June 2009; *BT* 23 June 2009.

[3] *BNL* 24 Oct. 2007.

[4] *SL* 7 June 2009; *BT* 18 Dec. 2007.

[5] The writ issued by Carson McDowell solicitors was clear in stating that the IFA was "not entitled to terminate the 1984 Agreement". Considerable groundwork undertaken by the Board had placed the club in a position ready to refute IFA accusations that Linfield had neglected its duty in upkeep of the stadium. Writ issued by Carson McDowell's on behalf of the Trustees of Linfield Football & Athletic Club, 9 Oct. 2007; *BT* 22 Oct. 2008; *BT* 17 July 2007.

[6] Not long after the Maze project was ruled out, the *Sunday Life* became a cheerleader for the Blanchflower stadium in East Belfast. *SL* 22 June 2008; *SL* 26 Apr. 2009; *BNL* 23 Apr. 2008; *BT* 23 June 2009; *BNL* 8 Sept. 2009.

[7] *LAL* 12 Sept. 2009; LFC minute book 2007-10, entry 12 Oct. 2009.

[8] Michel Platini gave little credence to the correspondence sent by Glentoran. Indeed, less than half a year after receiving the letter he authorised a grant of £306,000 for necessary repair work at Windsor. *BT* 22 Jan. 2010; *SL* 13 Sept. 2009; *BNL* 23 Oct. 2009.

[9] *BT* 7 Oct. 2009.

[10] *BT* 19 Oct. 2009.

[11] *SL* 23 Sept. 2007; *BT* 9 Sept. 2009; *BT* 25 Sept. 2007.

[12] Demonstrative of just how demanding the Linfield job is, was a letter received by the Management Committee after the trophyless 2008/09 campaign, suggesting it was "time for a change of Manager". LFC minute book 2007-10, entries 12 May 2009, 21 Dec. 2009.

[13] *BT* 21 Dec. 2009; David Jeffrey interview with author 22 July 2014.

[14] *BT* 21 Dec. 2009.

[15] *SL* 17 Jan. 2010; *BT* 8 Jan. 2010.

[16] The financial difficulties that afflicted Stockport during Thompson's time had a serious impact on the club. In 2011, County was relegated from the Football League. By 2016, the club had slumped into the sixth tier of English Football – the Conference North. *BT* 8 Jan. 2010; Peter Thompson interview with author 19 Oct. 2016; *WSC* Feb. 2013; *TG* 29 Mar. 2013.

[17] *BT* 22 Jan. 2010; *BNL* 26 Jan. 2010.

[18] *BNL* 24 Apr. 2010.

[19] *LAL* 25 Aug. 1989.

[20] In April 2011 Noel Bailie was recognised for his long service to Linfield, by Lord Mayor Pat Convery at Belfast City Hall. Then in June 2013 he was awarded an MBE. Even though he had achieved so much in his career, Bailie was never one to seek the limelight. Indeed, at the end of the 2009/10 campaign he turned down "the possibility of the Club holding a Dinner in his honour". LFC minute book 2007-10, entry 12 May 2010; Noel Bailie interview with author 22 Apr. 2014; *SL* 25 Apr. 2010.

[21] *BT* 28 Apr. 2010; *BT* 29 Apr. 2010.

[22] *BT* 29 Apr. 2010; *BT* 10 May 2010.

[23] Thompson's permanent return to Linfield was confirmed at the start of July. *BT* 2 July 2010.

24 *BT* 8 Apr. 2011.

25 *SL* 1 May 2011; David Jeffrey interview with author 29 July 2014.

26 David Jeffrey interview with author 29 July 2014; Michael Gault interview with author 6 Jan. 2014.

27 *IN* 10 Aug. 2011; Michael Gault interview with author 6 Jan. 2014.

28 The decision to phase out full-time playing contracts was taken by the Management Committee in April 2010. LFC minute book 2007-10, entry 12 Apr. 2010.

29 In 2006 Derry City also made it through the qualifying rounds of European competition. That year the outfit progressed to a UEFA Cup first-round tie against Paris St Germain. This was an achievement that defender Darren Kelly (who had played in the Irish League with Portadown) put down to full-time football. He explained: "In the Irish League it is hard to get a balance between trying to maintain a high level of fitness and work on areas of your game as well as prepare for the opposition on a Saturday and I think that is reflected in results in Europe [whereas] at Derry we can work on every aspect of our game throughout the week… we are Ireland's sole representative in Europe and being full-time is a major part of that." *BT* 14 Sept. 2006.

30 *BT* 4 Sept. 2007; David Jeffrey interview with author 22 July 2014.

31 Peter Thompson interview with author 24 Feb. 2014; Michael Gault interview with author 6 Jan. 2014.

32 The 2011/12 games against Glentoran (which all ended in defeat) had added spice after Glens forward Daryl Fordyce moved to Linfield in May 2011.

33 David Jeffrey interview with author 22 July 2014.

34 David Jeffrey interview with author 22 July 2014.

35 David Jeffrey interview with author 22 July 2014; *BNL* 4 Apr. 2012.

36 *BNL* 29 Oct. 2009; *BT* 23 June 2010; LFC minute book 2007-10, entry 14 June 2010.

37 LFC minute book 2007-10, entry 14 June 2010; *BT* 3 July 2010; *BT* 13 Nov. 2009; *BT* 24 Aug. 2010.

38 After the controversial sacking of Howard Wells and the costly settlement, the Stormont government was adamant that IFA president Raymond Kennedy and vice-president David Martin should resign. The government would eventually get their way, but this rumbled on throughout the summer and autumn of 2010. Then once Kennedy and Martin had left their positions, Sports Minister Nelson McCausland called for a review of the Association before money could be handed over. *BNL* 27 Aug. 2010; *BNL* 1 Oct. 2010; *BT* 18 Oct. 2010; *BT* 16 Dec. 2010; *BNL* 11 Mar. 2012.

39 When the contract with the IFA was settled in February 2012, a letter was sent to all club members explaining the terms of agreement. LFC minute book 2007-10, entry 27 Feb. 2012; *BNL* 23 Feb. 2012; *LAL* 3 Mar. 2012.

**Chapter 13**

1 *BT* 26 June 2012.

2 *BNL* 3 July 2012; *BNL* 4 July 2012.

3 *BNL* 11 July 2012; *BT* 11 July 2012.

4 *BNL* 11 Aug. 2012; LFC minute book 2011-16, entry 2 July 2012.

5 David Jeffrey interview with author 28 July 2014.

6 *BT* 8 Oct. 2012.

7 *BT* 12 Nov. 2012; *LAL* 24 Nov. 2012.

8 *BNL* 29 Nov. 2012; *BT* 30 Nov. 2012; David Jeffrey interview with author 28 July 2014.

9 LFC minute book 2011-16, entry, 10 Dec. 2012; David Jeffrey interview with author 28 July 2014.

10 David Jeffrey interview with author 28 July 2014.

11 *BT* 6 Mar. 2013.

12 *BT* 18 May 2005; *BT* 10 Dec. 2013.

13 *LAL* 14 Dec. 2013.

14 *IN* 6 Mar. 2013; *BT* 6 Mar. 2013; *LAL* 14 Dec. 2013.

15 Post-liquidation of Glasgow Rangers, debate has surrounded whether the club that currently exists is the same football club as prior to liquidation. It should be noted that both FIFA and the Scottish Professional Football League have stated that Rangers is the same club. *Herald* 24 May 2015; Wilson and PieKarz, *Sports Management*, p. 23; *BT* 8 May 2012; *LAL* 23 Feb. 2013.

16 The four Rangers players that started both games were Lee McCullough, Lee Wallace, Neil Alexander and goalscorer Chris Hegarty; *BNL* 11 Apr. 2013; *BT* 11 Apr. 2013.

17 *Evening Times* 11 Apr. 2013; *LAL* 20 Apr. 2013.

18 *Scotsman*, 2 Feb. 2013; *BT* 31 Jan. 2013; *BT* 14 Jan. 2008.

19 In tribute to Brodie it was decided that when the new Windsor was finished, the pressroom would be named after him. *BT* 1 Feb. 2013; *BT* 25 Aug. 2012; *BT* 12 Dec. 2012.

20 *LAL* 23 Feb. 2013; *BT* 12 Dec. 2012; *BNL* 18 Apr. 2013.

21 LFC minute book 2011-16, entry 22 Apr. 2013; *BNL* 29 Apr. 2013.

22 *BNL* 23 May 2013; *BT* 23 May 2013; LFC minute book 2011-16, entry 27 May 2013.

23 *BT* 23 May 2013; *BT* 3 June 2013.

24 *BT* 15 May 2013; *BNL* 16 July 2013; *BT* 16 July 2013.

25 *BT* 16 July 2013; *BT* 17 July 2013.

26 *SL* 25 Aug. 2013.

27 *BT* 4 July 2013; *BNL* 25 July 2013.

28 *LAL* 10 July 2013; *LAL* 17 Aug. 2013; David Jeffrey interview with author 22 July 2014.

29 *BT* 1 July 2013; *LAL* 10 July 2013; *LAL* 17 Aug. 2013.

30 *BNL* 19 July 2013; *BNL* 25 July 2013; *SL* 28 July 2013.

31 *BT* 26 July 2013.

32 *BT* 26 July 2016; *SL* 28 July 2013.

33 Amidst the pressure on the pitch, David Jeffrey was also coming under fire for a video that had appeared on social media. In December 2013 a clip of the Blues boss surfaced in which he was singing "Thank you very much for Jimmy Callacher". Callacher was a Glentoran player looking to leave the East Belfast club and it was believed Linfield was interested. *BT* 17 Dec. 2013; *BT* 28 Dec. 2013; *BT* 14 Dec. 2013; *BNL* 29 Jan. 2014; *BT* 14 Jan. 2014.

34 *BNL* 30 Jan. 2014; *SL* 2 Feb. 2014.

35 *BT* 7 Feb. 2014; *The Sun*, 10 Feb. 2104.

36 *BT* 25 Oct. 2012; David Jeffrey interview with author 28 July 2014.

37 Jeffrey had become the longest-serving Linfield manager back in June 2011. Before then, Roy Coyle held the record. At the Board meeting held on 15 Feb. 2014, club officials were informed that the "Team Manager [had] indicated he wished to retire from his position at the close of the present season". LFC minute book 2011-16, entry 15 Feb.

2014; David Jeffrey interview with author 28 July 2014.

[38] David Jeffrey interview with author 28 July 2014; Jamie Mulgrew interview with author 17 May 2016; Michael Gault interview with author 5 Jan. 2016; Michael Gault interview with author 6 Jan. 2014; Sean Ward interview with author 13 May 2016.

[39] Andy Waterworth interview with author 23 May 2016; Sean Ward interview with author 13 May 2016; Michael Gault interview with author 6 Jan. 2014; Jamie Mulgrew interview with author 17 May 2016.

[40] David Jeffrey interview with author 28 July 2014; Sean Ward interview with author 13 May 2016; Michael Gault interview with author 6 Jan. 2014; Jamie Mulgrew interview with author 17 May 2016.

[41] Michael Gault interview with author 5 Jan. 2016; *SL* 16 Feb. 2014.

[42] *LAL* 15 Mar. 2014; *SL* 30 Mar. 2014.

[43] *BNL* 3 Apr. 2014; *BT* 23 Apr. 2014.

[44] David Jeffrey interview with author 28 July 2014.

## Chapter 14

[1] The *News Letter* commented that timing of the Feeney announcement (straight after Jeffrey's last game) "left a lot to be desired". *BNL* 28 Apr. 2014.

[2] *SL* 12 July 2013.

[3] Warren Feeney interview with author 11 Sept. 2014; *SL* 27 Apr. 2014.

[4] *LAL* 8 July 2014.

[5] *BT* 9 May 2014; *LAL* 8 July 2014; *BT* 7 Aug. 2014.

[6] Andy Waterworth interview with author 23 May 2016; *BT* 10 July 2014; *SL* 20 July 2014; *BT* 18 July 2014.

[7] *SL* 20 July 2014.

[8] According to Stefan Szymanski, overseas rights generated by the 2015 English Premier League's television deal had the potential to double the domestic monies brought in. Szymanski, *Money and Football*, p. 104; *BT* 10 Sept. 2014.

[9] The almost 13 per cent increase in Irish League attendances was not sustained throughout the campaign. That said, by the end of the season attendances were up 8.5 per cent on the previous year. That season 18,363 extra people watched Irish League games, representing a significant increase in punters through the gates. *BT* 8 Aug. 2015; *BT* 1 Aug. 2014; *BT* 7 Mar. 2015.

[10] *BNL* 12 Aug. 2013.

[11] A document entitled 'Creating A Soccer Strategy for Northern Ireland' was published as part of the early-2000s Task Force established by Stormont. *BT* 30 Oct. 2001; *ISN* 8 Feb. 2003; *ISN* 17 Aug. 1985.

[12] *SL* 8 Dec. 2013.

[13] *BNL* 5 Dec. 2013; *SL* 8 Dec. 2013; *BT* 26 June 2014.

[14] At Windsor the average attendance by the beginning of January 2015 was just shy of 2,500. This was significantly up on previous campaigns. LFC minute book 2011-16, entry 12 Jan. 2015. Part of the surprise at the positive reception of the NIFL proposals was due to the fact that the Irish League's three tiers would be reduced from 42 teams to 36, significantly dropping the number of junior teams. It had not been expected that this would be endorsed with such a clear mandate. *BT* 26 June 2014; *BT* 7 Mar. 2015.

[15] *BT* 15 Jan. 2015.

[16] *SL* 1 Mar. 2015.

[17] *SL* 29 Mar. 2015.

[18] *DT* 30 Mar. 2015; *BT* 7 Nov. 2015; *BT* 1 Apr. 2015; *BT* 21 Apr. 2015; *BNL* 21 Apr. 2015.

[19] LFC minute book 2011-16, entry 9 Feb. 2015; *BT* 22 Apr. 2015.

[20] Warren Feeney interview with author 10 Sept. 2015.

[21] Jamie Mulgrew interview with author 17 May 2016; Andy Waterworth interview with author 23 May 2016.

[22] *SL* 2 Apr. 2015.

[23] *BNL* 21 Apr. 2015; *BNL* 10 June 2015.

[24] *SL* 21 June 2015; *BT* 16 Mar. 2016.

[25] Warren Feeney interview with author 10 Sept. 2015; *BT* 16 Mar. 2016.

[26] LFC minute book 2011-16, entry 12 Feb. 2015; *BT* 16 Mar. 2016.

[27] Warren Feeney interview with author 10 Sept. 2015; *LAL* 23 July 2015; *LAL* 2 July 2015.

[28] *BNL* 14 Sept. 2015; *SL* 13 Sept. 2015; *BT* 7 Oct. 2015.

[29] *BT* 7 Oct. 2015; *LAL* 10 Oct. 2015.

[30] *BT* 6 Oct. 2015.

[31] *BT* 15 Oct. 2015; David Healy interview with author 21 July 2016.

[32] David Healy interview with author 21 July 2016.

[33] David Healy interview with author 21 July 2016.

[34] David Healy interview with author 21 July 2016.

[35] David Healy interview with author 21 July 2016; *SL* 18 Oct. 2015.

[36] David Healy interview with author 21 July 2016.

[37] *SL* 29 Nov. 2015.

[38] *BNL* 11 Apr. 2016.

[39] Andy Waterworth interview with author 23 May 2016; Sean Ward interview with author 13 May 2016; Jamie Mulgrew interview with author 17 May 2016.

[40] *SL* 8 May 2016; *BT* 24 May 2016.

[41] It should be noted that although there were some parallels between Carroll and Caughey's moves to and from Linfield, Carroll's transfer did not provoke any acrimony, as Caughey's had done. See *BT* 28 June 2014.

[42] *ISN* 17 Aug. 1985; *BT* 6 Nov. 2015.

[43] *BT* 6 May 2016.

[44] One thing that has changed at Linfield in the years between the 1986 centenary and 2016, is the club's status. In February 2010, the club membership voted to become a Limited Company instead of a Private Members' Club. *BNL* 19 Feb. 2010.

# Bibliography

## Primary Source Material

### Manuscript Sources

Linfield Football Club minute book 1985-93

Linfield Football Club minute book 1993-99

Linfield Football Club minute book 1999-2003

Linfield Football Club minute book 2003-06

Linfield Football Club minute book 2007-10

Linfield Football Club minute book 2011-16

### Government Publications

European Commission, The European Model of Sport: Consultation Document of DG X 1998.

Northern Ireland Executive, Advisory Panel to the Minister for Culture, Arts and Leisure report on Creating A Soccer Strategy for Northern Ireland 2001.

Home Office, Committee of Inquiry into Crowd Safety and Control at Sports Grounds: Interim Report 1985.

House of Commons Culture Media and Sport Committee, Racism in Football Second Report of Session Volume 1 2012

## Contemporary Books, Pamphlets and Articles

ABC Ltd, *Standard Certificate of Circulation for the 146 issues distributed between 1ˢᵗ July 2002 and 29ᵗʰ December 2002 Belfast Telegraph – Evening* (Berkhamsted, 2003).

Co-operation Ireland, *Committed to Change: 20 Short Stories* (2000).

## Newspapers and Periodicals

*An Phoblacht*

*Andersonstown News*

*Belfast News Letter*

*Belfast Telegraph*

*Birmingham Mail*

*Daily Mail*

*Daily Telegraph*

*Derry Journal*

*Evening Times (Glasgow)*

*Economist*

*Guardian*

*Herald (Glasgow)*

*Independent*

*Ireland's Saturday Night*

*Irish News*

*Irish Times*

*FCK Magasinet*

*Londonderry Sentinel*

*London Evening Standard*

*Look at Linfield*

*Moscow Times*

*Observer*

*One Team In Ulster*

*Scotsman*

*Sunday Life*

*Sunday News*

*Sunday World*

*The Blues Brothers*

*The Sun (Northern Ireland edition)*

*Ulster Star*

*When Saturday Comes*

# Secondary Source Material

### Books

Black, L. Crabbe, T. and Solomos, J., *The Changing Face of Football: Racism, Identity and Multiculture in the English Game* (Oxford, 2001).

Bose, M., *Game Changer: How the English Premier League Came to Dominate the World* (Singapore, 2012).

Brewer, J.D. Higgins, G.I. and Teeney, F., *Religion, Civil Society & Peace in Northern Ireland* (Oxford, 2011).

Brodie, M., *Linfield: 100 Years* (Belfast, 1985).

Bryan, D., *Orange Parades: The Politics of Ritual, Tradition and Control* (London, 2000).

Coyle, P., *Paradise Lost and Found: The Story of Belfast Celtic* (Edinburgh, 1999).

Donovan, D. and Murphy, A.E., *The Fall of the Celtic Tiger: Ireland and the Euro Debt Crisis* (Oxford, 2013).

Duke, V. and Crolley, L., *Football, Nationality and the State* (New York, 2014).

Ferguson, R., *Here for a Season: Black Diamonds and the Blue Brazil* (Ellon, 1993).

Fink, C. Hadler, F. and Schramm, T. (eds), *1956: European and Global Perspectives* (Leipzig, 2006).

Flynn, B., *Political Football: The Life & Death of Belfast Celtic* (Dublin, 2009).

Football Friends Media, *Two Left Feet* (Kent, 2011).

Gillespie, G., *Years of Darkness: The Troubles Remembered* (Dublin, 2008).

Goldblatt, D., *The Game of Our Lives: The Meaning and Making of English Football* (St Ives, 2015).

Hennessey, T., *A History of Northern Ireland: 1920-1996* (Basingstoke, 1997).

Hill, D., *Out of His Skin: The John Barnes Phenomenon* (London, 2001).

Honigstein, R., *Englischer Fussball: A German View of Our Beautiful Game* (London, 2009).

Hornby, N., *Fever Pitch* (London, 1994).

Horton, E., *The Best World Cup Money Can Buy: The World Cup of 1994 and the World of Football* (Oxford, 1995).

Jefferys, K., *Sport and Politics in Modern Britain: The Road to 2012* (New York, 2012).

Jenkins, D., and Holly J. (eds), *Survival of the Fattest: An Alternative Review of the '94-95 Football Season* (London, 1995).

Keane, R. and Dunphy E., *Keane: The Autobiography* (London, 2002).

Lendvai, P., *One day that shook the Communist World: The 1956 Hungarian Uprising and its legacy* (New Jersey, 2008).

Markovits, A.S. and Hellerman, S.L., *Offside: Soccer and American Exceptionalism* (Princeton, 2001).

McKittrick, D. and McVea, D., *Making Sense of the Troubles: A History of the Northern Ireland Conflict* (London, 2012).

McLaughlin P. (ed.), *The Malcolm Brodie Northern Ireland Soccer Yearbook 16/17* (Belfast 2016).

McManus, S., *The MacBride Principles: Genesis and History and Story to Date* (Washington DC, 1993).

Mortimer, G., *A History of Football in 100 Objects* (London, 2012).

Murray, B., *Bhoys, Bears and Bigotry: The Old Firm in the new age* (Edinburgh, 1998).

O'Dochartaigh, P., *Germany Since 1945* (London, 2004).

Ponton, G., *The Soviet Era: Soviet Politics from Lenin to Yeltsin,* (Cambridge, 1994).

Phillips, T., *Fit to Bust: How Great Companies Fail* (London, 2011).

Ridley, I., *There's a Golden Sky: How Twenty Years of the Premier League has Changed Football Forever* (London, 2012).

Rodríguez, P. Késenne, S. and Koning, R. (eds), *The Economics of Competitive Sport* (Cheltenham 2015).

Rowbottom, M., *Foul Play: The Dark Arts of Cheating in Sport* (London, 2013).

Scott, L., *End to End Stuff: The Essential Football Book* (London, 2008).

Scraton, P., *Hillsborough: The Truth* (Edinburgh, 1999).

Selznick, B.J., *Global Television: Co-Producing Culture* (Philadelphia, 2008).

Smith, G., *The Post-Soviet States: Mapping the Politics of Transformation* (London, 1999).

Spaaij, R., *Understanding Football Hooliganism: A Comparison of Six Western European Football Clubs* (Amsterdam, 2006).

Szymanski, S., *Money and Football: A Soccernomics Guide* (New York, 2015).

Taylor, M., *The Association Game: A History of British Football* (Abingdon, 2013).

Walker, G., *The Politics of Frustration: Harry Midgley and the Failure of the Labour Party in Northern Ireland* (Manchester, 1985).

Walvin, J., *The People's Game: The History of Football Revisited* (Edinburgh, 2000).

Wangerin, D., *Soccer in A Football World*: The Story of America's Forgotten Game (London, 2006).

Wilson, J., *Behind the Curtain: Travels in Eastern European Football* (London, 2006).

Wilson, R. and PieKarz, M., *Sports Management: The Basics* (Abingdon, 2016).

Woods, A., *A Manufactured Plague: The History of Foot-and-mouth Disease in Britain* (Trowbridge, 2004).

Zürcher, C., *The Post-Soviet Wars: Rebellion, Ethnic Conflict, and Nationhood in the Caucasus* (New York, 2007).

**Articles**

Ashe, F., 'From Paramilitaries to Peacemakers: The Gender Dynamics of Community-Based Restorative Justice in Northern Ireland' *The British Journal of Politics & International Relations* 11:2 (May, 2009) pp. 289-314.

Bairner, A. and Walker, G., 'Football and Society in Northern Ireland: Linfield Football Club and the Case of Gerry Morgan' *Soccer and Society* 2:1 (Spring, 2001) pp. 81-98.

Behlmer, G.K., 'Introduction' in G.K. Behlmer and F.M. Leventhal (eds), *Singular Identities: Tradition, Nostalgia and Identity in Modern British Culture* (Stanford, 2009) pp. 1-10.

Cain, L.P. and Haddock, D.D., 'Similar Economic Histories, Different Industrial Structures: Transatlantic Contrasts in the Evolution of Professional Sports Leagues' *The Journal of Economic History* 65:4 (Dec., 2005) pp. 1116-47.

Cornwall, P., 'The Making of Saint Michael' in M. Perryman (ed.), *The Ingerland Factor: Home Truths from Football* (Edinburgh, 1999) pp. 97-108.

Cox, M., 'The Search for Space: How a theory of political polling explains why New Labour was like Dennis Bergkamp' *The Blizzard Issue Zero* (Mar., 2011) pp. 78-82.

Cronin, M., 'Catholics and sport in Northern Ireland: exclusiveness or inclusiveness' in T. Magdalinski and T.J.L. Chandler (eds), *With God on Their Side: Sport in the Service of Religion* (London, 2002) pp. 20-36.

Esplin, R., and Walker, G., 'Introduction' in R. Esplin and G. Walker (eds), *It's Rangers for Me?: New Perspectives on a Scottish Institution* (Ayr, 2008) pp. 5-9.

Groeneveld, M., 'Matters of the Heart: The business of English Rugby League' in S. Ardener and F. Moore (eds), *Professional Identities: Policy and Practice in Business and Bureaucracy* (Oxford, 2007) pp. 27-46.

Jary, D. Horne, J. and Bucke, T., 'Football "Fanzines" and Football Culture: A Case of Successful "Cultural Contestation"' *Sociological Review* 39:3 (Aug., 1991) pp. 581-97.

Johnes, M., '"Every day when I wake up I thank the Lord I'm Welsh"; Sport and Identity in post-war Wales' in A. Smith and D. Porter (eds), *Sport and National Identity in the Post-War World* (London, 2004) pp. 52-68.

Magee, D., 'English Beer and American Football: Exporting American Football as a Cultural Commodity to the British Isles' *Irish Journal of American Studies* 7 (1998) pp. 121-48.

McCann, E., 'Two Tribes on the Terraces?' *Fortnight* 274 (June, 1989) p. 25.

McKeown, L., 'Bulldozing History?' *History Ireland* 13:6 (Nov., 2006) pp. 5-6.

McLlister, R., 'The Red Army Invades the Brandywell' *Fortnight* 234 (Mar., 1986) pp. 11-12.

O'Hara, D., 'Other Foot' *Fortnight* 314 (Feb., 1993) p. 11.

Rookwood, J. and Chan, N., 'The 39th game: fan responses to the Premier League's proposal to globalize the English game' *Soccer and Society* 12:6 (Oct., 2011) pp. 897-913.

Sondaal, T., 'Football's grobalization or globalization? The lessons of Liverpool Football Club's evolution in the Premier League era' *Soccer and Society* 14:4 (July, 2013) pp. 485-501.

Storey, D., 'Football, Place and Migration: Foreign footballers in the FA Premier League' *Geography* 96:2 (Summer, 2011) pp. 86-94.

Wagg S., 'Nowt for Being Second: Leeds, Leeds United and the Ghost of Don Revie' in P. Bramham and S. Wagg (eds), *Sport, Leisure and Culture in the Postmodern City* (Farnham, 2009) pp. 129-52.

Welsh, I., 'Introduction' in M. King and M. Knight, *The Naughty Nineties: Football's Coming Home?* (Edinburgh, 1999) pp. 9-19.


## Unpublished Articles

Gillespie, G., 'Northern Ireland Fanzines', held at Linen Hall Library Belfast, 2000.


## Television

*ITN News Report*, 17 Feb. 1990


## Websites

Tennessee Athletics. 'Neyland Stadium', utsports.com, http://www.utsports.com/facilities/neyland/